The First Canary

Sheldon Baverstock

Copyright © Sheldon Baverstock (2022)

The right of Sheldon Baverstock to be identified as author of this work has been asserted by him in accordance with section 77 and 78 of the Copyright, Designs and Patents Act 1988.

All rights reserved. No part of this publication may be reproduced, stored in a retrieval system, or transmitted in any form or by any means, electronic, mechanical, photocopying, recording, or otherwise, without the prior permission of the publishers.

Any person who commits any unauthorised act in relation to this publication may be liable to criminal prosecution and civil claims for damages.

This book is a work of fiction. Names, characters, places and incidents are either products of the author's imagination or are used fictitiously. Any resemblance to actual events or locales or persons, living or dead, is entirely coincidental.

ISBN 978-1-7635535-1-4

First Published (2022) Cranthorpe Milner

Current Publication (2024) Nextsearch

Prologue

High Road and Low Road

The nurse in the maternity ward, soon to be wearing the uniform of a World War II nurse, had seen it all before – the young girl in the bed, barely seventeen, feeling a lot older after the last few hours, now holding her newborn baby daughter in her arms. Her facial expression was something between disbelief and wonderment at the sight.

She showed the girl how to offer the bottle's teat to the baby. *Let the baby's lips find it so she can start suckling*, the nurse thought. In adoption cases it was best to introduce bottle feeding as soon as possible. Such a method allowed the birth mother to feed her baby if she so desired. This was often when the tears would flow, as they were doing now down the cheeks of this young girl. She handed the girl a tissue so she could wipe her nose before she dripped on the baby.

The nurse looked up at the sound coming from the doorway. There stood a man – the girl's father – and a senior midwife. The matron had informed the nurse earlier that they would be coming for the baby but she hadn't realised it would be so soon.

"Pa, Pa please! Let me keep her. I promise I will finish school. It will be OK. Please Pa!"

The nurse watched as the man nodded at the woman alongside him and she stepped forward to take the baby from the girl's arms. His daughter resisted and the midwife looked at the nurse for assistance, but she ignored the request, instead sitting down on the bed beside the girl, cradling her sobbing shoulders.

The editor leaned back in his chair, feeling like he had just won the lottery. The graduate of Natal University's class of 1961 before him was everything the newspaper's human resources team had promised. Along with her outstanding grades in literature and journalism, he detected a tenacious personality and a passion for a story.

Clearly she was very smart and had a wonderful sense of humour. The psychometric test had indicated what they referred to as an 'underlying anxiety trait' but this was nothing serious, her score falling just outside the parameters of 'normal'.

Every year, the newspaper competed with others for an outstanding candidate to fill their graduate program. This year the editor felt sure they had found a good one. The formal interview was over and now it was time to get to know a bit more about the candidate's personal life.

He leant forward slowly and carefully, remembering that when he got too animated his leather chair made a farting sound.

"Have you lived in Durban all your life? Were you born here?"

He smiled, his upper lip almost hidden by his abundant moustache perched below a large nose and big green eyes.

"I have no idea where I was born, actually," the young woman said with a shrug and a grin, hands held open.

They both laughed aloud.

The young student, who was crammed behind the pile of miners' overalls, helmets and gum boots in the trunk of the battered Ford, held his breath. His racing mind projected images onto the lids of his tightly closed eyes; a slow-motion movie where boots crunched across the gravel around the car, certain to approach the trunk, before the wearer paused to yank it open.

As fearful as he was, he perversely relished the

thought of the freshness that would descend into the trunk with the cold night air; relief from the over-powering stench of oil and old sweat ingrained in the dirty overalls he was now burrowing into like a mouse trying feebly to escape a cat.

Through the thin metal of the vehicle's panels, he had heard the surprise in their voices.

"Black people driving at this hour?"

It was after the curfew time indicated in their passbook – the hated *dompas* they were forced to carry.

"What the hell are you people doing travelling so late?" The question was asked by one of the policemen manning the roadblock they had been stopped at. On-road security checks were becoming increasingly common since Nelson Mandela's armed ANC wing – <u>Umkhonto weSizwe</u> ('Spear of the Nation'), more commonly known as MK – had started its domestic bombing campaign in the Sixties.

"Sir, I am taking my friends to catch the bus to Lesotho – the one that takes the miners. It goes from Harrismith station tonight. They are new mine workers."

A torch flashed across each of the nervous young black faces in the car, their eyes wide and pupils dilated like those of an anxious cat placed on a vet's treatment table.

"Open!"

The voice snapped like a rasp over the policeman's shoulder; a command from his superior.

"*Maak oop*," the captain snarled, this time in Afrikaans. He waved the barrel of the automatic weapon he clasped in his large hands; the action stretching the strap over his shoulder as he gestured towards the rear of the vehicle and its trunk.

The driver could smell gun oil, the well-lubricated weapon inches from his face. He heaved himself quickly from his seat.

Hearing the commands, the young student inside the trunk tried to make himself as small as possible. Trembling, he buried his face in the unwashed work clothes and held his breath as the trunk lid creaked slowly open, the rusty hinges squeaking in protest.

If he had dared look up from his hiding place, he would have seen the slim outline of the driver illuminated by the car's taillights. His dark, red-tinged frame shook slightly through fear and cold; both arms raised above his head as they held the trunk lid open.

Suddenly a two-way radio crackled loudly in the darkness nearby. The burly figure beside the Ford's driver spun around, looking back down the dark road, listening intently.

"Vehicle approaching at speed. Over," came the scratchy voice from the radio. The voice came again, louder and more urgent. "Repeat. Car approaching fast. Over."

"OK go. You lot go!" The captain gave his command, his hand waving at the car and its driver in dismissal.

Looking back into the darkness, he gave hasty orders to the officers around him before turning back to the car's driver, irritated at the sight of the immobile statue standing in the taillight glow with arms still raised, his eyes wide and white against his black face.

"Did you hear me? Bugger off!" he shouted.

The lid crashed down suddenly, making the trunk's occupant jump. Gears grated before the driver had even fully closed his door and the old Ford moved off while behind, the helmeted security force manning the roadblock moved quickly, taking up new positions as instructed by their captain.

Their weapons were now pointed down the road into the darkness, towards the distant oncoming car in the valley below; its headlights slashing through the blackness this way and that at each sharp turn, like the search lights that lit up London's skyline during World War II in search of enemy aircraft.

Tyres screeched from time to time as the oncoming vehicle's driver negotiated the steep, contoured road up Van Reenen's Pass at what the high-pitched revving engine indicated was great speed.

Previously illuminated by the old Ford's rear lights, the reflective police emblem on the backs of the dark figures manning the roadblock faded as the car moved slowly forward, heading up the hill; its aging engine thumping erratically as it went. The passengers were far too terrified to look back through the cracked rear window.

The occupier of the trunk, relieved to feel the car moving again, removed his face from the stinking overalls and tried to shut out the image of being hauled from the trunk by burly policemen and how their fists would have felt; the sound of flesh on flesh.

*

Earlier that day, the student's mind had been filled with other unwanted images as he travelled by bus from his university campus to his home in Kwa Mashu, a sprawling high-density township on the outskirts of Durban. The narrow road into the township was lined two or three-deep with workers returning home from their jobs. They were walking because at this time of the week there was no money left from their meagre wages to pay for the bus or an overcrowded taxi.

The bus jolted and accelerated intermittently as the driver jammed on brakes, avoiding pedestrians who stumbled from the safety of the road's edge, tripping on crumbling macadam into the bus's path. Mongrel dogs chased each other across the road, appearing without warning between walkers' legs.

The passengers yelled at the driver each time they were thrown forward, hands stabbing at the seat-back in front of them when he braked, the smell of exhaust fumes wafting through the open windows.

"*Qaphela, qaphela.* Watch out!"

The cursing driver ignored them as he ground the gears, yelling at the pedestrians in his path even though they were unable to hear him.

Deep in thought, the student had been staring through the windscreen. He sat in a front-row seat across the aisle from the driver, but he wasn't really taking in what he was seeing. He wasn't even aware of the stinking carbon monoxide that was being sucked in through windows, left opened in an effort to encourage a breeze to counter Durban's oppressive February humidity.

His mind was re-playing the day's events and he tried to suppress the dread he felt growing inside him for what was likely to be the outcome of this morning's campus protest. Being a young activist is easy, when you're part of a chanting crowd; a face lost amongst many, backing into those behind you as the snarling police dogs strain at their leashes to reach you. Then suddenly you're singled out. Maybe you tripped? Now you're pounced on and now it's personal.

He didn't see the approaching car or the mongrel dog – her extended teats from many births swaying like erratic pendulums as she trotted along the side of the road in his direction, leading her identically-coloured pup. There were more pressing images flashing through the student's mind at that moment than the everyday ones outside: his mother's face expressing fear and concern; his father's, frustration and anger. Then there was the anger and hatred of the policeman's face, and his snarling Alsatian with the saliva dripping from lips curled above white fangs.

He was jolted back to the present as the mongrel dog, faithfully followed by her pup, suddenly veered onto the road for no apparent reason and into the path of the approaching car. Mother and puppy both disappeared from view as the car drove straight over them.

The young student turned his face – a mask of horror – aside in an effort to avoid the image, when both dogs re-appeared unscathed from the rear of the car's underside as its driver screeched to a halt.

"*Inhlanhla mama inja* (lucky mother dog)!" laughed the bus driver, as he began to speed up again, passing the now stationery car whose driver was heaving himself out from behind the steering wheel, expecting to see the worst.

Grinning at the bus driver, the young student

wondered to himself if he too had, in a way, been run over earlier at the university when he'd walked into the path of Prime Minister Botha's police force. Would he emerge unscathed, like these dogs?

By now at least one of his father's friends, who worked in the office at the university, would have fully appraised his concerned parents of the trouble their student activist son was in as a result of the day's unfolding campus drama.

Unbeknown to the student however, they had also proposed a solution for their friend's son who was now a *non*-student activist without official identity, having had his passbook confiscated by the police during his arrest and expelled that same day by the faculty for inciting a riot at the university.

After his arrest, he had managed to escape from the police by slipping through the rear door of the police van and ducking through the milling crowd where he could hide unseen amid the confusion. Yet it would only be a matter of hours before a police truck would rattle down the dusty township road and stop in front of their small house.

Later, packing a small bag, the teenager could hear his mother weeping quietly in the other room – the only other in their house – as his father's earlier words echoed in his mind.

"Your mother and I used all our savings for your education, but you can only think about Nelson

Mandela and 'Amandla' so here is what you must do: tonight, you go to join Madiba's army before the police arrive to put you in jail. My friend will take you with him. He is taking new recruits for MK to Lesotho, this evening. You are lucky to have such an escape."

*

The aspirant miners and their car finally crested the last steep section of road that snaked up the Pass. Looking back down into the dark valley, they could see a train's long line of window lights against the black slopes. Climbing up through the valley, the train seemed to wind back on itself as the track followed the contours of the surrounding hills, making it appear like an illuminated caterpillar following its own tail.

In the distance, high above the train's moving line of lights and the hillside it climbed, they could see a jagged black outline against a starlit sky. It was the peaks of the Drakensberg Mountains, and by tomorrow morning they would be there.

It was not too much longer before they turned into the parking area at Harrismith station. The car jolted over the entrance speed hump with a *thump* that left the trunk's occupant rubbing his head, as he fought off the toppled mining gear that was now threatening to suffocate him with its smell.

The old car crunched to a stop on the gravel, and after a few seconds the trunk's lid creaked open. Three young faces appeared above the mining gear, which they dragged out while helping their comrade into the open. He was so stiff he could hardly stand up straight.

"The new Spear of the Nation is already bent," said their Zulu driver, with a grin. Time had elapsed since his ordeal at the roadblock and he had re-gained his composure now they were off the road.

The young men all laughed nervously over the earlier experience and began putting on their mining overalls and helmets. The driver led them to a spot in the thick bush on top of a small railway embankment alongside the deserted station. Here they could watch for the arrival of the bus without being seen from the road. On the other side, to the rear and below them, was the railway track so they would not be surprised by any unexpected arrival from behind.

As they settled down, their driver said quietly in Zulu, "Now we wait for the bus from Johannesburg with the miners going home to Lesotho."

*

Lost in thought about an uncertain future, the four of them, together with their MK recruiter, had been sitting in total silence except for the sound of crickets in the darkness around them and the occasional croak of a frog (that was probably looking for the crickets).

A sudden blast of an air horn made them all jump.

It was so close it seemed to be almost on top of them; the locomotive with its loud warning and its intensely bright headlight streaming down the track, appearing out of the blackness. It was probably the train they had seen earlier coming up the Pass, now announcing its arrival at the station.

Moving at a reduced speed for its entry into the station, the locomotive and its brightly lit carriages trundled past them with a rhythmic *clickety-clack* as the steel wheels bridged the expansion joints in the tracks. The train continued to slow down and the increasingly longer pause between each *clack*, sounded to them like the train was weary from the long haul up Van Reenens's Pass.

The five men gazed into each window sliding by, their heads moving like tennis spectators as their eyes flicked back and forth to follow the occupants of the passing compartment windows a few metres from them. Each carriage was filled with young white men in their late teens; the same age as the comrades sitting in the dark watching them go slowly by.

They realised as the train slowed it was obviously not a normal passenger train, for in each carriage, older men in army uniforms walked stiffly up and down the aisle, leaning into compartments and pointing in different directions. Although they could not be heard by the onlookers, it was obvious that the officials were barking out orders, presumably relating to their imminent stop at Harrismith station.

Behind the four recruits their driver whispered to them in Zulu. "They are also going to army training. One day you will shoot at each other."

The boys thought they could hear him chuckling quietly in the dark.

His young recruits were transfixed as the troop train came to a stop. Being much longer than a normal passenger train, the platform wasn't able to support all the carriages. Consequently, one of them halted directly opposite where the comrades were hidden in the bush, alongside the track. They could hear the young men in the carriage, laughing and joking.

Some were playing cards while others were already lying on bunks they had eased down from their latches on the compartment walls. Some leant out of the windows, joking and yelling playful insults at their fellow conscripts either side of them who were also leaning out of their carriages.

These young men looked more like they were

going on holiday than to army training. The four young men crouching in the bush with their recruiter had already faced risks today, and they were only just starting the journey towards their training as soldiers. They would not see a comfortable bunk or a hot meal for some time.

Peering into the carriage opposite, his legs still aching from hours in the Ford's trunk, Zeb wondered what things these young guys might be passionate about; what cause they might have to risk their lives for. He had not really had an opportunity to get to know any white boys at the university.

*

As progressive as Natal University was in the Apartheid era in the early Sixties – allowing black people (albeit only a small number) to gain entry to the university – classes were nonetheless segregated. Outside class Zeb spent most of his time on a bus, travelling between the township he lived in with his parents and the campus, which was a great distance away near the city where black people were not allowed to have homes. There was no time left for social activities or to meet people after class.

Zeb had however met some white boys when he stayed with his mother, Muriel Hani, during the school holidays when she worked as a live-in maid for a woman in Pietermaritzburg. He'd played soccer in the backyard with the homeowner's son, Cliff, and his friend, Josh. He remembered his mother's tiny room in the garden at the back of the main house that she kept as spotless as the large house she cleaned and cooked in for her employer.

He was unable to go to the local park with the two white boys because black people were not allowed there. Yet the boys wanted to involve him because he was their friend and so they had been happy to use the backyard as their football field.

During term time, Zeb stayed with his father in Durban. His father had decided to move to the bigger city of Durban where there were more opportunities for work. Also, they could stay with his sister, Zeb's aunt, while he looked for a job that would pay enough for him to rent a home for his wife and son.

Zeb, Cliff and Josh became good friends over many school holidays. However, Zeb had not seen them since his father had found a really good job in Durban, and his mother, no longer having to work, had joined them both in the house Zeb's father had rented in Kwa Mashu, a high-density township suburb of Durban.

*

Zeb held onto a branch to help support him as he leant out of the bush that hid them at the top of the embankment, peering up and down the long line of carriages of the stationary train. He wondered whether Cliff or Josh might be one of the passengers on board.

Shortly, the train would move off and across the flat plains of the Orange Free State to a training camp somewhere, whilst Zeb and his fellow recruits would be crammed into an old bus filled with surly (and mostly drunk) old miners. Their transportation would then rattle off towards Maseru, high in the mountains of Lesotho, before flying on to Zambia to start their overland journey to their training camp in Angola.

After they completed their training, they would begin risking their lives in the fight for democracy. Meanwhile, their white counterparts on the train would complete their training and, for the present, simply return to their homes in the suburbs, back to their families and jobs.

Suddenly their hiding place in the bush was filled with light from bouncing beams. An old bus, belching black smoke into the security lights that surrounded the station, clattered off the road over the speed bump and executed a wide U-turn in the dusty parking area that was empty, except for the old Ford that the previous occupants would abandon there.

The driver whispered, "Here is the bus. The mountains and an airplane to Zambia await you."

Brenda could not believe how fast the day of Cliff's departure to basic training had arrived. She felt extremely resentful towards a government that had taken her young man from her so soon after they had started a relationship. Her anger was exacerbated by the conversations she overheard in the office amongst the senior journalists. She was still a junior so didn't offer her own comments or thoughts, but she listened with great interest to theirs.

The consensus amongst them was that the conscription of young white boys, some just school leavers, to help support their Apartheid regime was just another inhumane, albeit legal, Government policy. Except for the Afrikaans newspapers, the South African Government considered the press to be left-wing Liberals who were 'probably all commies'.

Without a real family all her life, Brenda had only recently begun to feel the joy of having someone close to her to share things with. Now, she was standing distraught on a station platform watching a train full of young men peering out of carriage windows, disappearing into the darkness at the end of the platform.

On the way home sitting in silence beside Beryl, Cliff's mother, Brenda resolved to make the most of Cliff's time away. Having an insider in the camp would enable her to gather first-hand information that could form the basis of an army conscription *exposé*. She could pitch the idea to her editor, or just work on it in her spare time. Such a scoop would certainly impress the senior journalists at the paper! Or maybe she could even write a book; she had always wanted to write a novel.

Part 1

Chapter 1

Beryl's Brothers

Even before the World War II generals came calling for her brothers, Beryl noticed them being enticed away by her next-door neighbour Madge, who was determined to marry one of the good-looking Barkerfield boys.

She fell firstly for Gerry – the youngest and thinnest of the brothers. She loved how he was always smartly dressed. He wore long-sleeved shirts, even on hot days; never rolling them up. Madge wondered if he did so when he went on his solitary fishing trips to the local dam.

*

Their marriage ended on their wedding night when Madge opened the door of their en suite. With her eyelids drooping seductively, she slowly slid into their bedroom.

There, in the bright light he had forgot to dim, Gerry waited for his bride with a shy smile on his face. His thin white legs protruded out from beneath oversized bright red satin under shorts; so large she mistook them for a skirt. Part of his chest was hidden under the wide elastic holding them up. Madge was an avid birdwatcher and the image of a Lesser Red-breasted Meadowlark crossed her mind at that moment.

Seeing Gerry shirtless for the first time was a shock for Madge. Psoriasis covered the entire length of his arms and shoulders. Madge imagined flakes falling from the skinny arms he held out to her; her boxer husband in his satin shorts waiting for his gloves to be slipped on.

An image of her and Gerry in a shaken snow globe suddenly came to mind, and it started a giggling fit that all but destroyed Gerry and certainly their wedding night.

*

Gerry cursed himself and God for having to bear the affliction he had; one that Madge was convinced was contagious. As a result he had had to forgo making it to Madge's bed – not only on his wedding night but thereafter – other than to briefly seek out his cat, Binge, who preferred her warm bed to the small couch Gerry slept on.

After a week Gerry left Madge's apartment with

a suitcase gripped in each hand and Binge under his arm, his legs dangling.

When Gerry went fishing, Binge would wait at the gate for him to return, his patience later rewarded with a whole fish. Gerry smiled to himself on the days he returned empty-handed and Binge was not at the gate. The cat would purr loudly when Gerry found him later and scratched him behind the ear.

"You always know, somehow boy, when the fish won't bite."

*

The next activity that seemed to have a fish association to become part of Gerry's life was not one that was of interest to Binge, or at least not initially. It was something he had already contemplated in the past, and convinced his aborted marriage confirmed he was unsuited to mainstream family life, Gerry decided to seek out a different family.

He applied to become an ordained minister of the church, conscious there was no need to get naked in front of anybody in God's family. He relished the opportunity to conceal his arms in a long-sleeved robe (or whatever priests wore when in public). *God owes me*, he thought.

*

Not long after the near-drowning of his circuit supervisor in the seminary fishpond, Gerry had been promoted from probationer and ordained as a minister of the church (much to the disgust of the aforementioned circuit supervisor).

The supervisor blamed Gerry and his cat for the incident but despite his strong recommendation to do so, the church council had refused to sanction Gerry over the drowning incident; Bing, as they knew him then, being a firm favourite of theirs as a result of his mouse-catching prowess. When he had first arrived the circuit supervisor had, after begrudgingly allowing Gerry to have Binge in his apartment, insisted he change the cat's name.

"It has an alcohol connotation, my son."

So Binge, who didn't care what he was called as long as he got fed and had a warm place to sleep, became Bing. The name change prompted Gerry's fellow probationer, whom he shared an apartment with at the seminary and fancied himself as a comedian, to sing "I'm dreaming of a white Christmas," under his breath whenever Bing padded slowly into view.

What irked the supervisor was the fact that with his recent promotion, Gerry had found the confidence to disobey his boss and re-name his cat Binge again.

"I've prayed on it and God says the name is OK," he informed the supervisor, with a grin.

*

The apartments housing the on-campus probationers at the seminary were set out in a semi-circle that overlooked a large fishpond about the width and depth of a suburban swimming pool, which was its original purpose. However halfway through the build, the pool was condemned by the church council as being unseemly for the seminary since they had decided to allow women to be admitted as probationers.

"I don't want male probationers peering down at scantily clad women through cracks in their curtains," the head of the council had said, with a hand gesture that made the other council members grin.

So after some discussion it had become a fishpond, and notwithstanding the rock features and stepping-stones that had been added, a deep one. Latterly, it also became the pride and joy of Gerry's circuit supervisor who took it upon himself to nurture the pond's plants, as well as the goldfish and carp that lived in it. Nurturing included chasing Binge away whenever he saw him wandering nearby.

Given his new vocation and duties, Gerry no longer went fishing so Binge had decided to take advantage of the local facilities to do so himself. Gerry only discovered this when he and his roommate occasionally found dead goldfish on the kitchen floor.

"I've seen him at it. He has the patience of Job. Maybe you should change his name again?" he deadpanned.

The supervisor knew the cat visited his pond as he had seen him deftly skip across the steppingstones to the central island of reeds. However, he had no idea what Binge got up to there. Then one afternoon, as he strolled past admiring his pond, he was aghast to see Binge on one of the steppingstones wrestling with a large carp, its tail clenched in his jaws.

Binge had got lucky with this catch and was determined to land it. He crouched, back arched up in the air, claws extended, digging into the mossy rock to steady himself from falling into the water as the fish flapped; the motion jerking the cat's head back and forth.

With a yell in protest, the supervisor grabbed his robe. Pulling the heavy black cloth up to his knees, he stepped over the child-proof fence and entered the pond, advancing one hesitant step at a time across the stones.

"Let it go! Let go you fucking bastard," he hissed in a quiet voice he hoped wouldn't be heard by any passing probationer.

Binge, spotting the advancing human out the corner of his eye, was acutely aware of the threat that had been added to his already challenging task of getting his catch under control. Finally, with a swift change of grip, he had the fish where he wanted it. Now locked in his teeth, the cat retreated with his catch back across the stones.

Having only one escape route, the cat had no option but to slip between the skinny white legs that were nearly on top of him. The hand that reached down to grab Binge served no purpose other than to unbalance its non-swimming owner. With his other hand holding up his robe, he was left without a means of balancing and, like a felled oak, he toppled slowly into the water with a splash and a water-choked cry, "Hulp!" The supervisor was rescued by probationers rushing out of their rooms from where they had mirthfully followed the incident through cracks in their curtains.

Later, after the pandemonium had died down, in the silence of their room Gerry and his roommate stood looking at the dead carp on their kitchen floor. Binge crouched beside it, staring up at them, stoical.

"So where are the five loaves, boy?" Gerry's roommate asked, leaning down to scratch the cat's ear.

*

With his newfound status as an ordained minister, Gerry resolved to try to enlist again; this time in the navy as a chaplain. He quite fancied the white robes the navy chaplains wore that would act as camouflage for his psoriasis flakes, which had resulted in him being turned down before. The enlistment office would be his first 'port' of call and if successful, the next stop would be to ask Beryl if she would look after Binge while he provided spiritual comfort to the soldiers at war.

Following her aborted marriage, Madge found solace in the company of Beryl's middle brother, Raymond, who offered his support during the annulment process. They never discussed what had happened between her and Gerry. They only spoke of him once, to laugh about him telling Beryl that the church circuit supervisor had advised him that as he was now a probationer in the church, his cat's name was not appropriate.

Raymond and Madge would spend hours together chatting, sharing each other's dreams about the future, but to Madge's annoyance the two of them never had the same dreams. Impatient to get the platonic relationship onto a romantic footing, Madge resolved to take the initiative.

In a second disaster with a Barkerfield brother, she lost Raymond's support and his company the evening she took his hand and said in her most seductive voice,

"Raymond, we talk about our desires so often, I have come to believe *you* are the one that could fulfil my desires, my dreams. I want to have a family. Why don't we get married?"

Beryl was just seven when she walked home from school on her own for the first time. Normally she had to wait for her mom or one of her brothers to fetch her but today her mom had said she could make her own way home. It was a short distance with no roads to cross, and Raymond was at home to look after her. Supposedly he had a cold and couldn't go to school even though he was missing a mathematics test.

"How unfortunate." His brother Frank had smirked, winking at Gerry across the breakfast table.

Feeling very grown-up on her arrival home, Beryl waved to their neighbour as she turned into her driveway and headed for the back door. Slipping off her shoes she walked quietly down the hall, hoping Raymond had made her a sandwich as instructed by their mother that morning.

The music from the radio coming up the hallway

as she headed for the kitchen was definitely not her mother's. She walked into the kitchen expecting to see Raymond but instead was surprised to see whom she thought at first glance *was* her mother, at the sink busy filling the kettle and swaying to the music.

"Hi Mom, thought you were—"

The figure stiffened at her greeting, and as Beryl took the remaining few steps across the kitchen to smile up into what she thought was her mother's face, what came into view instead was the shocked, panic-filled face of her brother Raymond; his wide eyes accentuated by the badly applied mascara and eye shadow.

"Raymond!" Beryl screeched with delighted surprise. "Are you going to a dress up? You look so funny in Mom's dress and wig." Beryl held her tummy as she laughed uncontrollably. "I have to pee, I have to pee!" she cried, as she ran, bent over, for the toilet down the hall.

Raymond, flushed with embarrassment but relieved at the window of escape Beryl's enforced departure presented, seized the opportunity to pull off the wig and run in the opposite direction to his mother's bedroom. While he shed her clothes, he thought of a plausible explanation to tell Beryl (and what he could bribe her with to keep it quiet).

"Shit. How could I have forgotten about her coming home early today? Shit, shit, shit," he said to his reflection in the bathroom mirror, as he washed eyeshadow from his face and wiped roughly at the pink lipstick.

*

Raymond's request to be a nurse in the army provided the kind-faced recruiting officer with a way out. It was difficult to turn away a young person brave enough to do his duty; one who was willing to give his life for his country. On the other hand, he had to be realistic as to who could handle a battle situation and who couldn't.

"This is the second one I have had this week. They are just not suited to combat," he murmured under his breath. His fellow recruiting officer raised an eyebrow and drew his lips into a tight line. Shaking his head slightly, he glanced heavenward.

However, nurses were desperately needed. The rules didn't allow a man to be given the title of nurse – instead they were called orderlies – but the roles were similar in a war zone so Raymond proudly signed on the dotted line. He was looking forward to the following week when he would report for basic training and acquire his army uniform.

It was third time lucky for Madge and Beryl's

oldest brother, Frank. When Beryl was told when their first child was due, she thought to herself, *Madge took no chances this time.*

Not long after his first child was born, Frank was caught up in the wave of patriotism sweeping the country. Hitler's troops were on the march, and something had to be done. Frank passed his medical examinations with ease. Beryl had reminded him several times to make sure he did not belch loudly at any time during them.

It looked like Madge's desire to have another baby would be put on hold again. She had begun initiating intimacy by wearing her most revealing dresses at the dinner table, while alluding to the fact that Michael would be lonely as an only child. However, before she could enact her plan, Frank came home from work one evening to tell her he and his brothers had enlisted. She took him to bed immediately after dinner that night.

A few weeks later, two of the Barkerfield brothers sailed together from Durban harbour. Frank headed directly to the Middle East, while Raymond and the other nurses were bound for Cape Town, where they would disembark for intensive medical training before continuing onwards.

Gerry and Madge, together with Beryl and her parents, waved from the quayside far below the rails of the giant troop carrier, with hundreds of others bidding farewell to loved ones too. Tugboats moved the ship's steel sides slowly away from the concrete quay; many with faces turned skyward felt tears slip down their cheeks.

One by one, the paper streamers snapped their connection to those leaning on the ship's rails above. The paper curled away; fragile links floating slowly downwards to join the growing grey mush underfoot while the sound of encouraging cheers faded and the giant hulk moved away slowly through the dark water.

Earlier before the new recruits had embarked, struggling up the long rising gangplank with overloaded backpacks, Beryl had lined her brothers up for a family photograph. All three of them were dwarfed by the giant ship's dark grey hull in front of which they stood; her name emblazoned on her bow far above their heads – HMS *Imminent*. This seemed to be a foreboding backdrop for the two fresh-faced young soldiers in their brand-new uniforms.

Alongside them Gerry, wearing his black church probationer's robes, was presumed by most to be exempt from active service because of his calling to God, and had been invited there to bless these two men departing for war. However, it was in fact his psoriasis that curtailed another 'marriage' – this time to the army. Several months before, his unsightly skin condition had caused the recruiting and medical officers to gape in astonishment as they hastily handed him back his shirt.

It was also still an issue for Madge. As heavy as the twelve-month-old Michael was becoming in her arms, she turned down Gerry's offer to hold her son. She preferred to support the baby's weight with one aching arm while waving to her departing husband with the other.

The first time Beryl allowed her son Cliff to stay over at Josh's house (with his Uncle Frank and Aunt Madge, along with his numerous cousins) was when he was twelve. The siblings included two boys – Michael and Josh, who was the younger of the two at twelve years old. Josh and Cliff were the same age and already 'big buddies'. As well as Michael and Josh, there were two younger girls of six and five, and twin boys of three.

His mother often referred to the siblings as 'an avalanche of kids' who were all crammed together into two small bedrooms that were even more cluttered and chaotic than the rest of the house. The backyard chickens used the kitchen as part of their foraging range; occasionally even clucking their way into the dining room during meal times in search of anything that may have fallen from the table.

When Auntie Madge, at her son Josh's suggestion, had phoned Beryl to invite Cliff to stay over that weekend, Cliff just happened to be in the hallway where he picked up the gist of the conversation. His exaggerated throat-cutting signals and tugging at her dress were ignored as his mother was just too embarrassed to say, "No."

Cliff banged his fists theatrically on the wall in exasperation when he heard his mother accept the invitation on his behalf.

"It will be ever so good for you to stay away for one night, Cliff. Make you more confident; develop your independence."

"But Mom, Uncle Frank talks to their chickens all the time, like they're his kids, it's weird. And there's no lock on the toilet door. I will probably have to share a bed with Josh!" he complained. Stamping on a hapless passing ant in his frustration, Cliff continued. "Can't I just go for the day like I normally do? Or I know – why doesn't Josh come here for the weekend?"

Beryl put her arm around him and gave him a hug. "You'll be fine. It's just a bit cluttered there because there's just not a lot of money to go around, what with all those brothers and sisters. It will teach you to appreciate home, my darling."

"I already do, Mom. Maybe not any more though! Not after you making me do this," Cliff added, with a pout.

"Poor Josh. He would be so hurt if he knew you didn't want to be in his home or with him. He's just trying to be a good friend; showing you how much he likes you."

"Mom! You're just trying to make me feel guilty, aren't you?"

*

What was Josh thinking? Just wait till I get my hands on him! Cliff often rode his bike across to the neighbouring suburb to play with Josh, but at the end of the day he would climb back onto his bike and return to the quiet, orderly sanctity of his own home.

When he arrived at Josh's house that weekend, Cliff was relieved to find he had been provided with a small fold-out bed in the lounge. So after a dysfunctional family supper, when the others went to their rooms to sleep or read, he and Josh had the luxury of playing card games alone in the lounge room; alone that is except for Uncle Frank, who sat on a dining room chair with his foot resting on another while he cut his toenails with an instrument that reminded Cliff of his mother's gardening shears. Uncle Frank was a study of concentration as he closed the blades across each of his toenails. *Click, click* went the scissors. Cliff watched wide-eyed over the cards in his hands. Then *ting* – a toenail clipping ricocheted off a hard object. Maybe it was Uncle Frank's glass of brandy beside him on the table? No, the large spinning blue-black nail clipping landed further down the table's surface, stopping between the two card players.

Earlier, when Uncle Frank had first taken his socks off, Cliff had gasped while Josh held his own nose theatrically, using his finger to make vomiting gestures. For Cliff it was not only the ghastly aroma that drifted through the room that repelled him, but the sight of the toes; black and contorted like they had been bashed with a hammer.

"That's what wearing rubbish army boots for six years in the war does to your feet, son," Frank said. "Marching miles through the desert in the hot sun. Did I ever tell you about the forced march we had to do the night Tobruk fell?"

With his back to his dad, Josh looked at Cliff and raised his eyes to the ceiling. "At least this time it's not a story about digging holes in the hot desert sand so they could go to the toilet," he whispered.

While Frank set the scene for his story, Cliff surreptitiously flicked Uncle Frank's toenail clipping off the table with his seven of diamonds.

*

That Sunday evening on his return home Cliff left his bike at the back door before stomping down the hallway, pausing briefly to hurl his rucksack into his bedroom. He found his mother in the lounge having tea with a visitor – his auntie Raechel –

whom he adored, as did his mom.

"Auntie 'Chel! Yay! Are you staying over?" he cried, hugging her.

"No, no. Work tomorrow," Raechel responded. "Picking and packing. Just brought you guys some fruit. Most of my trees are full. Have a look in the bag in the kitchen, then come and tell me about your weekend adventure."

Cliff made a face at both women as he left the room, "Do I have to?" He hoped there were peaches rather than apples in the bag.

*

Raechel lived a short distance from town on a smallholding with several orchards. Cliff loved going there and his aunt invited him and Josh over regularly. They would play games for hours, finding hiding places in the orchards. His aunt often joined in with their games and would laugh when they chased her with the beetles held between thumb and forefinger. She never screamed like other girls did.

Cliff thought she must be lonely on her own and that was why she invited them so often. One day, Raechel was preparing the boys a snack of bread and jam (made from her own fruit of course) in the kitchen when Cliff and Josh came in after playing in the orchards for hours. While they washed their hands in the sink, the boys came across an open photograph album lying on the worktop nearby.

One picture caught their attention: two young men in uniform and a priest standing alongside.

"That's a dog's collar," Josh enlightened Cliff.

The priest was standing near to what looked like the gangway of a ship – its grey hull in the background –while high up in the distance, the name of the ship could be seen above the men's heads.

"Hey, isn't that your dad, Josh?" Cliff said.

"Yes, and the man with the dog's collar is Uncle Gerry," Josh answered, repeating his information with relish.

"Who's that standing with them Auntie 'Chel?"

Glancing at the photograph, Raechel replied after a long pause, "It's your Uncle Raymond."

"Didn't know we had another uncle!" The boys laughed together.

"Well, it was a long time ago." She stared out through the kitchen window to the view across the fields and orchards. "I'm not sure where Raymond ended up," she murmured. "People forget. They don't talk about stuff," she added.

Josh and Cliff knew this was not the prelude to yet another war story as, unlike their uncles, Auntie 'Chel seldom said anything to them about the war. However, the boys had already forgotten the photograph and were ravenously tucking into their sandwiches, unaware of the tears in their aunt's eyes.

Chapter 2

Aerial Equilibrium

The lioness and her two cubs lay on the edge of the gravel. They were trying to escape the sun in the sparse shade of the monkey thorn trees that grew up to the edge of the game ranger's track, seemingly keen to reclaim it.

The day was oppressively hot and quiet; the only sounds the grunts and immature growls of the wrestling cubs provoking each other unenthusiastically and the forlorn calls of a turtle dove on an unseen branch in the surrounding canopy. Even the huge clouds building like mountains in the distance offered no sound of thunder.

In one quick seamless movement the lioness raised herself to a sitting position. Turning her head, she looked down the track to where it disappeared into the distance, curving away behind the thorn trees. She sniffed the air, her ears rotating slowly as she assessed whether a sound might be an intruder.

A fly landed on an unhealed wound near her eye – the consequence of a recent flailing zebra hoof – and when a slow blink did not move the insect, she shook her head without shifting her gaze from the track. At the flapping sound of her shaking head, the cubs looked up briefly from their game, ever conscious they needed to take heed of every move and sound she made.

It wasn't a ranger's vehicle – she knew that sound as they still patrolled the area occasionally even though the park had been closed to tourists in 1971, over a year ago. This was new, and any strange sound was treated as a threat unless it proved to be otherwise. She stood up now, the cubs instinctively attentive. Their game-playing was over and they immediately came to her side. Standing still, they just watched, unsure how to react. They waited for a sign from their mother.

The sudden agitated chattering of monkeys in the distance and the sound of fluttering birds leaving the canopy were all the confirmation she needed. With a growl and a quick look over her shoulder to make sure her cubs followed she moved silently into the bush. Instantaneously, all three were hidden from view within the thick undergrowth.

The sound of the three-ton Bedford army troop carrier clattered into earshot several seconds before its rounded, camouflaged snout appeared. The wide shoulders and back of a man in camouflage fatigues protruding from its cab roof soon came into view around the curve in the road. Engine thumping, its wheels rolled slowly, crunching through the loose gravel of the path as it moved. The large vehicle, which was carrying twenty-two infantrymen, took up all the space beneath the canopy of the thorn trees that stretched across the dusty track.

Advancing slowly, the vehicle pushed aside the spiky thorn-covered branches that squealed in protest against the open metal frame. The truck forced its way through the narrow channel designed to accommodate a game warden's Land Rover or the occasional family of elephants, rather than the bulky Bedford.

Given the vehicle's slow pace, there was little dust from its wheels and after a few quick steps to try and counter the truck's momentum, each recruit threw himself off the rear of the truck into clear air. From the comfort of his Land Rover behind them, Cliff was able to clearly see the contorted expression on each of their faces as they focused on landing upright.

The permanent force instructor, Sergeant Swartberg, stood on the Bedford's passenger seat; his knees level with the driver's head as his body poked out through the circular observation hatch in the roof of the cab. Every few seconds his whole body seemed to contort as he yelled his command, "Go! Go! Go!"

The instruction sent a recruit on the back of the open truck at a stamping trot towards the rear of the vehicle and into open space.

The force of each man being propelled upright off the back of the vehicle hopefully matched exactly the residual opposite force of the truck's forward motion. The timing had to be just right.

The one force not having a counter in this 'equal and opposite' equation was gravity. This meant the recruit, after momentarily being suspended with his head and shoulders level with the canopy either side of him, dropped gently upright to the ground with knees bent for impact. His rifle held diagonally at chest height, from his landing spot he could deploy like a frightened rabbit into the shelter of the bush, hopefully before being blown to bits by enemy fire. In a live situation, that was the theory at least.

The facial expressions of the jumping recruits ranged from bravado to downright terror as each set of army boots clattered towards the end of the truck's metal flatbed; its open clanging tailgate signalling their launch point. Cliff tensed with each leap as if he was doing the jump himself. It was like sitting in a car as a passenger and involuntarily stamping on a non-existent brake at the first sign of trouble.

This is probably an anecdote Brenda would like

for her book, Cliff thought. He remembered during his basic training that she had started writing, although she hadn't mentioned anything about that lately

"Nothing else to do in the evenings," she had written in a letter at the time. "I am writing a book about the futility of conscription."

She had insisted he always include a description of any funny or bizarre incident that had taken place whenever he wrote one of his letters home. To Cliff, all his army days seemed to be 'catch twenty-two' stuff so he had plenty of anecdotes.

With Brenda on his mind, while watching the spectacle before him, he found himself musing. Maybe this is how marriage worked – a leap of faith. Too much forward momentum when you landed, like an over-confident yet suddenly out-of-control skier, and you fell on your face. However, if entering the relationship tentatively and without enough commitment, the negative momentum dragged you stumbling backwards, like an amateur skier exiting a chair lift without conviction or confidence. You had to get it just right. Brenda often said he lacked commitment to their relationship. She liked to use the analogy of the chicken and the pig and say, "If not a commitment, at least make a contribution, Cliff. You're just along for the ride. At least the eggs please, I'm not asking for the bacon."

Muscle memory learnt in basic training four

years ago, from doing the same exercise from a vehicle crunching across the camp's dusty parade ground, served these recruits well now. Notwithstanding the odd stumble, most of them landed safely, scrambling left and right with their knees pumping high as they ran into the tall grass and bush, cursing the long thorns snagging their camouflage fatigues.

The loud blast of the locomotive's horn brought Cliff out of his motion-induced doze. He straightened in his seat, wondering how often his nodding head had slumped forward. When they travelled together on a bus or train Brenda always giggled when a sleepy passenger started nodding off near them.

"He's going... he's going... there he goes... and... he's back!" She would whisper in his ear between giggles, her long hair sometimes tickling the side of his face that made him laugh too. Cliff was always surprised at Brenda's sense of humour. Given the upbringing she had endured, he expected her to be more serious than she was. Yet Brenda was a keen observer who found the funny side to things that simply irritated him. Maybe it was her journalistic nature to see a different angle?

Sometimes she would be caught out by people

who would become suspicious she was laughing at them. Yet while he cringed in embarrassment, her smile-wrinkled blue eyes and grin somehow always got her out of trouble. If the subject of her amusement felt compelled to glare, they always glared at Cliff.

Recently there had been increasingly less fun in their relationship. She appeared to be preoccupied with something. Reflecting upon how distracted she seemed to be nowadays, Cliff stared out of the window at the tops of the thorn trees flashing by in a constant stream of green. Swaying gently with the train's movement, his eyelids started to droop.

*

The giraffe, in Cliff's dream, seemed to rock with the train's movement as it munched on the foliage of a thorn tree's uppermost branches, oblivious to the long thorns accompanying the greenery now being herded into its mouth by a large grey tongue. Occasionally the munching jaws and large black eyes would swoop down on the end of the long neck, eyes peering into Cliff's. He could feel the warmth of its breath as it whispered, in Brenda's voice.

"And... he's back."

*

Heaving himself upright once again, Cliff glanced at his fellow passengers, many of whom wore army fatigues. He wiped his hand surreptitiously across his chin in case he had dribbled saliva while he slept and wondered if his mouth had gaped open? *Not very becoming for an officer*, he thought. His grandma used to gape when she dozed on the couch in his mom's lounge. Her tongue was grey like the giraffe's, with whiskers on her chin too.

Through the train's window the closest thorn trees were passing by again; their distant cousins almost stationary. His thoughts returned to Brenda's response to his announcement that he had received notification from the army. He had been summoned to attend a training camp for three months; a summons he had dreaded receiving for years. After completing his 'basic' training, he never wanted anything to do with the army again. He knew this one would be the first of many that followed basic; the one this very train was taking him towards. Cliff had been a little disconcerted when, upon reading the letter, Brenda's mood had seemed to lift.

There was a sudden flash of white railings across the glass opening he stared through, accompanied by the momentary loud clanging of a bell. The train sped through the level crossing that the earlier horn blast had warned it was hurtling towards. He wondered if her reaction to the summons was also a warning – an indication that their relationship was not what it had been; that a crossroads was approaching.

Her demeanour had certainly been different when he had gone off to basic training a few years before. Then, she had tears in her eyes as the train pulled out of the station, holding onto Beryl for comfort. As for him, while standing at the window of the moving train, he had received a supportive pat on the back from his lifelong friend and cousin, Josh, who had also been called up in the same army training draft.

Brenda's first thought as she read Cliff's notification of call up had been that she would have some space, which was unexpected but not unwelcomed. Cliff being away would give her some time to think, and to try to understand the growing anxiety she was feeling. At first, she had assumed it was simply that her marriage had not fulfilled her expectations. She had thought their relationship would improve as the years went by, even though she knew this didn't include children; such was Cliff's reluctance. She had thought long and hard about that and had reached the conclusion that having children didn't necessarily mean fulfilment. *Would having them right the wrong that was done to me?*

Brenda felt that Cliff's disinterest in having a

child was more about his characteristic lack of commitment to anything, rather than specifically a lack of inclination to parenthood. She got the feeling he was going through the motions with their marriage; more to please his mother than her, she thought sometimes. Then she considered that no, it was not her marriage that was the problem. Rather, she began to suspect her discontent was more likely attributed to her lack of a mother or father and this was making her long for answers.

Brenda had no idea who her birth parents were. Her only true memories, and the formal records that existed, were of the foster homes she had been in. It was like she had been dropped from the sky into an orphanage before being placed in her first foster home. She must have been very young because she had no recollection of her first family at all. The next two foster homes came to an end as a result of foster parents getting divorced. Then a fourth placement ended because her foster mother could not tolerate her husband's insistence that their ten-year-old foster daughter sit on his lap in the driver's seat and learn to steer the car every day.

Fortunately, Brenda had already won a scholarship to go to university when her final foster home arrangement came to an end. This occurred after her foster father took her for a driving lesson shortly after she turned seventeen.

After seating her behind the steering wheel and taking ages to make sure his old-fashioned seat belts were fitting over her snugly, he closed the door and went around to the passenger seat.

Before letting Brenda drive, he slid across the bench seat of his old Chevrolet, putting his arms around her to make sure she knew how to hold the steering wheel correctly. He was very pedantic about where she placed her hands on the wheel, giving instructions quietly, his mouth close to her ear.

Brenda's awkwardness was growing into fear when suddenly a loud rapping on the driver's window made them both jump. The curled lips of her foster mother's snarl would remain in Brenda's mind forever.

Cliff never forgot his first afternoon in basic training. The bright blue Orange Free State sky had clouded over earlier and within a few hours it had become quite cold in the barracks where they sat waiting to be told what was happening next. They would learn quickly that there would be a lot of this in the army. Suddenly over the tannoy there were a few crackles of static and then an announcement.

"All recruits are instructed to change into warm clothing. Cardigan or other appropriate clothing.

No exceptions."

It was the forerunner to how their lives would now become nothing more than responding to one instruction after another. Fresh from a life where for as far back as he could remember he had been encouraged to think for himself and to show initiative, Cliff found this new way of life demeaning. Repetitive saluting, snapping to attention, marching and polishing brass buttons was the new normal; using starch and an electric iron – a first for most of them – to get the folds of a sleeping bag's inner sheet to appear perfectly square where it sat at the head of your barracks bed, was the new challenge.

*

On the parade ground three weeks into their basic training, Company Sergeant Major van Plettenhof was reading out who was going where for specialised training – who would be drivers, paratroopers and candidate officers, and who would remain as ordinary soldiers (or troopies as they were called by their instructors).

To pass the time during the train journey to camp, what role to choose was discussed at length, with recommendations coming from older brothers and others who had gone before. The sergeant major's first option of being a driver was highly sought after. The advice was to make yourself look busy in the vehicle pool all day, with a mostly unused cleaning rag in your hand, employed only if an instructor approached and you had to hastily slip your dog-eared paperback into your pocket and start wiping diligently at your truck's bodywork.

Having called out all the drivers' names, Sergeant Major van Plettenhof moved on to option two: paratrooper basic training. This role opened up the possibility for a recruit to potentially become one of the army's heroes as a 'maroon beret', facing the dangers of being dropped behind enemy lines, except there were no enemy lines at this point in time. Interested recruits had been taken on a tour of the paratrooper training facility nearby.

During their first week at basic training, several times a day Cliff and the others had noticed parallel lines of maroon berets either side of a moving, horizontal tree trunk in the distance, crossing the veld outside their perimeter fence. Arms encircled the tree trunk that had worn shiny from many years of being carried in such a way, and they watched as it bounced on the shoulders carrying it aloft.

Clomping forward like Lipizzaner stallions, these paratroopers-in-training proudly sang their team-building chant in time to the beat of their boots as they stamped across the stony ground towards seemingly nowhere in particular.

"Hidee hay, hidee ho, parabats are on the go. Hidee hay, hidee ho, parabats are on the go. Hidee hay, hidee ho, parabats are on the go."

*

The aspiring paratroopers, who had just returned from their tour, talked animatedly over each other in their haste to speak. Cliff and others in the barracks felt relieved they had not chosen the same path after what they heard.

The first thing they saw as they alighted from the troop carriers on their visit to Parachute Battalion HQ was the *aapkas* (monkey box) towering above them.

Weeks ago, on arrival at their training camp, they had noticed a mysterious tall steel structure in the distance. Up close it was foreboding, as high as a ten-storey building, with its crisscross steel girders making it look like something out of a King Kong movie. A dark doorway in the cabin, affixed to a small steel platform at the top of the tower, seemed as though it was staring down at them.

All the way up one side, a steel caged spiral staircase was attached to the frame of the tower. *Climbing that must be a challenge in itself*, Cliff thought, as he listened to the details of the visit now being recounted. The thick metal cable attached to a heavy steel plate above the doorway dropped almost vertically to the assembled group on the ground, before curving away from its steep descent to a suspended horizontal position a few metres above their upturned faces. The instructor leading their 'tour' had announced, "This is the jump you will do during assessment to see if you are serious about being in this unit."

He had barely finished speaking when a figure appeared at the opening. A thick steel wire was attached to the harness he wore that in turn was attached to a pulley contraption that ran along the top of the cable, dropping towards them and the ground.

Leaning slowly forward and downward into space, with his arms crossed over his upper chest he left the platform like a falling domino, dropping towards the gaping mouths and wide eyes of the faces below him.

The pilot and his co-pilot exchanged looks of dismay in the adrenalin-filled World War II C47 cockpit as they observed the solid cloud bank at penetration altitude. It obscured the entire western half of the thirty-five-kilometre-wide peninsula of the Normandy coast – their target.

Had radio silence not been imposed upon them during flight (surprise being the key element of the D-day strategy – preventing warnings of adverse weather), they would have known there was an opaque ground fog over many drop zones. As it was, they were already concerned without this knowledge.

The ashen-faced paratroopers waiting further back behind the crew in the interior of the C47 fuselage were even more ignorant of what awaited them that night, as were thousands of their comrades sitting in similar positions, in hundreds of neighbouring aircraft edging towards the French coastline through the black sky above the English Channel.

In the darkness, the planes seemed to spread endlessly towards the horizon, like a colony of flying foxes seeking food in an Australian evening sky.

*

The C47's appeared just as relentless as they droned toward the coast, equally single-minded about their intention: to deposit thousands of infantrymen behind the German lines of Omaha Beach.

Their mission was to destroy bridges and roads approaching the coast. This plan would prevent the Germans from sending reinforcements to stop the surprise invasion that was about to take place on the beaches they were soon to cross at high altitude. The paratroopers squirmed uncomfortably on the hard seats of the transporter, weighted down by their rifles, backpacks and explosives strapped to them.

The opaque ground fog over many drop zones not only meant that the accuracy of their aircraft's position was brought into question, but the pilots had no idea that the Germans had flooded vast areas of farmland. Their certainty of having arrived safely over France and crossed the coastline could prove to be misguided.

There was no turning back. Surprise was what the D-day strategy was about. Dispatchers in countless flying metal tubes across the dark skies of the Normandy coast sprang to their positions as 'go' warning lights were switched on by pilots.

The dark figures attached to static lines stamped towards the howling opening and sprang into the night. They appeared, for a brief time, to be in free-fall before their parachutes were jerked from their backpacks, leaving them to float, into the lights of flashing gun barrels below them.

When their bullets hit the backpacks of their descending enemy, German troops on the ground were delighted to watch the explosives detonating mid-air rather than on one of their bridges.

Many of the parachutists managed to land safely in the cold waters of the sea or the flooded farmlands, but then drowned under the weight of their explosives.

When Company Sergeant Major van Plettenhof reached the names on his clipboard allocated to option three – officer training –there were carefully disguised smirks and ridicule from the majority of recruits who felt those wanting this third option were taking the army too seriously; wanting to be a leader of men who had no interest in being there and just wanted to go home.

In reality, they were all like ducks out of water. None of them had any idea why they were in the army in the first place. All they knew was that announcing their call-up to parents after opening their official brown envelope unleashed a torrent of anecdotes from wartime fathers or uncles (and sometimes wartime nurse mothers too) about their time in World War II and how good this experience would be for them.

As the sergeant major called out names, the recruits fell out to join their various groups. Glancing around, Cliff noted that the number of recruits who had volunteered for the paratrooper qualification had dwindled dramatically since their visit to Parachute Battalion HQ and their introduction to the *aapkas*.

The company sergeant major gave the rest of them a broad grin. "Now for the leftovers. Unfortunately for you guys not all of you can be plain old troopies even if you are FAFIs and would love to be one."

They all grinned at his acronym – Fuck-all Ambition Fuck-all Interest. After a long pause while he preened his moustache, the company sergeant major continued in his guttural Afrikaans accent.

"Because there were not enough applications for officer hey, we have decided everyone with a matric is going to be on this officer training – whether you like it or not. You will all be blerry ice cream boys!" He grinned again, referring to the white epaulettes (candy stripes) worn by junior officers during their training. "Only those without matric who are not drivers or paratroopers... yes, I know, some of you didn't even go to blerry school... will be my troopies."

After another pause, which Cliff thought was done for dramatic effect, the company sergeant major yelled the command for some of them to step forward.

"Those with matric... forward... step."

There were not that many who had completed their schooling with a matriculation in this remaining group. Cliff had discovered one or two who could not even write and who had had to pay a willing person in their barracks to be the ghost-writer of their compulsory weekly letter home. Cliff unfortunately met the qualification for officer training and he allowed himself a small sigh of resignation. *Firstly having to reconcile with Josh's lucky escape and now this.* He came to attention and stepped forward smartly.

"Don't look so miserable men. Won't you enjoy it when you have pips on your shoulders and I have to salute *you*? That is why we will make your life a blerry misery for three months!" The company sergeant major growled; his accent accentuating the menace in his voice. "If I have to blerry salute you, you can blerry well earn it," the company sergeant major concluded.

He looked over his shoulder towards the horizon in response to an aside from his staff sergeant standing next to him. Behind them, across the dusty parade ground in the distance, a gigantic rolling dust cloud moved rapidly towards them, swallowing distant buildings while the sky above remained a clear blue. It seemed more than just an imminent dust storm to the newly assembled candidate officers. Finding themselves suddenly in a strange orange twilight, the company sergeant major's words echoed in their ears and it felt like an omen of hard times ahead.

Looking back, the company sergeant major stood smartly to attention himself, "Companee! Companee! Attenn... shun! Diiss... missed."

*

As he and the others broke away and ran to their barracks to tear washing off clothes lines and close windows against the impending dust storm, Cliff reflected that his friend Josh had been fortunate to be given an unexpected fourth option: honourable early discharge.

Through his broad grin, Josh's words had reached them as he ambled across to where they had stood waiting for him. He had been called to the administration office by a panting camp orderly as they were about to start their after-work soccer game.

"Something about the urine test I did. They say I need to see a specialist ASAP. Said I should go home. Discharged me as not fit for duty. Train tomorrow morning."

His slim frame rocked as his barracks mates around him shoved him and slapped his back in congratulation.

"Lucky bugger. Dammit!"

"What mixture did you concoct to get that result you conniving bugger?"

"We need some of that!"

Cliff felt a twinge of guilt now, remembering that instead of concern for Josh's health he felt only envy that his old friend had escaped what he still had to face.

Josh hadn't gone to his own doctor as instructed... not until he had to.

A few months before he had found himself sitting in a Land Rover watching people throw themselves off the back of a truck, Cliff had been sitting on the bus to work, staring at the crumpled envelope he had carried in his pocket for the last three days. The stamp of the South African Defence Force (the government's name for its armed forces) told him it was from the army. Without a doubt it was the dreaded call-up to one of the training camps that followed basic training; each three months long in some God forsaken place on one of South Africa's borders. There had been increasingly more reports in the newspapers lately about insurgent activities on the country's northern border with Angola. By not opening it he could continue to enjoy the state of denial he was in.

Cliff knew that the ANC's military wing – Umkhonto we Sizwe – had begun to establish training camps in Angola in the early 70s, under guidance from Cuban and Russian 'advisors'. Infiltration through South Africa's vast northern borders by heavily armed insurgents was increasing.

He and others who had been conscripted into training were now being called up not only for additional training but to support the country's police posted to outlying borders to ensure its sovereignty was not threatened by those opposing the apartheid regime.

His fellow passenger gave him an irritated glance as he leant against her to get the letter back into his pocket.

*

Brenda found the crumpled letter in his pocket as they prepared to load the washing machine one Saturday morning. After emptying more than one load of wet washing speckled with soggy tissue confetti, she never trusted him to check his own pockets.

"Really Cliff? This hasn't even been opened," she said, as she handed him the wrinkled envelope. "Read your post for God's sake!"

Tearing the envelope open he expected the worst, but it wasn't what he feared. It was just a letter from the administration office of the Chief of the Defence Force.

*

The only other letter from the Defence Force Brenda had ever seen in her home was when Cliff had been called up for basic training. Not having older brothers, Brenda had no idea what conscription was about, so when that letter had arrived to threaten her newly established relationship she was upset and surprised.

Cliff had explained that the Defence Force had created a largely part-time unit of conscripts who he supposed were being trained in case there was ever another war similar to the one his uncles had volunteered for before he was even born. He remembered them sharing countless anecdotes about it, recounted again by his mother, who had written about her memories of that time in letters to him during training.

"I am learning more about my uncles as young men in Mom's letters than I ever did when I was living at home," he told Brenda in one of his letters. "Desert, and tanks and digging trenches. And endless waiting. I'm surprised on my first day I did not find a shovel included with my kit."

*

The letter he now read alongside Brenda, accompanied by the pulsating sound of their washing machine, stated that as he had not received his commission at basic training, even though he had successfully completed his officer training during that time (*they got that wrong*, thought Cliff), he was thereby retrospectively commissioned in the rank of lieutenant. A formal letter of appointment would follow via registered post including a certificate of commission, and list of insignia depicting his rank that he should order, to attach to his uniform.

Although Cliff had been coerced into officer training during his basic training, he had never completed the course, managing to get himself transferred to an army camp nearer home for some exaggerated 'family crisis' his family did not know they were having. Therefore, the promotion was clearly an error by a clerk at Defence Force headquarters.

The following morning Cliff awoke feeling groggy, having tossed and turned all night in a mild panic that he might be found out to be an imposter. Rising from the sofa he had been sent to by Brenda, Cliff phoned Defence Force HQ. After being put on hold and transferred countless times, he was finally put through to a staff sergeant who handled such matters. Cliff explained his concern regarding the notification he had received in the last few days and how it related to what had transpired in basic training.

"I'm sorry Lieutenant..."

My God, he's already calling me lieutenant!

"But our records only show you were enrolled in the officer training. There is nothing about you being transferred out before completion."

The more Cliff protested the more irritated the staff sergeant became, asking Cliff angrily at one point if he was implying he was stupid or lying. Cliff grimaced into the phone and bit his lip.

"The record shows what it shows. That's all

there is to it. If you don't want to be an officer, you can resign your commission."

"OK, great," said Cliff, momentarily relieved and his hopes lifted. "How do I do that?"

"Well, you can't resign your commission until you have actually been active as an officer... which you haven't."

Cliff could almost hear the smirk in his voice.

"But I don't even know what an officer does, what his duties are. I'm not trained!" Cliff tried not to sound like he was pleading. "How can I be active if I don't know how?"

"Our records say you *are* trained, so you won't have a problem, *Lieutenant*." The staff sergeant was clearly enjoying himself now. "Wait for your first camp, and at the end of it you will have been active enough to resign."

Thinking he had done all he could to rectify his predicament and resigning himself to his fate Cliff decided, upon reflection, that seniority might actually make life easier for the duration of his training. Oh, what the hell! He would go along with it until such time as they found him out. He wondered when a call-up to his first three-month post-basic camp would follow.

That evening, when she came home, Brenda just shrugged when he told her about his unearned promotion and said it must be encouraging to be such a high-ranking clerical error.

"Your mother will be pleased," she said.

Cliff had always loved the way Brenda moved her shoulders as a form of expression. Unless she was actually laughing, the beautiful features of her face were always composed. He always felt he had somehow been gifted with an intimate gesture when she shrugged.

"Maybe there's a book in the library on how to be an officer," she said with a straight face, but he caught the look in her eyes. She shook her head in disbelief. *How does a man lead when he goes through life trailing behind whoever he can find to follow?* she thought.

Sighing, she reached for the notebook in her briefcase. She used it for making notes for the book she had started when Cliff was in basic training but had yet to complete.

"One day Brenda... one day," she murmured to herself.

"What? What did you say?" Cliff asked, but she just smiled and shook her head slightly.

As their Land Rover followed slowly behind the troop carrier, Cliff and his driver could see there was one recruit who had still not made the leap into space. The last troop remaining on the carrier seemed transfixed, like a deer caught in headlights, leaning his back against the truck's cab staring blankly towards the tailgate as if it was the edge of an abyss.

He had managed to ease himself towards the rear of the waiting line of jumpers whenever his turn had come, but now there was no one left to hide behind. Even from his position in the Land Rover, Cliff could see how fragile the young man looked. He had a slight build, his face pale against his short black curly hair. He wore a terrified expression, and his slender white fingers seemed incongruous as they trembled around the butt and barrel of his rifle.

"He's never going to jump. Not that moffie," mumbled Cliff's driver, Sam, with a grin. Cliff pointedly ignored the derogatory comment sometimes used by Afrikaans speakers to describe anyone who looked effeminate and was therefore presumed to be gay.

The instructor was now leaning far out over the ledge of the cab's circular hatch, stretching to get close to the hesitant recruit's ear. His position gave him the appearance of a scrawny-necked vulture, reaching to feed a returned fledgling perched on the edge of the nest.

"GO!" He shouted so suddenly next to the boy's ear that it made the recruit jump. His command was in fact so loud they were even startled in the Land Rover.

"Uh-oh, Sarge Swartberg is getting angry," Sam said in Afrikaans. Cliff supposed he was speaking in the other main language of the country to make the point that, as the instructor was permanent force, he therefore had to be Afrikaans-speaking.

Never mind the loud command. The red face is enough to show he's worked up all right, Cliff thought. The young recruit did not move. Cliff could see a wet patch spreading in his fatigues below the butt of the rifle he held against his body.

Oh God. Cliff waited for his driver to spot it.

Sam chortled, "I *knew* it."

Cliff glanced sideways at him, smiling. His large beak-like nose had been the first thing Cliff noticed about Sam that night at basic training years ago when it had first appeared above their Bedford's rear flap. It followed the rest of the gear he, still out of sight, had pushed over the tailgate into the back of the security guard-carrying truck Cliff and the others were already seated in.

With nothing more than rifles clamped between their legs and rolled up sleeping bags on their laps, they had stared agog at the paraphernalia that followed Sam's rifle as it clattered to the steel floor: a pillow, sleeping bag, small portable radio, packet of crisps and a large bottle of Coca-Cola.

Cliff remembered thinking that as Sam clambered onto their truck, somehow this recruit was going to make their inaugural night of guard duty somewhat memorable...

Behind them, a five-metre-high razor-wire fence towered above the recruits standing to attention under the security flood lights, their sleeping bags on the ground in front of them. They were about to begin the first guard duty mission of their basic training. Behind the surly-faced instructor before them, stood a small guard's tent, backed against a replica of the fence they stood below. Inside it were eight tiny steel beds to accommodate the recruits during their shift pattern of two hours on, four hours off.

The strip of ground between the fences, large enough to accommodate a pair of Land Rovers, was going to be their focus for the night. It surrounded a huge square parking area with a concrete tower at each corner upon which hundreds of armoured vehicles were stationed. The silent, ominous heavy calibre barrels poked out from them in various directions, waiting for a war.

Cliff and the others had all laughed when Sam had climbed into their truck with all his paraphernalia, but it didn't seem funny now as they all stood to attention, stony-faced. The instructor prodded the toe of his boot into the bulging sleeping bag and pillow lying in front of Sam, before launching into a diatribe about the perils of sleeping whilst on guard duty. Cliff imagined their faces were just a few inches apart but not daring to look to his side, he pictured a profile of the two heads instead – Sam's nose dwarfing that of the instructor's. *No match for Sam's*, he had thought to himself and smiled while keeping his own face forward.

*

It was midnight and it seemed like he had only just closed his eyes when Cliff felt his shoulder being grabbed roughly. A loud voice told him to *move it*. How was he going to survive not sleeping for the next two hours? Before ducking through the tent flap, anxiety replaced tiredness when he saw his partner for his guard stint that night was Sam who was still resisting the steel grip of the human alarm clock trying to shake him awake. Outside the tent, having left his rolled up sleeping bag piled in a corner with everyone else's, Cliff stood to attention. With his rifle held to his shoulder he was ready to march in a single column of two – one behind the other – to his allocated tower.

Finally, a bleary-eyed, tousled-haired Sam stumbled out of the guard tent, rifle slung awkwardly over his shoulder. His pillow and hastily crumpled up sleeping bag were tucked under one arm; a large bag of crisps and a bottle of Coca-Cola under the other.

"This is bullshit," he yawned. "I'm a driver not a fucking security guard!" He burped loudly, grinning at Cliff. "Sorry."

Leaving an open-mouthed Cliff still standing stiffly to attention, Sam yawned loudly again before strolling off between the rows of floodlights that lit the route to their guard tower. Cliff followed, rifle held to his shoulder, marching stiffly, like the wooden toy soldiers he and Josh used to play with as children. With his free arm swinging as straight as a die, he felt silly following behind an ambling Sam who was yawning repeatedly and loudly.

Clanging slowly up the steel ladder to the top of their lookout tower, Cliff smiled to himself as his guard duty partner below lay out his sleeping bag on the dusty concrete floor forming the base of the guard tower. Cliff knew this was an anecdote Brenda would want for her book.

"Help yourself to the crisps, Cliff. Wake me if you hear the instructor's Land Rover coming, hey mate."

It wasn't long before Sam's snores echoed up the concrete tube of the guard tower that a vigilant Cliff peered out from.

Now in their Land Rover, as they watched the unfolding drama on the back of the truck, that same beak-nose that introduced Sam to Cliff during basic overlooked a large bushy moustache.

The facial hair did not seem to belong on his face, almost as though it had been grown for the occasion to create a caricature of an authority figure.

His moustache was decorated with crumbs from the sandwich he had held onto earlier while his other had alternated erratically between steering wheel and gearstick. Sam showed no sympathy for the unfortunate recruit in the truck before them, only scorn for his frustrated instructor; his head nodding knowingly in I-told-you-so amusement. Sam had dealt with his fair share of authority figures in the army and would have given them all the finger if he could.

Reading *this is what you get* into Sam's nodding gesture, one of the letters his mother had written to him during his basic training came into Cliff's mind. It had been about her brother Raymond, who had been discharged shortly after enlisting and starting his training during World War II because he was deemed 'unfit for service'.

Cliff had never known him but his auntie 'Chel had told him and Josh about Raymond once, when they were children. He supposed his mother had mentioned her brother in response to his letter about Josh's sudden departure in the first few days of basic training, when he'd told her about Josh's discharge due to him being 'unfit for service'. Though Josh had been discharged on medical grounds, Cliff didn't doubt that there were conscripts out there now who had been deemed 'unfit for service' for the same reason as Raymond. He wondered how the unfortunate recruit in front of them had not suffered the same fate at his basic training.

On the troop carrier, looking down through the circular turret opening he stood in, the instructor yelled, "Stop! Stop!" to the driver. The vulture disappeared back down into its nest, only to reappear through the cab door as he hauled himself onto the back of the now stationary truck. He grabbed the recruit by the arm and dragged him towards the tailgate. "Now, you can try it while we are stopped," he growled. "JUMP... JUMP!"

Poised at the edge of the truck's tailgate, the thin frame seemed to lean forward slightly in slow motion and then accelerate as the hand at the end of a burly arm thrust it forward. There was a brief mid-flight scream that was stifled as boots landed awkwardly on the gravel.

His outstretched arms and small hands with a white-knuckled-grip on the rifle did little to stabilise his toppling body before it crashed forward into the gravel. His helmet spun away like an empty bowl knocked onto a kitchen floor while his elbows and knees received scant protection from the army-issue fatigues as they smashed into the gravel.

The sergeant jumped down from the truck. He bent over the prostrate recruit who was now on all fours struggling to right himself without releasing his grip on the rifle. His basic training had taught him that dropping his rifle in front of a permanent force instructor was a death wish, no matter the circumstances.

The scene was being observed a little way off by the last few troops already deployed, who were now partly obscured by tall grass and thorn trees. They were not sure whether to laugh or feel sorry for their fellow recruit, even though there had been a few asides in the first days of the camp about him being 'effeminate', and his solitary swim in the lake every evening in the fading light. He was still one of them though, not a fucking permanent force prick.

"Stand up! Opstaan! Get up!" the sergeant yelled again. "You will do it again and again and again until you get it right!"

"No! That's enough, Sergeant." Cliff heard himself shout the command as he climbed from the Land Rover with more authority than he expected.

Having never had to say, let alone shout, anything with authority before, it sounded foreign to him. His authority had been assigned through the 'pip' – the silver star pinned on each of his shoulder epaulettes.

"That's enough, Sergeant," Cliff repeated quietly, now that he had the instructor's attention. "This troopie is going to badly injure himself if he keeps trying to do what he is not capable of."

The instructor looked incandescent with rage but he brought himself smartly to attention as he was required to do before an officer. Controlling his voice he said, "But sir, he has to complete this exercise. It's his duty."

The recruit was standing up now; pale-faced and trying to hide the wet and fortunately now dusty patch in his fatigues with the butt of his rifle.

"Then give him a job in the mail tent or radio tent or wherever it might be more likely he *will* do his duty. You can see as well as I can that he will never be able to do this exercise."

The sergeant had been told by the commanding officer Colonel Roverstone that this lieutenant was assigned to the training camp by Defence Force HQ to observe and report on army training activities and their effectiveness; even to make recommendations. He decided it was not worth risking a negative note in a report by continuing to push back.

*

Brenda had shaken her head in amazement when Cliff had told her what his assignment was for the camp. *An officer promoted through a clerical error is going to make recommendations on training? Time to get out that manuscript I started when our 'officer' was in his basic training.*

*

Growling inwardly, the sergeant realised it was best to let this go. *These civvy boys, coming from their jobs in the city to play soldiers for a few months are a joke. Thirty years I've been in this army, including a war.*

"Yes, sir," said Sergeant Swartberg. He turned back to the waiting recruit who jumped, as did Cliff, when the sergeant bellowed suddenly, "DEPLOY! DEPLOY!" The sergeant raised his arm, pointing to where the other recruits had taken up positions amongst the thorn trees. "DEPLOY!"

In the Land Rover, Sam smiled to himself and thought, *I wonder how much of that bellow was for the recruit and how much was for the general?* He had taken to calling Cliff 'General' since finding he had been promoted to lieutenant.

Walking back to his Land Rover, the 'general' was having the same thought. *You've made an enemy there, Lieutenant.*

Chapter 3

Communals: Old and New

It was the unmistakable smell of canvas that reminded Cliff where he was as he surfaced, eyes still closed, from a deep sleep on the first morning of his post-basic training camp. He lay motionless, trying to suppress the mounting dismay as the realisation he was not at home returned to him. He was in the middle of nowhere for three months at the camp a train and thereafter an uncomfortable troop carrier had brought him to the night before.

This was the first of many post-basic training camps he would be called up for. It was also one that would give him the chance to be active as an officer in order to earn the right to resign his unwanted and unearned commission.

When he allowed his eyelids to part, he discovered it was just as dark with his eyes open. Through the thin canvas walls of his tent he could clearly hear the intermittent waking calls of nearby birds in the bush around him. Each call was different – a feathered orchestra tuning its instruments – awaiting the conductor to appear above the horizon in the east and release them to the day.

Towards the end of that first day, the adjutant, with a wry smile at Cliff, pointed out a wooden shack to him. It had a rusty iron roof, a single window and a door that hung half ajar on a solitary rusty hinge. "Your office, Lieutenant," he proclaimed.

It was one of the few permanent buildings – now reserved for administration – in this mainly tent town set up in the middle of the bush south of the border between Namibia and Angola. It had been initially constructed for police contingents.

The surrounding bush, part of a game park, had been a hot spot in the past, favoured by freedom fighters because of its dense cover. In recent years, however, it had been avoided by them due to the dangers posed by the park's lions as these insurgents made their way on foot towards their targets. After some messy encounters, activity had tapered off, much to the relief of the army conscripts who became the game park's new guests. The camp was now used mainly for training activities, although it was still not far from the red zone.

Cliff's designated office had a makeshift toilet

and shower tacked onto it, accessed through a narrow door in the corner of the room. When he discovered he had his own private facilities as he inspected the tiny, dusty office, he mentally patted himself on the back for his decision to make the best of his serendipitous promotion.

Army life suddenly seemed more pleasant. Even with no doubt a cold-water shower on offer, this was still a lot better than using the open-air communal showers or bathing in the nearby lake. He wouldn't miss sharing a six-seater wooden bench communal toilet either, perched above a trench dug in the ground surrounded by meagre waist-high hessian walls for privacy.

Before discovering this facility was available, Cliff had resolved to schedule his ablution time for the dawn hours so as to avoid any awkwardness with fellow campmates as well as the countless flies dominating proceedings in this hot bushland, known for seeking out the most inconvenient places to land.

The Romans considered shared open stone toilets with running water to be part and parcel of life. They facilitated social interaction, especially for the poor, so would probably not have felt awkward, Cliff thought, as he clomped down the steps of his new office to collect the military standard computer and other equipment the adjutant said the quartermaster had ready for him.

One evening, during basic training, the underlying design principle of Roman sanitary infrastructure proved effective for the modern recruits too in their hour of need. Earlier that evening while sitting on his bed, pen poised above paper as his mind wandered, Cliff had an uninterrupted view through the open door of his barracks to the ablution block entrance across the way. He had made a comment once in a letter to his mother: 'from my bed, across the road, I have a view to die for!'. Beryl had since repeated this many times over tea with her friends as a funny anecdote.

A few minutes later, his letter writing had been interrupted suddenly by an intense twinge in his lower abdomen, making him look up with a grimace. He noticed there seemed to be a line forming at the toilet entrance now. In fact it was already as far back as the brick walkway between the lines of barracks.

Never seen a queue for the toilets before, he thought, as the griping pain passed and he looked back down to his letter with an ironic smile. *It was quite an exciting day today, Brenda. A line formed for the toilets!* Weekly compulsory letter writing was the bane of every recruit's life as they tried to find interesting content amid their drab, repetitive routines.

Cliff sometimes felt he was under additional

pressure as he knew Brenda treated his letters as research. After his very first anecdotes about being instructed over the tannoy to put a cardigan on and their heads being shaved during their first few days at camp, she had responded positively, telling him to include anything he thought she would find funny in his letters.

"There's a book in there somewhere, Cliff."

Staring at his writing, Cliff had shaken his head, wondering what she would find funny.

*

"Wow, there's custard with dessert tonight," exclaimed someone in the line in front of him, as they shuffled forward, each clasping a steel mess tray with pressed-out compartments onto which their evening meal would be plonked by permanent force mess workers. The eyes of these impassive faces dared them to make a comment about the food they were dishing up. "Come on, just one moan, troopie," they seemed to say.

Normally dessert was just a tin of mixed fruit, served to round off an equally uninteresting main meal. The accompanying side dish always consisted of two slices of bread with a frozen square of butter firmly stuck in between. If you were in a hurry to eat a slice of your bread, no matter how surgically you parted it from its Siamese twin, it ended up with a matching square hole in its centre.

This evening was the first meal after calling off their hunger strike; one that started on the basis of a World War II anecdote: 'my dad was a prisoner of war and they were sent chocolate by the Red Cross to supplement their diet, so how healthy must it be for you? And aren't babies brought up on milk?'. This assertion had seemed to support the rationale behind their decision to go on a food strike or, more accurately, a chocolate-eating, milk-drinking binge.

For a week they sat in the mess each evening with unused mess trays in front of them, eating chocolate and drinking milk purchased from the kiosk adjoining the mess hall, convinced they were on a diet that could sustain them during their protest; a protest the mess workers seemed oblivious of.

The strike, although soon enjoying the support of many other barracks, had made absolutely no difference to the quality of the food or the attitude of those preparing it, and had been prematurely terminated due to the rampant constipation it caused! Perhaps tonight though, the introduction of custard was an indication their message had got through?

Cliff watched the faces in front of him to confirm his taste buds were not playing a trick on him. Although it was a nice change to have the custard mixed with the fruit, it had a distinct chalky mint flavour.

The range of expressions around him seemed to agree with his consensus and he was just on his last spoonful when suddenly one of the late starters dropped his spoon on his tray with a clang.

"I came to army training to get 'mother's revenge?'. I know this taste," he went on. "This is milk of magnesia! My mother always gave it to us as kids, my brother and I, when we were constipated. She camouflaged it with custard, just like this."

"Nah, it's just mint-flavoured custard. Bit old though," came a counter observation.

"They probably buy the custard powder in bulk. Store it for years," laughed another recruit.

"You mean the rats have been shitting in it?" laughed another.

"Yes, because they ate it in the first place!"

"Talk about shitting," said the first recruit. "My mom used to give us just a tablespoon full but this tastes like it has about ten spoons in it!"

By the time they had deposited their pans in the racks of the large washer alongside the exit, most had already forgotten their custard experience and were engaged in other conversations as they strolled up the brick walkway between the long line of barracks. Some, like Cliff, were already back in their barracks, sitting with pen in hand on adjacent steel beds, hunched over their obligatory weekly letter home.

*

The second griping pain to hit Cliff was intense enough to clarify in his mind the reason why there was a growing line outside the toilets, and why there were so few people on the beds around him.

As he strode hastily across the walkway to the ablution block, he looked up and down the rows of barracks and saw long lines had formed outside all the other toilet block entrances too.

His line consisted of grimacing young men slightly bent over with hands on hips, shifting gingerly from one boot to the other. As Cliff joined the back of the line, conversation was limited, squeezed from lips held tightly in various contorted facial expressions.

"Can't... hold... on... much... longer."

"I'm going to explode!"

"Bad, bad, bad, bad."

"It's going to burn!"

"Hurry up in there!" someone else yelled.

A pale-faced recruit emerged and informed the waiting line of men about the carnage inside.

"Smells really, really bad in there. Couple of guys never made it in time. They can't clean up because there are guys even crouching in the communal showers now, running the water."

Cliff heard a murmur from the recruit behind

him. "Yup, that's good thinking and appropriate signage."

He turned around to see what he meant. A red fire bucket had been placed on the gravel below its hanging latch on the barrack wall. It was partially hidden under two large white buttocks but the word FIRE written on the side was visible.

"Whoever brings me a toilet roll gets to use my bucket next," the owner called over his shoulder.

However, those nearest him had already hobbled off, stooping like old men, sliding one boot after the other, as they sought to commandeer their own fire buckets from the corners of other barrack walls.

Now, thinking laterally about their pressing needs, the victims of what came to be known as 'the charge of the shite brigade' cast around for something that would offer a higher volume solution than the limited number of fire buckets on offer. It came when a desperate recruit simply pulled down his fatigues and squatted over the brick storm water drain that ran parallel to the walkway between the rows of barracks. Walking, doubled over, Cliff joined several others. With their fatigues around their ankles, each crouched on the edge of the drain, shoulder to shoulder, like birds on an overhead telephone wire.

An enterprising recruit, already free of his burden, had unwound a fire hose from its reel on a barracks wall and positioned it so that water gushed along the bricks in the drain. Others further down the line of barracks did the same with their hoses, and with fresh water surging across the bricks of the drain, a rudimentary sewerage system was soon in play.

Within a few minutes, available space along this spontaneous Romanesque toilet drain was at a premium (as were the toilet rolls being passed up and down the squatting line of recruits). Even entertainment was on hand as a recently relieved recruit marched up the walkway, glaring down dramatically at the faces of those crouched below him along the drain while doing an impression of Company Sergeant Major van Plettenhof.

"So, you blerry FAFIs. Say you don't like my food, hey?" he said loudly, in an exaggerated Afrikaans accent. "So, you think you can eat your blerry chocolate on my shiny vark panne, hey? Now, you know what happens when you disrespect my chef, hey? You like my mint surprise, hey? I make your life a blerry misery, hey!"

"Fuck off and get some toilet rolls, smart arse." This was the only response he got from his strained, captive audience who were focused on passing the few precious toilet rolls they had up and down the line, and concentrating on not falling backwards into the fetid stream now gushing below them.

Sitting at the one rickety desk in the office the adjutant had allocated him and rifling through his dusty notes from his last few field observations, Cliff wondered if anybody in a Defence Force department would ever actually read what he was compiling. He transcribed his notes in the format stated in the dossier that was handed to him by the adjutant on his arrival, making an educated guess when he did not have the facts.

A tentative knock on the open door made him look up.

"Yes?"

Cliff saw it was the young recruit from the day before. Other than his fatigues being ripped at the knees, he seemed unharmed by his ordeal. Under his black curly fringe and thick eyebrows were the bluest eyes Cliff had ever seen. He felt for a moment like they were piercing his innermost thoughts.

"Your mail, sir. They collect letters each day from an army mail collection point in the local town," he said by way of an explanation, as he handed Cliff an envelope. Cliff took the envelope from a hand with badly grazed knuckles.

Glancing at the envelope, he smiled to see the precise handwriting of his mother. *Unreal! I've only been here a few days and she has already got a letter to me. She has reinitiated her army training camp letter routine*, he thought.

"Thank you. Recovered from yesterday's spacewalk I see."

The recruit nodded.

"Good. So, they gave you a mail room job then?"

"Not really sir. Sergeant Swartberg asked me to bring that letter with me because I had to report to you anyway, sir."

It appeared Sergeant Swartberg knew more about the processes relating to junior officers than Cliff did, which was not surprising. The sergeant had reconciled himself with Cliff's orders. It was best to rid himself of a recruit who was going to struggle to keep up with the physical regime, especially when his instructional technique was being monitored.

It was a standard regulation that junior officers were assigned a batman – an orderly – for daily duties deemed inappropriate for an officer. As Cliff was the only junior officer on camp, it seemed he was to have a batman all to himself. However, he was not sure what to ask him to do. He did not see himself asking the young recruit to clean his boots. *Maybe he could take over this damned paperwork*, he thought.

"Well let's start with your name. Private..."

"It's Peter, sir. Peter Pike. I know sir – who would give their child initials like that?"

"I've heard worse. Well, if we are going to work together every day we will need to dispense with army jargon. Unless other officers are around, it's

Peter and Cliff, OK?"

"Sure. What are my duties then sir? Sorry – Cliff."

"You can start by typing up all my notes and correcting the grammar and spelling too. Can you do that? Firstly though you better ask the adjutant if he can find you a desk. Oh yes, and our driver is Sam. You'll *love* him," Cliff said quietly to himself, as Peter negotiated the steps outside. Turning his eyes from his orderly's departing back, Cliff smiled to himself as he opened his mother's letter.

When her only son went off to basic training Beryl Barkerfield had decided to support her boy by sending him regular letters to keep up his spirits, just as she had done with her brothers when they joined the army during World War II. She had been just a teenager when her three big brothers enlisted to go to war.

So once a fortnight, her letter to Cliff included a World War II anecdote and indeed any other memory that came to mind.

Beryl's letter told of how one afternoon, pausing as he passed through the assembled men, their supreme commander happened to look directly at Frank and called out to him:

"How are you doing soldier?"

Uncle Frank had snapped to attention,

somewhat flustered, and to the delight of his mirthful comrades, he had blurted out, "Not so fucking dusty, sir."

His mother had used a few asterisks to disguise the profanity.

*

Josh and he had also exchanged letters during basic training. The rule stated that recruits had to write two letters home every fortnight: one to a parent or spouse and the other to a friend. Failure to do so could mean extra guard duty or a cancelled weekend pass. Josh's letters were always addressed to him as Combat General C. Barkerfield VC or similar variations, which earned Cliff a few scowls from his PF instructors as they distributed the mail.

As a result of being handed back a year of his life he thought he had lost to the army, when Josh returned after his unexpected discharge, he found himself at a loss for something to do. He had recently completed university but with a year of army training looming, he had not given much thought to a career thereafter. Now he was home however, and a chance meeting with Brenda proved to be serendipitous. Listening to her describe the day-to-day activities and challenges of her job had re-ignited his enthusiasm for journalism.

He had always enjoyed putting together reports and essays at university, and during one of his semesters had completed a short course on journalism. His excitement at having discovered a possible career however had been diminished somewhat by the cynical lecturer who ran the course.

"And don't forget – if any of you want to get a job as a journalist, good luck. You've got more chance of finding that needle in the proverbial haystack." This was how he always concluded his lectures and he would snigger at his remark.

"Well, he is not far off, I'm afraid," Brenda laughed, as he relayed his experience. "But as with all things, it's who you know not what you know. Let me see what I can do, Joshie."

When she called a few days later he was delighted to hear her words.

"Want to start at the bottom Josh? You may be sweeping the office floor some days."

I finally got around to going to a specialist. Remember it was recommended by our camp hospital doctor? And recently I had some guidance from my kidneys, ha ha. Since getting back I had

been doing quite a bit of partying, as you do, and I thought all I needed to do was to cut back and get a bit healthier in order to stop feeling shit all the time.

It turns out I have a problem with my kidneys so have been having a whole lot of tests with more to come. They have given me some really good meds though, so feeling a lot better.

Just thought I would let you know so you don't feel too bad about my 'Great Escape'. Wink, wink did you like that, hey? World War II connotation? Prisoners of war? Colditz? The book, Cliff! Duh!

I look forward to some of your boring army news!

Your faithful servant and likely Pulitzer Prize winner,
Josh

Chapter 4

Discovering

Most days, Cliff was away from camp with his driver, Sam, monitoring patrols or training exercises. He would return with dusty and crumpled notebooks for Peter to decipher and transcribe. He generally stayed on after the day had officially ended, to work through Cliff's 'scrawl' (as Brenda called it).

Cliff presumed Peter stayed late because he was more comfortable in the office on his own than with a tent full of macho, cussing recruits. He was also aware that his batman had taken the liberty of using their office toilet and shower, which was fine with him. If Cliff felt uncomfortable with communal toilet seats and showers, what must it be like for Peter?

While observing Peter's slim shoulders hunched over the keyboard, Cliff had thought to himself that even if Private Pike was not gay, given his demeanour he was never going to be comfortable with a bunch of rat-bag young recruits, free from their behavioural limits set by wives and girlfriends; revelling in being able to carry on once again like obnoxious fifth-formers in a school dormitory or a changing room after a rugby game.

As the days went by and they became more familiar and comfortable with each other, their conversations turned to personal subjects. Cliff was surprised to find out that although Peter had missed the ballot-based draft that was employed in the days immediately before conscription was enforced, he had still volunteered for army training.

"Why on earth would you volunteer for this bullshit?" Cliff laughed, incredulous.

"Well to be honest I didn't really. My father volunteered me, basically – said it would make a man of me. He insisted army training would make me more physical. I would fill out, get stronger and develop an interest in sport. What he really meant was stop me from becoming a queer." Peter smiled at the look of embarrassment on his boss's face.

Peter's father, James Pike, had predictably had the nickname Fishie at kindergarten. At junior school, as the other boys grew and left him behind in stature, he became known as Jockey. Even now when he met his friends for a beer, he always made sure he sat on a bar stool. Standing at the bar was not for him; it always brought out dumb jokes from the barman, Fred.

Fred would smile at those standing alongside Jockey. "Enjoying your sit down over a beer hey, Jockey? Been a long day?" he would say, in his most innocent tone.

He wasn't especially sensitive about his physique and accepted the jibes from his friends good-naturedly. He knew he was well liked and respected. Notwithstanding his stature, they all knew that Jockey was a ferocious fighter not to be tangled with.

He was sensitive though – about the fact that in the bar his friends were always talking about their sons' escapades and sporting achievements, whereas Peter hated sports of any kind. This was unlike his outgoing, twin sister Jodie who did well at whatever sport she participated in. However, that fact didn't help when the men were discussing their sons. He didn't know if any of them even had daughters.

Both Jodie and Peter had inherited some of their father's genes, and although they weren't short like him, they had identical slim builds. James Pike worried terribly what his friends thought of his son. Worst still, as he had the same short curly hair and similar walk to his sister, from a distance Peter was often mistaken for her.

Even at kindergarten Jodie knew instinctively that her brother would need her protection. His gentle nature invited dominance – sometimes even aggression – from the other boys, so she kept a watchful eye on her sibling. If she spotted more than one boy at a time talking to Peter in the playground, she would sidle over to assess the tone of the interaction.

If there was a potential bullying incident brewing, she would intervene, for the most part diplomatically, but sometimes more forcefully when required. Jodie was not averse to swinging her school bag at the head of an aggressive schoolboy bully if they were pushing her brother around.

Once they reached an age when testosterone drove Peter's peers towards a new set of urges, the protective blanket Jodie employed took on a new form. By the time she reached her early teens Jodie had become a beautiful young girl; a natural leader who was good at all sports.

Jodie had influence so no boy in the school could afford to be ostracized by her, especially if the sanction was imposed simply for just teasing her brother or making a comment about him. Jodie leveraged this power to ensure her sibling's right of unencumbered passage through his schooldays.

To relieve the embarrassment he felt, Cliff sprung up from his desk.

"Oh, talking about pubs, I have to get myself down to the mess. It's nearly six. If I don't see you later, have a good day tomorrow, mate." He said, before stomping down the old wooden steps in his dusty boots. Looking down at them he thought, *the adjutant is going to moan about these again.*

As was the tradition, all officers met for drinks with the commanding officer each evening. This was where the politicking took place; where young officers had the wartime exploits of older, senior officers relayed to them. Cliff found a polite cough behind a raised fist could disguise most yawns of boredom.

Alden Nowlan's poem, *In the officers' mess* that the commanding officer insisted hang at the entrance to the mess, summed up most evenings:

> *Later the romantics will come back, wearing sweatshirts,*
> *to down three or four more doubles and refight with bottles,*
> *tumblers, matchboxes, cigarette lighters and swizzle sticks,*
> *the battles named on the regimental flag.*

Evening mess gatherings were an enshrined routine – a tradition never deviated from, even in the bush. It was said some regiments insisted officers took their formal dress (mess blues) to these camps for the event. *Thank God our CO never went that far,* Cliff thought.

Cliff stumbled down the rocky embankment in the growing darkness towards the tent that served as the officer's mess, the voices loud from within. Cliff's thoughts returned to the conversation he had just had in the office with Peter.

As he approached the pompous conversations coming from the mess tent, he tried to imagine what basic training must have been like for Peter. Cliff recalled his mother once telling him in one of her letters how she needn't have worried too much about Raymond, even though he was so 'different', and how he would fare in the war he departed for. He never even completed his basic training before being discharged. He arrived back home within a few months, having received a blue ticket issued under the World War II army regulation 'unfit for service'.

It is unknown exactly how many service members, including those who the army decided were 'homosexual', were given blue discharges under this regulation, but in 1946 it was estimated to be around five thousand; Raymond being one of the recipients.

Cliff's mother had written that having his army career aborted was traumatic for Raymond. He had felt his acceptance by the army to work as a nurse in the war was a stake in the ground for him; that he had been accepted for what he was. A few days after returning, after saying goodbye to her, Raymond left their home for good.

Sometime after her letter and when he was back home, Beryl told Cliff that she had never seen Raymond again. He had just disappeared. Leaving so suddenly and not knowing where to go, had led him to spend his first night away from the family home with Madge and her young son; a fact that Madge later confided to her.

"You must have been so sad," Cliff had said to his mother at the time, resisting the urge to ask what she had meant by 'so different' in her letter.

"Not really, I know he is fine. Madge hears from him occasionally although she has not seen him since that night. He's doing what he has to, and that's OK," Beryl murmured, unable to look at her son.

When his mother had avoided eye contact, Cliff tried to revive their conversation by saying he hoped that whatever demons Raymond was tackling would ultimately be defeated, so he could visit his sister one day. As he touched her hand tenderly, Cliff had wondered just how much more she was not telling him.

Arriving at the mess tent, Cliff paused to read the commanding officers' poem once again in the hope it would distract him from his thoughts. However, the distraction did not work and his thoughts only turned to another incident that had occurred during his own basic training.

A man in one of the barracks near Cliff's had a pretty awful time as a result of not conforming to what his co-barrack dwellers considered 'the norm'; for being an introvert. Cliff remembered the unfortunate individual had been accused of never showering, constantly being called dirty or smelly, and sometimes queer. The bullies decided to remedy the situation one evening.

With a towel around his waist in readiness for his shower, Cliff stumbled upon the assault by accident. Earlier when he was getting undressed, he had heard shouts and someone cry out but thought it was just normal raucous shower room behaviour. Therefore he was surprised and shocked to see the cruel schoolboy scene before him.

The poor victim had been shoved into the showers by several members of his barracks and made to strip naked. After dipping their brooms into buckets of soapy water, the bullies proceeded to scrub him down, He stood, covering his eyes, the tears slipping down his cheeks from under one slender hand while his other covered his genitals.

He was too terrified to move. Cliff thought it was almost as if the man felt guilty; that he deserved to be humiliated because he was not conforming.

He had relayed this incident to Beryl in one of his fortnightly letters. Usually struggling to find things to write about, for once he had something to say. However, his openness soon backfired as his mother's response made him feel guilty for weeks afterwards.

'What did you say to them? Did you give them a piece of your mind, Cliff? His poor mother. She must have been mortified when he told her. What happened to him?'

Cliff sighed when he read her words. He deserved to feel guilty. Then he wondered whether the young recruit would even tell his own mother about such an incident.

What had stuck in Cliff's mind about the shower scene was seeing the illegally utilized red fire buckets full of soapy water.

Cliff could only remember one occasion when he had seen those fire buckets actually being used for their intended purpose, and this had brought the wrath of the company sergeant major down upon them.

Company Sergeant Major van Plettenhof paced slowly up and down in front of the assembled ten platoons that made up C Company. His small moustache reminded Cliff of a satirical image; Adolf Hitler in a sombre, thoughtful mood, as he looked down with hands clasped behind his back, placing one shiny boot down in front of the other.

It was rumoured that they had been assembled to receive a reprimand for the fire incident that had taken place earlier that morning in one of the barracks. To Cliff's mind it had been more of a smoke incident than fire, and why the whole company had to be reprimanded rather than just the perpetrators, or maybe at most the occupants of the barracks the incident had taken place in, was beyond him.

When he reached the middle of the assembled row of platoons the company sergeant major stopped suddenly and turned to face the recruits. He came smartly to attention and, at a volume that could have been heard in the nearby city, he roared his command.

"Companee! Companee, stand at.............eeece."

Along with the sergeant major, the recruits raised their right leg, bent, waist high and stamped their boot attached down onto the dusty parade ground precisely twelve inches apart from the other, slapping their hands together behind their backs in the same movement. This was something they practiced every day. The company sergeant major wanted his audience to be comfortable.

He began his slow walk again. He smoothed his moustache with the back of his hand.

"So... you want to burn my blerry berracks down, hey?" he asked.

*

In one of the barracks that morning a platoon had been ready for daily inspection. Smoking was not allowed while waiting for an instructor to arrive, but a couple of recruits were sneakily doing so when the barracks' look-out spotted their instructor suddenly appear a short way off in the walkway between the barracks, striding towards them.

If a recruit was caught smoking it meant extinguishing the cigarette and eating it in front of the instructor – a horrendous experience. He had joked with Brenda that a good writer would try this as part of their research. He got the appropriate response in her next letter!

The two smokers noticed that there was a substantial crack in the floorboards where they stood, so they simply dropped their burning cigarettes through the gap. Halfway through inspection, smoke began to seep up through the floorboards. The planks were hastily ripped up, and fifty years' worth of accumulated smouldering rubbish was swiftly extinguished with fire buckets.

*

"You have been here only two blerry weeks and you already want to burn my blerry berracks down!" He shook his head slowly, an incredulous expression on his face.

Cliff resisted a shake of his own head at the company sergeant major's performance, which was like a cabaret. *He's loving this. That's why the whole company is here on parade*, he thought.

"Well if you burn my berracks down and tear up my floors, I will build a new blerry one. Thet's what will heppen. We will take your blerry wage peckit each week and *you* will pay for my beautiful new berracks! We will buy the best wood – no knots and holes like you have in your blerry heads!"

There were a few smiles from the recruits now and the company sergeant major did not seem to mind the loss of contrite expressions from some of the faces. He paced a bit more with his head down before looking up again. He groomed his moustache again and turned to them, with a wagging finger in the air.

"And you will blerry well buy me shiny new brass knobs for the doors and windows." He took a few more steps before stopping and turning sharply to face the assembled troops. "And you will shine those blerry knobs every day. Every blerry morning! They will shine like diamonds in a bleck pig's arsehole."

The recruits were now struggling to suppress their laughter.

He began pacing again. "You will get up very

early to do the shining. Very, very blerry early." He halted then turned and raised his finger to the sky. "You will be up to shine my blerry brass knobs before the first canary come down for a piss."

Even the instructors, who had heard it all before, could not stop themselves grinning at their recruits trying not to laugh; tears streaming down their cheeks.

*

In her letter Brenda simply asked, "Why a canary? Surely a sparrow or just a bird?"

A few of us have asked ourselves that same question, Brenda, Cliff mused.

Sergeant Swartberg was in the mess that night. Occasionally senior non-commissioned officers were invited to the officer's mess by the commanding officer as a matter of courtesy, particularly when there was no non-commissioned officer's mess facility, which was the case at this camp.

In the army, a commanding officer is traditionally the legal owner of every mess. The commanding officer had decided a non-commissioned officer's mess was not necessary for the camp; mainly because he wanted to use the only remaining large tent for his own personal accommodation. To keep the sergeants happy, they were invited into the officers' mess twice a week. Sergeant Swartberg was nonetheless still *grumpy* with the whole state of mess affairs (as he kept telling any officer who was prepared to listen).

He wasted no time in seeking out Cliff to ask how his batman was getting on. Although he saw the sergeant every day, he and Cliff exchanged very few words. With a drink in his hand, however, this changed, and it was a congenial Sergeant Swartberg who now stood before him.

"Ja, Lieutenant – how does it go with that moffie?" he smirked. "Why they let them into the army I don't know."

Cliff chose to ignore the sergeant's turn of phrase as though he had absolutely no idea what the Afrikaans word meant. "All good, Sergeant. Rifleman Pike is doing a great job compiling my reports. And the CO is pleased with the admin work he is doing for him."

"Oh, he is doing the CO's work as well?" said the sergeant, looking suddenly slightly crestfallen.

"Yes. The CO thinks the world of him," Cliff exaggerated. The commanding officer hadn't even spoken to Peter as it was the adjutant who handed out the work to him, but he enjoyed giving the sergeant something to reflect upon.

Cliff smiled to himself as the sergeant turned

away to order another beer and a large brandy from an orderly behind the makeshift bar. Before turning back to Cliff, he emptied the brandy into the beer and took a large gulp.

"I must give you a heads-up Lieutenant," he said, without bothering to raise his hand to disguise a burp. Taking Cliff aside with a tug on his arm, he lowered his voice. Cliff smelt the combination of beer and brandy as the sergeant spoke in what he thought was *sotto voce.*

"There is a night time exercise in a few weeks that will involve a simulated attack on this camp. No live ammunition of course, but thunder flashes and smoke grenades. As well you know, a blank at close range is very dangerous. I recommend you do not try to do an 'audit' on this exercise."

"Don't worry, Sergeant. I have done enough mock night time battle exercises to know they are complete chaos. Nobody knows what's going on in the dark —who's supposed to be the enemy and who isn't. Nothing I can observe in that scenario!" Cliff laughed.

"Not when *I'm* leading the exercise Lieutenant, s*ekerlik*, for sure."

"Thanks anyway, Sergeant, I will stay out of the way. Let me know which night, hey?"

"Sekerlik. Sekerlik," the sergeant grunted, as he headed back towards the bar.

Cliff knew he was being set up. *Don't go out that night Lieutenant. Lie quietly in your tent and wait*

for the thunder flash I am going to instruct someone to drop outside the thin canvas wall; leaving your ears to ring for days.
I don't think so Sergeant!

*

Later that evening, taking care not to stumble in the darkness and drop the bottle of wine he had sneaked out of the mess, Cliff made his way up the rocky slope back to his office. He was fed up with the army talk and looked forward to being alone.

At the top of the slope, he looked back to the mess tent. The silhouette movie playing on the side of the tent featured several stationary outlines; each one small alongside a large gesticulating figure with arms waving in all directions. *Careful sarge, you won't get invited back*, thought Cliff.

As he came level with the office window, he saw Peter sitting at his desk. He was barely visible, lit only by the dim lamp and the light from his computer screen. He was surprised, and a little self-conscious, at how pleased he was to see Peter there.

"Still at it?" he said, as he clumped up the steps in his heavy boots, waving his wine bottle in Peter's direction. "I bring gifts. Want one? Do we have any glasses?"

"We sure do!" Peter exclaimed. "You're a God

send." He grinned, "A *Greek* god send probably, if you bear a gift right? I was just feeling like a drink to cheer myself up. This army stuff is so boring. It's endless. I was starting to talk to the mosquitos."

"Must have been a 'buzz'!"

"Oh wow sir. I mean Cliff. That's worse than mine."

"Boring alright but not as bad as basic though, hey?" Cliff observed, as he poured wine into the two small jam jars Peter found. "How *was* your basic training, by the way Peter? I am always going on and on with my anecdotes. One only remembers the good times in the army, hey? Well, that's what my uncle Frank always said."

Cliff wondered if he was talking too much? He'd had several drinks at the mess. Cliff now considered that the chances of Peter having had a happy time in the army were not great, which suddenly made this an awkward question to ask as a conversational opener.

"Nothing funny like your experiences, Cliff. To be honest I try not to remember those times. People like me are not the best fit for the army. Thrown into the confined space of a barracks exacerbates the misfit. So-called 'normal' men feel awkward – even antagonized – by someone like me. It's like I'm a threat. If I invade their space, by association they will be considered to be like me."

Watching Peter's eyes, they seemed to Cliff to

fill with tears as he lowered his glass to the desktop.

"I have been meaning to say for a long time Cliff, that I really appreciated what you did for me that day on, or perhaps more accurately off, the truck... troop carrier... whatever it's called."

Cliff waved a hand dismissively. "Anybody with a bit of rank to throw around could have – *should* have – stopped bullying of that kind. He's not the sharpest knife in the drawer that one," he said, recalling his earlier conversation with Sergeant Swartberg.

"Well, what was just as important as saving me from further injury was showing me that I was not totally on my own here," Peter said. "Am I sorry for myself or what?" he grinned, raising the jam jar to his lips. "It helped to know there was *someone* who thought I was worth caring about."

Cliff was aware of the involuntary movement of Peter's hand that stretched towards his arm as he spoke; retracting it when he realised just how intimate the gesture to his lieutenant would be.

He camouflaged the half-gesture with a grin and waved in the direction of the door in the corner that led to the shower. "Not to mention the facilities you provide for your office workers. Lifesavers they are! And Sam – he has become a friend too as a result of working here with you," Peter went on.

Cliff pushed from his mind the sudden image of

himself and Sam in the Land Rover together and Sam's snide remarks about Peter.

"No problem," Cliff said, clearing his throat noisily to conceal any emotion in his voice. "More wine?" he managed.

Chapter 5

The Danger Zone

Cliff realised very early on in life that his mother was adept at making him feel guilty; playing the guilt card with the dexterity of a magician. Over the years, when he had felt resolute about a path he was embarking upon, she had changed his mind; changed it with an image she created and presented to him. He never contested these postulations. They were too graphic, too real; designed to tug at his heart strings that she plucked like a virtuoso.

His first experience of this was when he was ten years old. He had gallantly arrived home one day to proudly show her the sparrow he had shot with Josh's air gun, the pellet still lodged in its little chest and its wing torn apart.

Beryl looked at the dead bird and sighed deeply. "Tonight, mommy and daddy sparrow will be sitting in their nest, looking this way and that through the branches, wondering where, oh where, is their darling baby son? Why has he not come home?"

Cliff never touched a gun of any kind again until he joined the army. An army quartermaster, who handed out the kit during their first week at basic training, thrust a rifle into his hands. He told him to move one hand from the rifle's stock to the crotch of his fatigues.

"Say after me troop – this is my rifle, and this is my gun. This is my rifle, and this is my gun," he yelled.

Moving awkwardly to the next distribution point, Cliff shouted out the refrain as instructed.

"Never let anyone hear you call your rifle a gun," he heard from behind him. "Next."

Brenda met Beryl while on secondment at *The Witness*; a publication owned by the newspaper company Brenda had joined after leaving university. It was located in Beryl's hometown of Pietermaritzburg. She had done so well as a journalist over the last few years, that her editor had no hesitation in placing her in the role of acting chief editor while the current post-holder was on extended sick leave.

"It will be great experience for you. It's only a small publication, mainly local, but you will learn lots. Remember I will be here to back you up," her editor said, when she expressed reservations about being ready for such a role. "We've worked together for nearly three years now. You know how I operate. Just put yourself in my shoes for a while," he laughed. "Instead of being a pushy journo be a pedantic editor."

"I'm glad *you* said that," Brenda smiled.

The first person she met when she arrived at the new offices was Beryl. Beryl had been one of the receptionists at *The Witness* for longer than anyone could remember. It was well known that if you wanted to know anything, Beryl was the person to ask and Brenda instantly recognised this fact. She and Beryl shared the same sense of humour, which could be dark at times.

It wasn't long before having lunch together in the park opposite the office building became a daily routine. As the months went by, they became close friends. Brenda shared thoughts that she had never shared with anyone before. Beryl quickly became like a mother figure to her; more so than any of the foster mothers she had had growing up.

Cliff got used to the anecdotes of what Brenda had done or said, which his mother shared over the dinner table each evening or offered as unrelated asides while they listened to a play on the radio together afterwards. Over time, his mother gradually referred to her as 'poor Brenda' and he became wary; sensing the imminent placing down of a guilt card in front of him.

He knew his mother thought he should be 'getting on' with life, which to her meant finding a partner and moving out. Having qualified as an engineer, he could now easily afford a place of his own, especially if he shared with someone. His mother suggested he get a place with Josh, but while he was still eligible for conscription, it seemed pointless to move out yet.

"Poor Brenda. She just sits alone in that apartment every night. Never gets out. So sad," Beryl sighed over her knitting one evening.

He knew where this conversation might be going. He remained silent, sipping his tea, pretending to be absorbed in the radio's narrative. They were listening to a weekly play – a courtroom drama – called *Consider your verdict*. The jury was about to deliver its verdict while Beryl continued talking.

"She spent her whole childhood in foster homes. No wonder she has no idea how to meet boys. She was in tears once, telling me the story of her childhood. Maybe I should go to a movie with her? Not much fun for her going out with someone old enough to be her mother though. She's very smart and funny – acting editor at the paper – and she's basically still a kid. Bright as a button and gorgeous to go with it. Long blond hair. Gorgeous."

Cliff did not respond as just one word and he would be in the net. Finally, his mother seemed to tire of the subject. He listened to the *click, click,* of the colliding knitting needles over the voices from the radio, and his father's distant snoring.

"Poor thing. She must be so lonely."

"OK. OK!" Cliff gave a theatrical sigh of surrender.

The radio station paused for a commercial break, building the suspense during the interval. Each week during the break, Cliff and his mother disclosed their own verdict to each other before the true one was revealed. However, with his father's snores coming from the next room and his mother's endless talking he was struggling to concentrate.

"Invite her over here one evening and we will see how it goes. See if anything 'clicks'," Cliff said, watching his mother's long plastic needles, gyrating erratically. "Maybe she could hang out with Josh and I one evening? Safer that way – more informal. I don't do blind dates. I did once and it was a humiliating disaster. Hennie arranged it. You remember him? My friend from school. Fortunately, it was an afternoon thing at the zoo so I was able to lose her at the lion's cage, thank goodness!"

"She got eaten?" his mother giggled, which was something he did not see as often nowadays.

"Very funny, Mother."

"Shhhh... it's the verdict," she interjected, lowering her needles. "I say guilty," she said.

"You?"

Sitting opposite Peter in their old office, Cliff was absorbed in the letter he was writing to his mother when they heard rifle shots in the distance. Cliff presumed the sound was coming from Sergeant Swartberg's blanks. Peter's concerned frown relaxed when Cliff told him the source of the noise.

"Oh, I forgot to tell you: they have been planning a training exercise; repelling a simulated surprise attack on the camp. We're not involved. Just sit tight. There will be lots of noise and shouting. Total confusion if I know anything about these night time exercises."

Thinking about his suspicions regarding Sergeant Swartberg, Cliff was glad the exercise had started while he was in the office rather than his tent. A short while later they heard loud voices – commands being yelled and the crunch of boots on the slope below the office. The gun fire was much closer now. Blowing out the lamps, Cliff joined Peter at the small window. They watched the shadowy forms of men darting about in the darkness, sometimes illuminated by the bright flash from rifle barrels pointed this way and that, as blanks were fired into the night.

Even though they knew it was just a mock battle, the increasing noise of the fire fight was intense and disconcerting. Cliff watched as hunched dark figures moved rapidly between the tents in the direction of their office. One tripped over a guy rope and fell against the side of the tent it was attached to, collapsing a bunk bed inside. Its angry occupant rolled onto the floor with a surprised yell.

"What the fuck is going on out there? Thought you were supposed to be protecting us? Arseholes!"

A large shadowy figure appeared alongside the tent. It bent over the fallen recruit, who was still struggling to get up, and grabbed him by the arm.

"Opstaan. Opstaan!" came Sergeant Swartberg's loud voice, as he hauled the recruit to his feet.

Cliff saw the sergeant pick up something the recruit had dropped and, turning towards his office, his arm moved with a bowler's action. As the canister thudded against the wooden wall of the office and fell to the gravel, Cliff leapt back from the window, pulling Peter with him. There was a sudden ear-splitting *bang* as the thunder flash went off. It seemed to be right on top of them, shaking the old wooden frame of the office. They both jumped involuntarily. Peter let out a scream as he threw himself into Cliff's arms.

"Sorry. That was scary. Never actually jumped with fright before. At least I didn't pee my pants this time!" Cliff heard him shout, over the ringing in his ears.

*

As the weeks went by, increasingly Peter found that Cliff's driver was not the boorish character he had first thought. In fact, notwithstanding the occasional inappropriate remark (some of which made Peter laugh as well as angry), the two of them were getting on like old friends.

Sam repeatedly referred to himself and Peter as the general's 'odd couple'. It was not long before they were calling each other Felix and Oscar and sharing famous quotes from the *The Odd Couple* movie. Peter was Felix, the head-shaking tolerant one, who would chide Sam with, "Oscar, Oscar, Oscar."

When he was not driving Cliff, Sam was assigned as Peter's driver on the missions the adjutant sent him on for the commanding officer. This resulted in the two men spending hours together in the Land Rover, engaging in lengthy and noisy conversations, shouting to be heard above the wind and road noise.

*

Cliff had initially presumed his friend from basic training had not been called up to this particular camp as he was not on the train with them. Instead, Sam had been driven to the camp by one of his mother's drivers. She owned a large hotel and estate in the country near Pietermaritzburg; the city both he and Cliff lived in. Perish the thought her son would use public transport. Maybe a plane but certainly not a grubby train.

Upon arrival at the camp, Sam was told of Cliff's promotion. When he was assigned as his driver, Sam had immediately begun referring to his friend as 'General'. Given how Cliff felt about the army, he had played along with the irony but had told the grinning Sam to *piss off* when he suggested Cliff should sit in the rear of the Land Rover rather than alongside a lowly driver.

Having known Sam since basic training and his lack of respect for authority, Cliff knew it would only be a matter of time before there was an incident involving his driver and the pedantic Sergeant Swartberg. He was therefore not surprised when Sergeant Swartberg stumbled up the rickety steps of his office one afternoon, red-faced with anger. He saluted briefly before yelling loudly, causing a pair of Pied Crows to flap away from the office roof above the doorway.

"That blerry driver of yours! Demmit, Lieutenant!"

"Good afternoon to you too, Sergeant."

It appeared the enraged sergeant had just been to the vehicle pool to find his Land Rover had disappeared. After some detective work, which involved yelling at the young corporal responsible for the vehicle parking area, he had established the facts of the case. Upon finding Cliff's vehicle had a dead battery, Sam had taken it upon himself to commandeer the first working vehicle he found, reasoning that it was for the commanding officer's assignment after all.

Unfortunately he had chosen Sergeant Swartberg's Land Rover, but how was Sam to know that? Even if he had known, he would not have cared anyway. The sergeant was extremely possessive of his 'Landy', which he drove himself.

"Take mine," Cliff suggested to the fuming non-commissioned officer. "They will have replaced the battery by now, surely?"

"That's not the point Lieutenant! He can't just take a senior NCO's vehicle without permission. You will have to put him on a charge. What if there had been an emergency? We are in an active zone!"

"Really?" Cliff grinned. "Haven't seen much activity. Unless you count your night defence of *this* camp, a few weeks ago? I heard one of your men attacked some poor guy asleep in his tent."

Sergeant Swartberg appeared not to hear him. Cliff was enjoying this; a little revenge for the thunder flash.

"Doesn't matter. We have to be prepared at all times sir," the sergeant snapped back.

Over the sergeant's shoulder, in the distance about a kilometre away on a hill overlooking the camp, Cliff's eyes were drawn to dust rising up above the ridge. The dust billowed up behind a Land Rover appearing over a crest before driving down the track towards the camp. As he partly listened to the sergeant's World War II anecdote about consequences of not being prepared for an attack, Cliff watched the vehicle stop, dust swirling behind it as it did so.

Through the trailing dust now engulfing the stationary vehicle, a figure emerged from the passenger side and Cliff visualised Peter's slight figure easily sliding over the gear lever back to the passenger seat to make way for a new driver.

Even at this distance the burly figure was unmistakably Sam. *Driving lessons?* thought Cliff, as Sam took over for the approach to the camp.

Noticing Cliff's lack of eye contact and attention, Sergeant Swartberg turned slightly to follow his gaze. Looking back over his shoulder, he saw the now speeding vehicle approaching the camp down the twisty gravel road.

"That's him! Die bliksem," he growled, as he thumped down the office steps, nearly tripping in his haste to reach the vehicle parking area. Cliff looked from the oncoming vehicle to the marching sergeant, whose arms were swinging like a World War II storm trooper's, late for the invasion of Poland. Both the vehicle and the sergeant's thumping boots were kicking up dust along the collision course.

Now, standing in front of the entrance to the

makeshift car pool, which was nothing more than a football field-sized grass patch hacked from the bush in previous years, Sergeant Swartberg stood motionless with his hands on his hips as he glared at the approaching Land Rover.

Nearby, decomposing thorn tree trunks from the initial clearing work were stacked. On top of the pile stood an immobile solitary mongoose. The animal was not angry like the sergeant but certainly as upright and focused, as it gazed towards the approaching vehicle with what seemed to be deep concentration. Within a few moments a second then a third mongoose appeared; their little paws held in front making them as statue-like as the sergeant.

Rifleman Swartberg had joined the army because he believed it was the only avenue available to someone like him. Without having had an adequate education, he wanted to prove himself to his girlfriend's family; show them that he would be a worthy husband, and father to the child she was carrying.

He had left school too early but at the time it seemed to be the easy option. No school meant no homework and the freedom to go out whenever he liked. However, he could only see his girlfriend at the weekend as, unlike his own parents, hers were very strict about her school commitments.

He had barely started his apprenticeship as a cabinet maker when she fell pregnant. All hell broke loose; the telephone calls coming from her irate father to his. He was also called into his boss's office and fired. All this seemed to happen before he had even had a chance to reflect on the fact that he was going to be a father.

As was the custom at the time, his girlfriend was sent away to stay with an aunt in a different town on the pretext of furthering her education at a school that offered courses the local one did not. He had offered to do the honourable thing by marrying her, but her father had scoffed, sending him away and banning him from having any contact with his daughter.

So he joined the army, determined to establish himself as a military man. However, it would be sometime before he could return triumphant, resplendent in his uniform, to claim his bride and child. The letters they exchanged during his initial training declined as time went by. Her final letter was to inform him she had had the baby, and that it had been adopted at her father's insistence. She was to return to her studies in her hometown. She did not even say if the baby was a girl or boy.

He wrote back in response, describing how sad he was to lose his child, and asking if the baby was a girl or boy. Either way, they would reclaim their baby after he completed his training and married her. His letter was unanswered; so too all the others that followed.

Rifleman Cory Swartberg was broken-hearted and moped around for months. When his barracks mates questioned what he was doing staring into nothingness all the time, his only response was a shrug.

Finally, the sadness turned to anger – at her, at her father, and at himself for getting things so wrong. He was determined to use the opportunities the army gave him; use the army to turn things around; to become recognised and admired – someone his lost child would one day respect.

*

As well-trained regular soldiers, the newly promoted Sergeant Swartberg and his permanent force contingent had arrived in North Africa to join the war effort, alongside active citizen force World War II volunteers who outnumbered them by double.

Young and eager, he was determined to be recognised as a good fighter during battle but other than the odd skirmish, which required trying to keep up with the thundering tank they trotted behind like ducklings, ears ringing from its canon fire, it seemed to him they mostly did nothing more than long marches in the heat of the desert or sat around waiting. Such endless waiting. Then in June 1942 when Tobruk fell, he found himself a prisoner of war. This was to be his wartime contribution.

Sergeant Swartberg firmly believed his military career had hit a brick wall during that time. He had missed what he thought should have been a big opportunity to show his mettle and to advance up the ranks. On his return to his battalion without medals, he found himself ushered into an instructor role. He had remained there ever since.

"Blackie, those who can't do, teach, hey?" his commanding officer told him with a grin and a pat on the shoulder.

It was frustrating having to work with young men who simply did not take what they were doing seriously. They resented being drafted into the army for a year almost as much as Sergeant Swartberg resented having to train them.

Some days, scanning the faces of a platoon standing before him at attention, he wondered if one of them might be his long lost son. Was he the father they had never known? Or maybe it was a daughter he had lost? It was in moments like this that his resentment was momentarily replaced by nostalgia and then sadness.

What he resented most of all was the fact that with the increasing insurgency activity on South Africa's borders, rather than use the army, the government had deployed the police to take command of the situation. This left the army playing little more than a support role. *Another opportunity missed,* Sergeant Swartberg thought. *Stuck training citizen force kids who have no idea what a bush war entails or even know one exists.*

The approaching Land Rover slowed at the fork in the track.

This kid who thinks it's OK to commandeer an NCO's vehicle will find out what that's about when I commandeer his easy life as a driver... where does he think he's going now?

The sergeant loudly yelled. "Jou blicksem!"

He took off at a great pace, scattering the mongoose gathering with his sudden movement as well as sending a passing confusion of guinea fowl squawking down the road; their wings aloft looking like plump priests holding robes above their knees, running to escape the wrath of a vengeful God.

*

Cliff watched as the Land Rover bounced down the track towards the camp. At the fork in the road, instead of turning down towards the parking area where the sergeant now stood, hands on hips, Sam turned onto the track that snaked up towards

Cliff's office. The enraged sergeant ran back towards them, taking a shortcut across some bushland that formed an island between the two tracks.

Cliff had just stepped down from his office to meet the vehicle and to warn Sam of the impending storm behind him when the ground shook. A shockwave pounded his chest, winding him, as a loud explosion assailed his ears. At the same instant he felt sand and other fragments pepper his face and arms.

He staggered but managed to stay upright, screened from much of the explosion and shrapnel by the Land Rover. Nonetheless, he felt the intensity of the blast. Peter and Sam stared at him through the windscreen open-mouthed with shock, their faces a ghostly white.

With his hands on the warm car bonnet for support, Cliff stepped shakily to one side. He looked behind the Land Rover, through the black and acrid smoke of the explosion, towards the bush from where the sergeant had been approaching. He couldn't see him.

Finally, beyond the ringing in his ears, he heard him: agonised screams. He saw the tall grass moving as the vague outline of a man thrashed around in pain.

*

The anti-personnel mine Sergeant Swartberg stood on was one of many that had been deployed by insurgents in previous years. Most of them had been cleared when the camp was first established – some even earlier by unwitting wild animals – but for safety reasons, it was normally part of camp standing orders in border red zones that one did not stray onto disused tracks or bush bordering newly created tracks. Just in case.

The sergeant had been unlucky. He had let his guard down by being so angry about the situation regarding his vehicle. The lapse cost him his foot, as was the planter's intention. The idea behind such mines was to waste the enemy's time with the complex logistics of transporting and caring for the injured in a war zone, rather than to actually kill enemy personnel. Death of a recruit required no more than non-urgent transportation, or disposal.

Fortunately, this incident had at least happened at the camp where there were medics and treatment immediately available. Nonetheless, Sergeant Swartberg was air-lifted by a Defence Force helicopter within hours of the incident and flown to the nearby base at Grootfontein.

Cliff had been fortunate. Sergeant Swartberg's stolen Land Rover had shielded him from much of the peripheral blast and accompanying shrapnel. He had not wanted to distract the medics from their serious work with the sergeant so Peter insisted on cleaning all the small cuts on his face himself.

Now back in the office and sitting at his desk, Peter's delicate small hand held Cliff's chin as he dabbed his cuts with disinfectant. Cliff felt decidedly self-conscious. The rusty tweezers Peter found in his desk drawer and its application to the fragments in his face did nothing to distract from the awkwardness Cliff felt.

The fact that Sam did not utter a single word as he observed the medical attention Cliff was receiving, exacerbated his discomfort. *Say something sardonic, beak nose*, Cliff thought to himself, as he winced at Peter's gentle dabbing and watched Sam's face in his peripheral vision.

Sam was actually pre-occupied with thoughts of his own. The incident had thrown a different light on the time the army took from him. What Sam and many young men believed was a superficial period in their lives – a nuisance time, of being taught to be soldiers for what was a non-existent war – was emerging into the spotlight as a harsh reality.

The incident he had just witnessed was no accident – it was pre-meditated – the consequence of human beings consciously wanting to injure, even if not kill, others. There was nothing silly or ridiculous about this situation. This was sinister. The border war they read about in the newspapers (the fight against the so-called terrorists as the government referred to them in speeches) had just moved a step closer to him.

"Sam, is there a medical bag in the Rover?" Cliff asked, keen for him to leave, uneasy with his sudden stoic, uncharacteristic lack of comment.

"I'll have a look," he said, as he ambled off.

What happened to 'General'? Cliff thought.

*

The sergeant's untimely departure left the commanding officer with a dilemma. He had no trained permanent force instructor to deliver the rest of the scheduled training and had been told there was no chance of a replacement for at least three weeks.

His solution was to contact army headquarters and volunteer all three of his platoons for any mission requiring infantry support. *A bit of time deep in the red zone will keep idle hands occupied and get them focused,* he thought.

The red zone was where police on the ground were facing incursions regularly. In the 1970's the border war was perceived as a matter of law enforcement rather than a military conflict, reflecting a trend among Anglophone Commonwealth states to regard police as the principal force in the suppression of insurgencies. Hence why the police had set up posts throughout the Caprivi Strip, sending out patrols in search of bands of insurgents crossing the border after completing training under their Cuban and Russian 'advisors' at bases in Angola.

The mission the commanding officer was given by his superiors was to provide protection for a convoy of heavy vehicles heading from Rundu, north of their training camp on the Angolan border, to Katima Mulilo, deep in the eastern section of the Caprivi Strip; a landlocked peninsular of Namibia wedged between Angola, Zambia, Botswana and the tip of Zimbabwe.

Due to sanctions against South Africa, fuel was not allowed to be flown over these neighbouring countries. Instead, it had to be transported by road to the large military camp and airfield near Katima Mulilo on the banks of the Zambezi River.

Deployed in the cramped cabs of a kilometre-long, olive-green snake of trucks carrying hundreds of drums of fuel, for the next five days the commanding officer's somewhat apprehensive soldiers would trundle down hundreds of kilometres of narrow, sandy (and sometimes mined) road that was euphemistically referred to by those who had encountered it before as 'the Golden Highway'.

Chapter 6

The Golden Highway

In the total blackness, a lone flaring match was followed by the clang of metal and a frustrated curse, as a momentarily visible hand struggled with the catch on the troop carrier's rear flap.

"Extinguish that light immediately!" came the loud, pompous voice of the commanding officer from somewhere in the darkness.

Cliff thought he heard an exasperated adjutant alongside him say under his breath, "It's at times like this, sir," but in the dark he was not sure who said it. He did pick up on the frustration in the voice though.

Since he had struggled up from his rusty steel foldaway bed and fibre filled mattress, in what God only knows lived, Cliff had been guided by touch and sound only. Visibility was nil and there were not even any stars to relieve the moonless night.

Their commanding officer, Colonel Roverstone, had insisted they should handle their departure as authentically as possible, decreeing that there were to be no lights during mobilization to guide the enemy to their activity. It was chaos. Drivers were stumbling around trying to identify their vehicles, and troops struggled to find which vehicles they should load their own kit and other supplies onto. Their supplies included heavy boxes of ammunition that needed two men to lift them onto the back of trucks, invisible in the dark.

Under the cover of this darkness, the commanding officer's birthright was being brought into question over and over again, as were those of his ancestors, by increasingly frustrated recruits.

"Thinks he's a fucking bat."

Unlike Cliff, Colonel Roverstone had completed his officer training shortly after World War II for which, to his disgust, he was too young to enlist. Undeterred, he volunteered for the post-war citizen force army at a time when South Africa's armed forces were still referred to as the Union Defence Force. Back then, it was strongly British-oriented in usages, structures, uniforms and nomenclature until the mainly Afrikaans National Party got into power and decided to 'level the playing field' as they called it.

The young active citizen force officer thrived, developing strong ties with influential people within the senior ranks of the Union Defence Force's regular officers. Notwithstanding his refusal to speak Afrikaans (he had developed an authentic British officer's accent), in the increasingly Afrikaans hierarchy, he soon reached the rank of colonel and even commissioned a self-portrait wearing his khaki military jacket, leather Sam Brown and green beret. His choice of attire for the large painting was much to the annoyance of his wife as it clashed with the décor in their dining room.

When he was not engaged at a camp or other army activity, Colonel Roverstone could never quite leave the army, even when he was involved in his civilian job. Leaving the army meant leaving his ego behind too. In a day-to-day work environment he was a master at turning the conversation subtlety to all things military. He loved to take his service revolver from his briefcase and lay it front of anyone who showed interest in his extra mural military interests.

"Insist I carry it at all times, the SADF. Because of my seniority. Can't be too careful in these times they say."

The Colonel's blackout order meant Cliff and his

loyal staff of two found themselves stumbling around in the dark at two a.m. trying to find their Land Rover.

"Why so fucking early?" Sam moaned.

"Before the first canary come down for a piss, hey?" Peter contributed, with a passable impersonation of an Afrikaans accent.

"Not bad, Peter. Sergeant Major van Plettenhof would have been proud of him, hey Sam?" laughed Cliff in the darkness, not realising Sam had moved off down the line of Land Rovers, hand over hand on bodywork like a blind man.

He finally identified his vehicle amongst the others by feeling for the little indents the shrapnel had made in the back. He had kept the sergeant's Land Rover which was much better equipped than his. *He'll need an automatic now anyway*, he thought.

"Here it is," he called to Cliff and Peter.

As Peter and Cliff got closer to where Sam had found their Land Rover, they heard him groan.

"Shit, I hope that wasn't a foot I just stood on," he whispered in mock panic.

"Jesus, Sam, have a heart," Cliff whispered back. He could sense Peter trying to stifle a laugh in the blackness somewhere nearby.

"Oscar, Oscar, Oscar," Peter admonished.

"Sorry, General. And by the way – if I open the door, the vanity light is going to come on and the CO will shit himself." Borrowing an expression from basic training vernacular Sam continued. "That guy is the epitome of kop-toe. He would have his wife court martialled if she didn't salute him after sex! What's your call here, General?" he asked an unseen Cliff.

Cliff opened his mouth to say, "Just get in through the rear door then, duh," when suddenly the adjutant's raised voice boomed out in the night.

"Colonel, sir, we have to have some light. This is far too dangerous. The men are trying to load live ammunition in pitch blackness."

"They'll manage, they'll manage," the commanding officer replied curtly.

The adjutant tried another tactic. "Well yes but only until one of them gets disoriented in the dark and walks off onto a mine."

The previous incident involving the sergeant was too fresh in the commanding officer's memory and he was stopped in his tracks. "OK, torches but no camp generator lights."

Finally, after several minor accidents in the darkness, the troop carriers were lined up, ready to make their way to Rundu to meet up with the convoy. Before departure, the men from the three platoons had a briefing from the commanding officer.

He got the adjutant to hold a torch on him as he spoke. This elicited some snide remarks from those hidden in the darkness as he gave his orders. He spoke mainly about the fact they were heading for the red zone and that alertness was paramount.

Some contemplated whether this meant they were going into action and would be able to tell others afterwards that they had been to war. Sam mumbled something obtuse about where his last letter to his mother could be found.

*

They had been driving in pitch darkness for about two hours when, through drooping eyelids, they noticed the distant glow of a small town, demarcating where the horizon was in the darkness. As the glow slowly sharpened into individual lights, they realised it must be Rundu. Had it been later than four a.m. they might have seen the sun glistening on the waters of the mighty Cubango (as the Portuguese called the river) beyond the town.

"If that's Rundu, those big lights off to the side must be the airfield the CO was talking about – where we'll pick up the convoy," Cliff said.

"Angola is the other side of those lights and the Cubango guys," said Sam. "Welcome to the red zone."

"Just what I need," Peter sighed.

"Our bat-like CO will hate those big bright lights, won't he?" Sam murmured.

They had reached the outskirts of the town

when the commanding officer's Land Rover, which was ahead of them, suddenly showed a flashing indicator light and their convoy turned off away from Rundu, drawn like moths to the huge security lights lighting up the airfield and the slightly drooping wings of a dozen or so C130s. Had they been allowed into the airspace they could have carried the fuel in just a few hours. It would take their motorised convoy days to carry it to Katima Mulilo.

"One of those probably took the sergeant to Pretoria," Cliff said, as they circled around the airfield and its high anti-rocket launcher mesh fence, past the aircraft to the heavily guarded main entrance of the adjacent military base.

"Poor bugger," Sam murmured.

Thirty large olive-green trucks were parked alongside the airport fence. They were loaded with drums of fuel hidden under camouflage canvas canopies and were awaiting their chaperones.

After sitting in their vehicles for what seemed an age while Colonel Roverstone and the adjutant exchanged multiple salutes with the Rundu military and signed countless documents, the men were finally deployed along the long line of fuel-carrying vehicles.

It was not long before the double cab of each truck was occupied by two riflemen next to the waiting driver. In each, one of the men stood, poking out through the cab's round turret opening behind the light machine gun mounted on its roof. Despite the fact that the only light came from the huge security lights, each was resplendent in Raybans.

"Where did they get the sunglasses?" Cliff wondered aloud. "Who would think to take sunglasses to an army camp? All they need is a scarf each and we will have a line of Red Barons."

"Out of here," Peter informed him, patting a large and now partially empty cardboard box on the seat beside him. "We found it in the sergeant's Land Rover. They might be *knockoff* Raybans but better than nothing. I've heard there is lots of sun and 'glary' white sand where we're going."

"Maybe he was planning to make a few bucks? Who knows? Anyway we decided to bring them and hand them out to the needy. Like those turret guards there," Sam added, nodding in the direction of the convoy.

"Well maybe he knew something," Cliff said. "If I'm remembering my geography correctly, I think you're right, it is a bit like a desert. Perhaps he was looking after his boys, hey? Let's give Sergeant Swartberg the benefit of the doubt."

*

It was not yet dawn when the convoy started its journey towards Divundu, a town near its first stop on the way through the four-hundred-kilometre corridor of land. It was as little as thirty-two kilometres wide for much of its length. Known as the Caprivi Strip, it was created by the colonial land 'carve-up' of the Nineteenth Century.

This strip of land was not only used by elephants as a natural conduit between countries that bordered the Caprivi, but also by the armed wing of the African National Congress who were passing through it in their war against the South African Government. Notwithstanding the regular fire fights that were taking place between police units and insurgents in the bush along the border, the road itself was the site of injury and death caused by mines planted under its surface of deep, fine white sand.

Divundu was close to where they would cross the Cubango, after travelling parallel with the river and the Angolan border for a long way before entering the Caprivi Strip proper. Shining a torch onto the map he had found tucked into the backseat magazine holder, Peter gave regular updates regarding their position as they passed small signs indicating nearby towns.

"Katera to the left. If it were light enough we would be seeing a river probably. Can't see its name on this old map," he called out.

"Cubango," Sam said. "The Cubango River," he repeated in a louder voice.

In the beam of their headlights, swirling white clouds from the sand that formed the road billowed out into the darkness from behind the vehicles in front of them, depositing yet another layer onto the already dust-laden thorn trees they passed by. They looked a bit like snow-covered Christmas trees in the vehicle's bright beams. Even Sam's huge moustache was already showing signs of a 'dustyfrost' in the glow of the Land Rover's dashboard lights.

"You know, General, history shows the Germans made a total cock-up in the last century when they traded one of their colonies for this strip of land." He yelled over the noise of the Land Rover's engine and rattling chassis.

"Yeah? And why is that?" Cliff yelled back, wiping his eyebrows with the back of a finger in case they were turning white too.

"Grabbed it because they thought they could use the Zambezi as a transport link down the river to their ships anchored off Mozambique, but..."

"Didn't look at the map properly so they didn't notice the Victoria Falls on there, going downstream?" Peter smiled, leaning forward with his arms resting on their backrests.

"That's the one," Sam laughed.

*

All three were relieved to see the light increasing over the horizon hovering above the vast and endless black carpet of distant thorn trees. They had been acutely aware that the demeanour of the regular army personnel at the Rundu camp was the 'no nonsense' one displayed by those in a dangerous environment.

Once the lights of Rundu had completely disappeared from the horizon behind them, Cliff had drifted into a mood of increasing trepidation. At any moment, he was half expecting to see either side of him orange tracers from AK47s held by Russian-trained insurgents in the darkness. He hoped his imagination would be easier to control in the morning light.

Thrown from side to side by ruts in the soft surface of the road, Cliff and the other two did not seem to be as tired from their early morning start as he had expected they would be by now. It seemed that nervous energy kept them all wide awake and he gave up glancing to his right to check Sam wasn't falling asleep at the wheel. He had stopped asking him if he was OK too.

"You guys feeling a bit nervous, like I am?" he shouted.

"Nah. I always grip the steering wheel this tightly, General," Sam laughed.

*

With the increasing daylight their surroundings felt less threatening. They could see into the bush either side of the road now rather than just imagining what lay within it in the blackness. They had occasionally seen into the bush when the road curved and the trees were pierced by headlights. They would swear they saw camouflage-clad movement within.

Their vehicle was third in the convoy that was being led by a mine-protected Ratel; the army's custom-built infantry fighting vehicle. Second in line was the commanding officer and adjutant, with troop carriers interspersed behind them amongst the long line of fuel-carrying lorries.

In the morning light conversation had been limited between them while their inexperienced eyes still darted nervously left and right. In the last half hour the three of them had been silent, lulled into daydreams by the droning engine. All of a sudden the two-way radio, which Sergeant Swartberg must have had set to maximum volume when it woke from sleep mode, crackled loudly, jolting them from their thoughts.

"Jesus!" Sam gasped.

"Two zero, this is one zero. My signal strength? Over," came the adjutant's voice.

Sam looked at Cliff, nonplussed.

"Two zero, this is one zero. My signal strength? Over," came the crackling voice again.

Cliff pointed to the radio mic at the end of a cord, which was hooked onto the dashboard.

"Just say, one zero this is two zero. Good. Over," he said.

Sam unhooked the mic and raised it to his lips. "Zero one two. Also good. Over."

The adjutant ignored Sam's bungled radio technique and continued. "Convoy halt in one kilometre for rest and refreshment. Over."

Sam looked pleased with himself and with his moustache brushing the mic he replied. "Copy that sir. Over."

"What happened to radio silence?" Cliff asked.

"Well, when the commanding officer wants his breakfast..." laughed Sam, trying to re-clip the mic onto the dashboard and watch the road at the same time.

A few minutes later, one by one the convoy of trucks ground to a halt as each saw the hazard lights of the vehicle in front come on. They eased slowly up close to each other, big diesel engines clattering, their fumes competing with the fumes from the fuel loaded in drums behind their cabs. Riflemen descended from the backs of the trucks as they stopped, deploying as guards on either side.

Near the front of this long olive-green freight train *snake* the commanding officer's Land Rover had barely come to a stop on the side of the road before his batman, a young lance corporal who had experience with the commanding officer's breakfast stops, began hauling a portable gas burner and huge pot out of the back. He called Peter over to help.

Later, Cliff's curiosity as to why the commanding officer was hovering over the pot turned to concern when his batman explained a little about his superior's on-road cooking habits. The commanding officer assured them, as they stood around stamping their feet in the cold, that they would now be turning the drab tinned rations issued to each of them the previous day into a gourmet breakfast – whether they liked it or not.

All the way back down the line of stationary vehicles, men were rummaging in their backpacks, opening army-issue cans of various food varieties for consumption with their army-issue spoons. Some were bringing water from their webbing covered water bottles to the boil on small burners, before pouring onto the granules of instant coffee in their army-issue steel mugs. Into this they would dunk their circular army-issue 'dog biscuits', which were as thick and hard as rock.

When it came to eating on patrol, Cliff did not have good memories of training camp outdoor dining, and he had a feeling this open-air breakfast would be just as bad as the first one he had on a firing range during basic training.

His level of concern grew as, at the commanding officer's request they handed the open cans to the lance corporal who emptied them into the now steaming pot. Lamb curry, sausage, baked beans, sardines, tomato, salmon, corned beef and tuna found their way into what would soon become a 'gourmet' breakfast stew.

"Hang onto your cans; you'll need them to eat out of," the corporal said, as he re-distributed the empty cans.

"Here it comes – breakfast," the instructor at basic training informed them, over the intense ringing in their ears after their first morning on a firing range years before.

He pointed at the olive-green three-ton truck bouncing down the potholed corrugated track towards them. They had been on the firing range – a short distance from the main camp – since dawn. Although some of the recruits were handling a rifle loaded with live ammunition for the first time, the excitement had long since waned. It had been overtaken by what felt like permanently damaged hearing thanks to the failure of the army-issue cotton wool ear buds. Their stomachs ached with hunger too.

There had also been other body aches, as a result of their instructor's anger when their rifles had jammed on account of novice users being overly tentative with the cocking of the bolt. The resulting jam was repaired by an impatient instructor's sharp professional pull on the bolt, accompanied by an expletive, as the unspent live round was ejected into the air from the chamber.

Rising from his position beside the errant shooter, the instructor always followed the expletive by poking his toe-capped boot into the ribs of the dust-covered recruit lying prone on the ground.

"Don't pull it like you pull your own, troop!"

At stand down after firing at the five hundred metre mark, Cliff and his platoon stared longingly at the now stationary truck and its cigarette-smoking driver leaning against its side. They imagined their breakfast getting cold in the back of the truck. Finally, the sound of the sharp, repeated *cracks* heard all across the range gradually died away; the rest of the recruits ordered to stand down and form an orderly mess line.

Cliff was near the front of the line when they slammed open the steel rear doors to reveal the stacked metal containers. Unlike the normal mess trays recruits lined up with at camp mealtimes, what confronted them instead looked like metal school lunch boxes designed for easy transportation and distribution.

The instructors were clearly enjoying the moment as they handed down a lunchbox to each recruit. Cliff and the others soon found out why: their meal consisted of porridge, milk and sugar, fried eggs with sausage, tomato, bread and butter. However, the metal partitions in each container had not proved equal to the task of keeping the portions separate through the vibrations and rocking of the truck as it bounced its way down the track to the range. Looking with despair at the congealed image in his lunchbox, the work of artist Jackson Pollock came to Cliff's mind.

As the convoy resumed its journey towards the first of the rivers they would have to cross, Sam elbowed Peter playfully.

"See, my skinny friend, hunger *is* the best sauce. I quite enjoyed that 'one hundred and one varieties' stew. You should have had some – put some meat on those bones of yours."

"Speak for yourself. I slipped off and filled up on 'dog biscuits' to dunk in my coffee." Peter smiled. "I'm quite happy with my bones as they are thank you. Besides, I'm not keen on throwing up in front of people."

"I had no option but to eat it," Cliff complained from the back seat, where he was hoping to have a nap. "The CO insisted we 'enjoy' his anecdotes from his last trip to the Caprivi. I couldn't stand there with a can full of the stuff and not eat while he went on and on."

Sam exclaimed, "Yeah, and my God, the bit about the elephant standing on the mine, gross!"

"Oh no!" Peter cried. "Poor thing."

The convoy was still several hours from the

river crossing point. The adjutant had told them over 'breakfast' that they would ferry across via a large pontoon – each vehicle hauled one at a time across to the other side by a winch and cables anchored on either bank.

In their desert-like environment the early morning cold quickly morphed into intense dry heat. They had been taking ten minutes' convoy breaks every hour, during which they splashed themselves with water from their water bottles only to find their clothes were dry again within minutes. Now it looked like the commanding officer would not be calling any halts on this last stretch. Cliff presumed he wanted to push through so they could get all the vehicles across the river before nightfall.

Crossing the big river was going to take a while. Other than the Land Rovers, it would be one lorry on the pontoon at a time, and he needed to get them into the secure enclosure of the police camp before dark. They were apparently entering a very active area, and what better target for an insurgent than lorries carrying explosive fuel; fuel that would be used in vehicles and aircraft against them?

It was impossible to stay awake in the extreme heat and intense glare from the near-white sand of the road. They silently thanked the sergeant for his box of sunglasses, and each other, for grabbing a pair before handing what was left over to the adjutant.

The light was so intense though that even with the glasses, their dust-covered eyelids were still closing involuntarily. Cliff was losing his battle against drooping eyes so he told himself he should make loud conversation with Sam to keep them *both* from falling asleep but before he could he nodded off. Peter's head had already lolled forward before alighting on its final resting place – a windowpane beside him. Their early start that morning was finally taking its toll in the heat.

Cliff stepped down onto the platform two carriages up from where Brenda and his mom waited. He walked back towards them, looking up at the windows until he reached the place where Sam and Peter were pushing the windows down. He stopped, turning to face the two women who approached and shook hands with both stiffly.

"You must have really missed each other," Sam smirked over his shoulder, as he wrestled Cliff's heavy duffel bag off the rack above him and shoved it through the window.

"Brenda, Mom – this is Peter and Sam. We were the A-team at camp," he laughed, pointing to each in turn before extracting his boot from under the duffel bag Sam had dumped on the platform.

"Three's a crowd," smiled Peter, reaching down

to shake Brenda's hand as Cliff stamped his boot on the concrete trying to get the dent out of his boot's toe cap.

They held each other's gaze until Sam stuck out a hand and grinned, "You must have missed the General, Brenda?"

She shook Sam's hand before turning to Cliff. "What? Another promotion?"

"Brenda, can I have a quick word?" Peter said through the window, before he moved back to the door of the compartment and down the narrow passageway towards the main carriage exit door.

Heaving up the heavy bag Sam had pushed through the window, Cliff turned to hand it to his mother, which made her dog growl. He saw Peter leaning out from the bottom step, hanging on to the door rail of the carriage. He was whispering into Brenda's ear.

Brenda's head jerked up suddenly. For a moment, she looked directly at Peter before looking down again. She began digging around in her bag as the first blast of the conductor's whistle pierced through the other background sounds of the station. Cliff noticed people on the platform were laughing quietly while glancing at him.

The whistle made him look up at the station clock above them. It had a tiny little door above the face, and as the big hand clicked onto the twelve, it opened and a bright yellow canary appeared and flew off over the people on the station platform.

There was a second blast of the whistle, and the train started to move slowly away, taking the faces in the carriage windows with it. Walking briskly beside the moving train, Cliff shook his friends' hands through their open window; Peter now standing back in the compartment with Sam.

"Thanks Brenda. You're a life saver," Peter called, as he turned to look back and wave to Brenda. Beryl stood next to her daughter-in-law, unsteady, leaning forward thanks to the heavy duffel bag now on her shoulder.

"I don't think you need to have any more concerns about your friend being gay, Cliff," Brenda smiled.

His mother was giggling and pointing at him while moving her finger to the side of her head where she made a circular motion alongside her temple indicating he was peculiar, laughing as she struggled with his heavy duffel bag.

Brenda also started to laugh. He could see her lips forming words, and as she doubled over laughing while pointing up at the passing carriages, he could hear her say:

"Never mind the fact she has no Adam's apple – your dear friend just asked me for an emergency tampon!"

People on the station platform were laughing louder now, gathered behind his mother and Brenda, and pointing at him. Some pointed at the growling dog his mother had on a leash that bore the sign 'Am I a girl or a boy' around its neck.

Behind him, Cliff could hear everyone on the train laughing now as well. They were pointing at him too and leaning out of their windows to pat him on the head as they passed by. He was only half the height he had been when he arrived and was continuing to shrink. His diminishing size meant the train's passengers now had to lean out really far from their windows in order to reach him.

The dog was towering over him suddenly and growling. He tried to growl back but it came out a howl.

"Shit, General. Are you all right? You scared me half to death. Dreaming you were a wolf or what?" Sam cried, looking over his shoulder at Cliff.

Next to him Peter was still asleep, his head bouncing on the window as the Land Rover fought Sam's sweaty grip on the steering wheel. Cliff rubbed his eyes before taking a gulp from his water bottle.

"Wow!" he said to himself.

They were descending into a deep valley, and the ruts and ridges of the soft sand dragged the vehicles from side to side. The massive Cubango River lay before them measuring four hundred metres wide. Cliff imagined there was likely a mighty current under its calm surface that glistened almost black against the white sandy banks it flowed between. Far below them the winding road had occasionally come into view through the increasingly lush undergrowth but now it finally emerged in its entirety. The road stopped at a small building and sturdy-looking jetty jutting out over the water where a large pontoon was tied.

The Ratel that was leading the convoy stopped just past the building and did a three-point-turn to face the now stationary vehicles strung out up the hill. It would offer security while they were ferried across one by one. Sam stopped their Land Rover on the jetty behind the commanding officer's vehicle before several indigenous workers waved them forward onto the pontoon. They yelled instructions in a mixture of English, Afrikaans and their own native language but it was possible to understand the gist of what they were being asked to do.

Their wheels thudded up the short but steep ramp onto the pontoon. They immediately rocked as the large platform took the weight of the two vehicles while trying to resist the river's strong current at the same time.

"Oh my God, it doesn't even have any rails! We could just slide into the river," Sam observed.

"Please don't say that," Peter quavered. "I'm feeling seasick as it is."

Cliff was wondering if they were supposed to stay inside the vehicle or get out. He took his cue from the commanding officer and adjutant who had not moved so suggested they stay still too.

"I wasn't going anywhere," said Peter.

Cliff gave him a friendly slap on the shoulder to reassure him. "We'll be fine."

The shirtless workers shone like ebony in the sun; their skin taut over muscular arms and shoulders. They were busying themselves working around the two vehicles while laughing and talking loudly in Silozi – the Caprivi native language. Occasionally they looked directly at the vehicles' occupants through the windscreen but didn't extend any greeting. Cliff wondered if *they* should be making the effort to converse.

As though reading his mind, Sam reached into the glovebox and took out a packet before opening the door and getting out unsteadily; the rocking of the vessel taking him by surprise. He strolled over to the two workers unstably as if he was drunk. Just as he raised his hand in greeting, the movement of the pontoon caused him to lose his balance and he stumbled sideways.

A large hand reached out and grabbed his arm to save him from falling into the water. Sam laughed and seemed to be making a joke of it. He offered the packet to them, and they each took a cigarette with a grin. By the look of things, one of the workers spoke English, because Sam was responding to what he said. While they lit their cigarettes a conversation seemed to be underway between the three men; the second worker waiting after each exchange for a translation from his fellow worker.

During their chat, their arms pointed this way and that animatedly. Their conversation was interspersed with laughter, as well as deadpan shakes of their heads. Sam pointed towards the commanding officer's Land Rover and all three laughed together. The commanding officer and the adjutant had turned around in their seats and were making a gesture to Sam to return to his Land Rover. So after shaking both the workers' hands, he lurched back to Cliff and Peter.

"Well, that's a relief," Sam said, throwing the cigarette packet back into the glovebox as he climbed back in. "Jazzman and Nuka are about to start chaining our Land Rovers to those steel bollards bolted onto the deck."

"I didn't know you smoked Sam?" Cliff said.

"Nah I don't. It was the sarge who saved us again. They must be his. Made two friends with those. They say we are lucky we got here early. There's a lot of *Likwambuyu* – important visitors – in the area at the moment and the police camp over there is the best place for us to be safe."

Cliff grimaced. "I guess we know what they mean by visitors."

To their right, behind them, two thick steel

cables appeared from the small building they had seen as they descended down the track. These disappeared across the river to the distant bank; submerging themselves not far offshore as they sagged into the water.

The building housed a diesel engine and sat alongside the massive concrete base the two cables were attached to – one embedded in the concrete with the other wound around a huge pulley on an axle set into the concrete itself. Short cables were attached to the fixed cable by a series of pulleys so they could move with the pontoon and stop it from being pulled downstream by the current. The second cable around the pulley towed the pontoon.

A collective gasp came from all three of them as, with a sudden jerk like the one felt on departing a ski lift, the slack was taken up in the cable and they were on the move. The bank of the river appeared to drop away quickly as the cable, which slipped past above them after emerging from the water in front of the pontoon, dripped water onto the Land Rover's dusty windscreen, creating patterns as the large drops exploded on the glass.

Seeing the adjutant leave his Land Rover, the men decided it was now all right to do likewise. They got out and enjoyed the relatively cool air blowing across the river's surface onto their faces. However, not even the strong breeze could blow away the white dust that covered their hair. They gazed across what seemed to Cliff to be an ominous black surface, and beyond towards figures moving on the far bank.

"Is it my eyesight or are they naked?" Cliff asked aloud.

"They certainly are," came the voice of the adjutant, who had joined them at the foredeck of the pontoon. He had mentioned to Cliff earlier that this was his third convoy down the Caprivi Strip.

"These police guys are here in the bush for two years at a time. Their conditions are pretty tough. Days of boredom spiced with constant threat of attack, continuous presence of anti-personnel mines. And such intense heat. Regular night time fire fights. It's an environment that results in some strange behaviour that demands others to 'turn a blind eye'." The adjutant grinned. "Some would say they get 'bosbefok' from time to time."

They were hearing more frequently the border-war Afrikaans vernacular, which in this case, directly translated, meant: 'fucked by the bush'. The bush environment made one a bit crazy.

The adjutant continued. "You will notice, when we get nearer, that the one thing they seldom take off is the submachine gun slung over their shoulders. One of the few rules never disobeyed up here is to never be without your weapon."

The pontoon was closing in on the far bank. It glided across the surface silently, except for the swishing of the passing water having now left the thumping diesel engine that pulled their cable far behind them. The bizarre vision coming into focus before them reminded Cliff of the movie *Lord of the Flies.*

A dozen very suntanned naked men with shaven heads stood completely motionless. They stared directly at the approaching pontoon, their submachine guns slung over their shoulders. Their faces were expressionless – not welcoming, concerned, nor curious.

Cliff turned to Peter and Sam to discern from their expressions what they were thinking, but he discovered they had disappeared. Peter he saw had returned to the Land Rover where he sat focused on his old map; Sam, was busy moving even further forward, fascinated by what he was witnessing.

A hundred yards up the bank to their right they could see twenty large crocodiles lying motionless, like discarded tree trunks; their bodies dark against the white sand. Some of them lay with their mouths wide open, which it is believed they do to keep cool.

Suddenly one of the policemen thrust his submachine gun at his mate next to him and sprinted towards the crocodiles. A few metres before he reached the closest one, he veered off towards the water and dived in, taken immediately downstream by the fast-flowing current. Instantly alert, two of the crocodiles took a few quick steps on their short legs before slipping into the water behind him.

"Oh God! Are we seeing a ritual suicide of some kind?" Cliff asked, as he joined Sam.

"This is crazy," said Sam. "This is just fucking crazy, man."

Cliff turned back to their Land Rover, gesturing to Peter to look at what was happening. When he saw the head bobbing in the water, with arms thrashing either side of it, he put his hand to his mouth in astonishment even though Cliff doubted Peter could see that the swimmer had a pair of crocodiles in hot pursuit too.

The swimmer's colleagues were cheering now as he passed under the cables pulling the pontoon, the distance between him and the crocodile snouts reducing. Cliff and Sam were transfixed as they watched certain disaster unfolding before them. Cliff glanced at the adjutant who was smiling, seemingly unmoved by the events. He had seen this sort of thing before.

Suddenly the men on the bank, who had followed his course at a trot to keep up with the current, began to chant.

"Mooi so troepie, jy het you plig gedoen." This meant 'well done trooper, you have done your duty' and the chant was repeated over and over again.

Sam grimaced as their words reached him on the breeze. "Well if carrying out a death wish is a duty in the police force then yes, he has certainly done his duty," he said.

Their chants were the swimmer's signal that he could return to the bank and looking once over his shoulder at the snouts following him, he veered off course. When he had reached shallow water, he stood up and clambered up the steep sandy bank. The predators slipped from the water in pursuit of him mere moments later.

The men cheered as they hauled him up the last few metres of the bank before turning and making a hasty retreat from the slowing crocodiles struggling in the soft sand. They slapped the swimmer's back as he took his submachine gun and slung it over his wet shoulder.

Sam looked at Cliff. "Some kind of initiation?"

Chapter 7

On the Other Side

Cliff absent-mindedly rubbed at the texture of the waist-height hessian wall of the officer's mess as he stared out over the vast panorama below him. The outpost had been located at the top of a hill along a narrow track rising up from the Cubango below; the same one they had descended earlier on the opposite side of the valley to arrive at the river crossing point.

All the way up the valley he could see lush green foliage; evidence of the fertile soil and moisture either side of the river, a dramatic contrast to the dryness of the scattered thorn tree landscape it snaked through. High in the blueness above the valley a lone vulture was gliding in a circle that waned and waxed. Cliff marvelled at how with the slightest, almost invisible adjustment of its wing tips it could change direction, diving nearer to an object it wanted to inspect from a closer range. He wondered if it intuitively saw promise in the activities taking place in the bush around the camp.

Turning his gaze to the river below, he saw that the last lorry was on its way across. It was a surreal image – the vehicle taking up most of the pontoon looking like it was floating on the water, propelling itself across like some amphibious craft. Jazzman and Nuka must be happy their workday was nearly over.

On the bank, their submachine gun carrying welcoming committee were nowhere to be seen. Yet the crocodiles were still there, immobile. From this distance they looked like kayaks on the bank, waiting to be launched into the river. Cliff recalled when he and Brenda once went kayaking. He had moaned continually about his aching calves until she threatened to whack him with her oar.

The sleeves of Father Gerry's black robe hung open below the arms he held out to Brenda, inviting her to tell him what was troubling her. She tried not to stare at the sprinkling of white flakes on the inside of the sleeves. When he finally spoke, Gerry did so quietly, in what Brenda presumed was his priestly voice.

"You mentioned on the phone that you had been feeling down lately, Brenda. Is it Cliff being away perhaps?" he asked, having already spoken to Beryl.

Looking up at the painting of the crucifixion on the wall above him, Brenda smiled to hide her irritation at the immediate introduction of her husband into the conversation.

"No, this is not about Cliff."

She wondered why men tended to presume that most of the time the only thing that mattered to a woman was what their partner said or did.

She had recently confided in Beryl that she was feeling very anxious about where her life was heading, and that she was becoming increasingly resentful about being left in an orphanage as a baby.

While Cliff had been away at camp these last few months, Beryl had got the impression that Brenda had not missed him at all. She was beginning to think that the real problem here was their marriage. Maybe the lack of a baby was fuelling Brenda's discontent? She worried from time to time that although well intentioned, bringing Brenda and Cliff together might have been an ill-conceived idea. She knew her son; when pointed in a direction and given a slight nudge he kept floating in the same orbit, like space debris, until pushed off course. Beryl knew that a baby would push Cliff off his course of complacency. Make him take responsibility for once.

"Gerry has a lot of experience from his navy

days, Brenda. Stuck on a ship for months on end, young people had all kinds of anxieties. It might be worthwhile having a chat with him; get a different view on things. Also Gerry of course knows Cliff really well."

Brenda had wondered why Gerry knowing Cliff would be useful to her situation, but thanked Beryl for her suggestion and promised she would call the number given to her for Gerry's parish office.

Now, looking into Gerry's eyes, Brenda began describing her early childhood and the foster home experiences she had endured. Gerry seemed to listen intently but when she asked if he thought finding her birth parents might help her and if he could advise her on how best to go about finding them, she was not sure he had heard the questions. He was quiet for some time while he scratched at something inside his sleeve, and Brenda thought he must be reflecting on the best process she might embark upon.

When he did finally speak, his solution revolved around the joy and rewards of children in a marriage.

"Oh my God, I forgot my parking meter!" Brenda said, jumping up in haste. "I'll have to call you later. Thanks Gerry," she said in a fake panicky voice.

As bewildered as he was at the sudden end to their discussion, Gerry did look through some old papers after Brenda's departure, in search of the contact details of a probationer friend of his. The probationer in question had been adopted at birth and had successfully traced his own birth parents. Gerry remembered that what his friend had discovered during the process had in fact prompted him to enter the ministry.

Turning back from his view over the river, Cliff reflected that even in a danger zone the ritual of the evening officers' mess was adhered to. Here he was enjoying the view while sipping an ice-cold can of beer with a second cooling the palm of his other hand; the evening sun still powerful enough to burn down onto his back.

The mess's tradition apparently was that one drank beer in even numbers so Cliff was following this protocol tonight. The young policeman, who was the mess orderly for the night, also informed him that it was the local beer of Angola.

"When they're not shooting us sir, they're selling us their beer," he laughed. "Be careful – *Cuca* has a kick like a mule when drunk in this hot sun."

Over the waist-high hessian 'privacy' wall of the officers' mess, Cliff watched a post-work volleyball game. Probably due to the aggressive environment they found themselves in, the game was being played more as a contact sport, as an opportunity to relieve stress, Cliff surmised.

It had a distinct football flavour about it, as players barged into their own teammates or elbowed their way past to make ball contact. Several players were bleeding from grazes and cuts sustained through collisions.

Drinking beers with the other drivers, Cliff saw Sam and Peter in the background watching the performance with expressions of bemusement. Remembering Peter's embarrassment on the pontoon, Cliff was relieved for his sake that these hyperactive policemen were at least wearing shorts.

The camp adjutant had invited them to the mess and apologised for the absence of their commanding officer, Colonel van der Nel, who was still out on patrol. However, the colonel had just radioed that he was on approach. A few minutes later, as if responding to a starter's race gun, two constables broke from those gathered around the game and ran back towards the wide gate, located in the razor-wired perimeter fence that Cliff's Land Rover and the other vehicles had come through earlier. In the distance, trailing swirls of white dust indicated a vehicle was approaching at speed and its driver clearly expected the gates to be opened in time for his arrival.

Before the gates were even fully opened, the camouflaged four-wheel Land Cruiser raced through them with mere inches to spare either side of the vehicle. A few seconds later its oversized wheels skidded to a halt in the sandy parking area near the mess. Cliff was interested to see the passenger sitting alongside the driver was a black person. *I thought black people were the insurgents?* he mused.

He had heard vague rumours about Koevoet – an undercover South African Police unit operating in Angola comprised of former Ovambo Home Guard and SWAPO fighters. They were all black soldiers, led by top-class black *and* white officers from other organisations like Rhodesia's disbanded Selous Scouts. As the passenger alighted, the faded insignia sewn onto the shoulder epaulettes of his shirt looked like a major's crest. So here, it seemed, was a high-ranking officer.

Cliff observed that the large-framed, red-headed driver, who seemed to have prised himself down from the cab of the high-riding vehicle, did not wear any badges of rank on his shoulders. Instead of an army-issue handgun and webbing holster that Cliff and the other officers around him all currently wore, this man sported huge ivory-handled Magnums sitting in leather holsters on either hip, complete with leather thongs holding the holsters firmly to his upper thighs.

Getting down off his trusty steed, Twogun Red (John Wayne) strolled into the bar for a 'whuskey', Cliff thought, smiling to himself.

On the other side of the volleyball court, as he and Peter observed the same scene as Cliff, Sam was thinking more along the lines of World War II's General Patton and his famous ivory handled revolvers.

"Nothing like a few good slaps to get men loafing in hospital up and about," Sam quoted quietly to Peter, who gave him a quizzical look. "Later Felix, later," Sam smiled, without averting his gaze.

The tall colonel wasted little time on formalities. Looking down on them from his great height and while sipping the *Cuca* that had been handed to him by his adjutant, he shook hands and proceeded to inform their commanding officer and his officers what the camp standing orders for overnight visitors would be.

"Your men must sleep in the parking area, in the back of their trucks or ours and not leave them under any circumstances. Their weapons must be loaded and within reach at all times during darkness. If the camp is attacked or a firefight is underway nearby, they are to remain in their sleeping bags, flat, below the level of the top of the metal truck flaps. There is a SWAPO unit active in this area. We have had a few contacts and believe we have reduced their numbers, but they still keep having a go at the camp most nights."

Reduced their numbers? You mean killed them. Cliff was beginning to yearn for the safety of basic training, however much of a waste of time he considered it to be.

"Your Bedford's canvas sides are not going to stop a flying bullet. Stay down. Don't leave the vehicle for any reason. A single moving figure in the dark is going to be shot by one of my men. We only move in close contact – tight groups. A single, isolated figure is presumed to be an enemy, considered a threat and shot. You guys with Land Rovers can sleep in our trucks – the ones you are parked next to. Make sure your men have a few buckets in their trucks for emergencies. Getting off the truck for a piss or anything else will get them shot. Any questions?"

No one made a sound.

"Goed, dan. Let's drink together." He grinned, gesturing to the young barmen to hand out more beers – two apiece. "Oh, sorry I forgot to say – this is Major Hani," he said, introducing the officer who had been his passenger. "He has joined our unit for a special project."

The colonel didn't elaborate and neither did their own commanding officer, whose authority seemed to diminish in the colonel's presence. His officers were certainly going to ask him for more details later.

Cliff saluted the introduced officer and then shook the hand he offered in greeting before introducing himself.

"And when did you and Josh last enjoy a game

of backyard soccer, Cliff?" Major Hani asked, with a grin.

Cliff's mouth was agape; he was speechless.

"It's me – Zeb. I used to stay with my mother in the holidays, at your house." The major smiled.

"Oh my God, of course, Zeb! This place, the uniform and of course you're older. I didn't put it all together. I didn't remember your surname. It's been over ten years as well. I'm sorry."

"And all black faces look the same to you guys, hey?" Zeb said, no longer smiling. Then he laughed out loudly, pointing at Cliff's stricken face, before punching his arm gently. "Just teasing, my friend."

Unlike Chris Hani, who ran an operation against the Apartheid government from there, Zeb had only spent a few hours in mountainous Lesotho before he and his fellow recruits were flown out to Zambia. From there they had been taken by road to a training camp in Angola.

He had discovered that the majority of the recruits in the Umkhonto weSizwe training camps had been coerced into being there, much like he had after losing his ID document to the police that morning on the campus of Durban University. He had expected to be arrested later so he chose to flee, or rather his father chose for him. Zeb's abilities were especially noticeable amongst the unwilling soldiers, and his Cuban instructors, who were continually frustrated by the poor quality of recruits they had been given to work with, rewarded him accordingly.

As his rank and reputation grew so too did the conflict between his willingness to be a soldier for the cause and the rewards his growing status potentially offered him on a personal level. Assigned to a SWAPO unit just inside the Angolan border, his reputation as a leader of missions across the border grew with each contact. It was during an assignment with a SWAPO unit operating undercover within Namibia that he was approached for the first time to go over to the enemy.

*

Both the South African Defence Force and the South African Police launched parallel initiatives to create counter-insurgency units in the 1970s. The SADF's initiative resulted in 101 Battalion while the SAP formed the notorious undercover unit – Koevoet. Using the English translation of this unit's name – the crowbar – the minister of law and order, Louis le Grange, was credited for saying of Koevoet activities in the operational area, "(Koevoet) prises terrorists out of the bushveld like nails from rotten wood."

A captain from within the SAP's security branch was appointed to lead Koevoet. He had served with the SAP in Zimbabwe and used his operational experiences there in shaping Koevoet's mandate and organisational structure. Not long after its formation, even though he led the very insurgents they were trying to stop, Zeb's reputation amongst the captain's senior officers for being as good as any Selous Scout officer they knew, soon came to his attention.

He asked Colonel van der Nel (a red-headed giant who was himself infamous and who was operating in the area) to make contact with this enemy highflyer to see if he could be tempted to come over to Koevoet. The unit was to be patterned directly after the Selous Scouts – a Rhodesian Special Forces unit that included large numbers of former insurgents.

With SAP's intelligence people having learnt many were unhappy with risking their lives for no pay or security for their families as part of the SWAPO organisation, Zeb Hani would be invaluable in recruiting and training further converts from their enemy.

As was the rule in an operational area, mess finished at seven p.m. and everyone moved off to eat before retiring for the night. Cliff had enjoyed chatting to Zeb and hearing about some of his military experiences. Zeb's account had been a high-level view minus the details; especially about how he came to have moved from Umkhonto weSizwe to whatever he was now, some would have said this was a grey area.

It had been a long day and the *Cuca* beers had taken their toll. However, although he felt exhausted, Cliff lay awake in the darkness while Sam and Peter slept alongside. They lay in the back of one of the SAP trucks, and Cliff reflected for some time about his chance meeting with Zeb. *I bet he has a few stories to tell,* he thought.

Peter snored lightly and it reminded him of his dream. The dog with sign had been weird. He tried to remember more but big chunks of the dream had slipped away and he was soon asleep.

A few hours later they were instantly awoken from a deep sleep by the *crack* of a shot from a rifle followed by rapid machine gun fire. It seemed right on top of them and was deafening. This was definitely not one of Sergeant Swartberg's training exercises. Sensing Sam and Peter groping for their rifles in the darkness, Cliff reached down for his holstered handgun. He unclipped the cover strap and pulled at the butt. It wouldn't budge. The webbing holster had stiffened tight around the weapon after getting wet earlier in the pontoon's bow splashes. *That's just great Cliff. Aren't you the warrior?* he thought.

They lay there on their backs, as though frozen with fear, the fire fight continuing. Then it quietened down a bit and there was a thudding of boots passing behind their truck. Silence followed and the only thudding they could hear was the sound of their rapidly beating hearts. They lay inert for what seemed like an eternity.

Suddenly, there was whispering alongside the truck.

The Zulu accent identified the speaker as Zeb.

"Where the fuck is he?" he whispered.

"Behind those fuel drums, sir."

"Can we take him alive?".

"If he sticks his head up, I have a clear shot sir."

"No, not yet. I want him alive. Cover me. I want to try to talk to him. First, I will tell him to stay down. Take him if he sticks his head up after I start talking, OK?"

After this exchange, all the three men in the truck could hear was their own breathing. Then they jumped as a shot rang out right next to the canvas above them.

They heard the shooter say to the others around him, "Bastard had a grenade."

Cliff presumed the shooter had established this fact with the use of a night scope.

"Well he's not going to be doing much talking now. Let's go boys. Get them to bring body bags down from the camp," Zeb said in a matter-of-fact voice.

It would be many hours before any of them slept, and even then it would be only fitfully. As tired as they were from their two a.m. start that day, the fire fight had created enough adrenalin to keep them going for hours. In their own way, each man was coming to terms with the fact he had gone to war for the first time that night. They were also having to accept that they would never again think about their tiresome army camps in the same way.

Beryl sat alone on the front veranda of her small house overlooking the road, reflecting on some of the events of the past year. Through the window behind her she could hear the loud snores of Cliff's father who had 'retired to his boudoir' as he liked to say.

She always spoke of him as 'Cliff's father' and would refer to him as such in conversation. She never said 'my husband' or even called him by his name, except when speaking directly to him.

During each pause in the passing traffic she could hear the sound of her neighbour chatting to her old mother on their own veranda on the opposite side of the road. Her neighbour, Mrs Levy, had a speech defect that resulted in her unconsciously emphasising the letter 's' in every word. She sounded like a chick in a nest demanding food. The sound seemed to carry for miles on a quiet evening.

Mrs Levy's bird sounds coming across on the evening air made Beryl think of Cliff who always referred to her as 'the budgie'.

She wondered how he was. *I bet he's looking forward to getting back home. Only a few more weeks now*, she thought. Just then a bus belching smoke thundered past; its resultant noise drowning out Mrs Levy's chirps.

Beryl reflected on her conversation with Brenda. *I hope he is not going to come home to bad news. Cliff has never mentioned anything. Does he even know how she feels? Young people nowadays – they don't know how to get through hard times and make things work. They're always having to 'find themselves'. They would be better off finding ways to appreciate what they have. If I had had the same attitude, then what? How would Cliff have turned out if he had come from a broken home? They forget just how fortunate they are.*

Look at poor Frank. All the worry with Josh and his illness for the last few years, and then Madge's dreadful accident. Lucky he and the twins were able to stay with Raechel. I don't know what Frank would have done had he tried to look after the twins on his own with all his drinking. Raechel will put a stop to that I bet.

Must have taken him some getting used to – living with Raechel. I wonder if I should have told

Cliff about Josh's situation? I better write one last letter to him before he leaves the camp.

Across the road the 'budgie' said to her mother, "Time for sssleep don't you think?"

I agree, Beryl smiled to herself, getting to her feet.

As she closed the front door, she spotted Mrs Levy waving from her veranda, and waved back.

"Hop onto your perch, dear," she whispered to herself with a giggle, closing the door.

Madge and her youngest daughter, Mary, had been passengers in her friend's old car when the accident happened. Just as the driver was negotiating a sharp corner, Madge's back door flew open unexpectedly. She was not wearing a seatbelt and had been flung out into the path of a car going in the opposite direction. Their driver was shocked and distracted by what had just happened. Consequently, she lost control of the vehicle. She ended up going down an embankment, rolling the car and killing the remaining occupants.

The whole family was devastated. During the funeral Frank was completely lost and utterly inconsolable. At the graveside his twin boys clung to each other, crying for their mother and sister. Frank seemed at a loss as to how to console them as tears streamed down his own face.

Standing with his parents, Cliff wished he knew how to support the older siblings who stood weeping behind their father. Cliff saw his Auntie 'Chel, who seemed to appear from nowhere, bend down behind the twins.

She drew the two boys to her, holding them closely. She whispered in their ears as Madge's coffin was lowered gently into the grave alongside the coffin of their sister.

Chapter 8

On the Road Again

When they left the following morning, the Cubango River police camp they had stayed at was almost deserted. Several contingents had left at dawn to do a follow-up search for the SWAPO patrol – or what was left of it – that had attacked the camp the previous night.

There was no idle chat as the three set off. Cliff could see that Sam and Peter, like him, were still in a state of shock after the previous night. They had gone from a state of denial – based on ignorance to a large extent about just where their country was positioned as a result of its Apartheid regime – to the harsh reality of the potential consequences of its position.

The morning had not brought any lightness to their sombre moods, especially not when they entered the main camp for breakfast and saw the five bulky body bags being loaded onto the truck that had just trundled past them on their walk from the parking area.

"Oh God!" Peter said with a gasp. He visibly shrank back from where they were loading with tears in his eyes. "I can't do this. It's too much."

Sam put his arm around Peter's trembling shoulders. "It's OK. It's OK buddy. You'll be fine in a few hours. Once we're on the road." He looked at Cliff, indicating with his eyes that he too should say some words of comfort to the distraught Peter.

"Only a few weeks to go Peter, and we'll be back in Civvy Street. You'll have a few anecdotes to shut your dad's mates up with now, won't you? He'll be *bragging* about you now when he can say that his son was fighting on the border." Cliff laughed, giving Peter a pat on the shoulder.

Sam gave Cliff an inquiring look – he didn't understand the reference. Peter blew his nose and looking away towards the distant hills said, "It's not me. It's them. Probably our age, dying because they want what we have. Why don't we just share it with them?"

Cliff and Sam avoided each other's eyes.

As they drove into the rising sun, from behind the shade of his maybe stolen Raybans, Sam stared straight ahead in concentration so as not to drive into the back of the adjutant's vehicle. For the moment he had run out of jokes and jovial asides. In the skewed rear-view mirror Cliff could see Peter staring through the window beside him without focusing upon anything.

Their next crossing would be the Kwando River. It seemed they would reach it by late afternoon now. They had been delayed by a few over-heated vehicles; even having to leave one behind while it was fitted with a spare radiator. The commanding officer was keen to cross the river before nightfall as it was considered more secure on the far bank.

*

Notwithstanding they were missing a fuel truck, they arrived at the river without further mishap other than several badly sunburnt lookout recruits. Standing in the cab's turret it had seemed the obvious thing to do: dispense with one's fatigue top and enjoy the cooling wind.

"We gave them sunglasses. Did they want sunscreen as well?" the adjutant said, when the issue was reported to him. "I want them on charge for removing their uniforms. They're in a red zone, for God's sake!"

The crossing time was much shorter than the previous day's crossing. The Kwando was not as wide and the pontoon could take two vehicles at a time. The local operator made it clear however that he would be leaving with the last vehicles to cross and would not return until the following morning so they would have to bring the vehicle that had broken down across themselves when it arrived.

"Too dangerous this side at night, sir," the operator said as another two vehicles rattled off the pontoon.

He continued he was happy to give instructions to someone else so they could wait for the repaired truck to arrive and take it across themselves. Being in the vehicle immediately behind the commanding officer's was to Cliff's disadvantage, as he was the first officer Colonel Roverstone saw when he had finished speaking to the operator. He waved Cliff over to his Land Rover without delay.

"Lieutenant, I want you and your men to stay here until the vehicle we left behind catches up and bring it across. This gentleman is going to show you how to get the pontoon back to this side after we have the last vehicles across. Understood?"

Cliff could feel his stomach start to do strange things. He wanted to ask the colonel why the local man would not be available to do the job he was currently doing but thought better of it.

"Yes, sir."

"Draw extra ammunition from the supply vehicle behind you, just in case. You'll be fine, no activity reported here in my last sitrep."

"When was that, sir?" Cliff asked.

"Two weeks ago," interjected the adjutant, whose job it was to know such things. He gave Cliff a wry grin.

When Cliff relayed the orders to Sam and Peter their faces turned white.

"OK. We are going to need three submachine guns, hand grenades and a G5 cannon from that quartermaster behind us," Sam cried.

"Does he have any Sherman tanks? We could hide in them," Peter said humourlessly.

He looked stricken. Cliff patted him on the shoulder in comfort. "Look at it this way, your dad will be pleased. When you share these next few hours with him, he'll know the army made a man of you."

Peter grimaced. "I'll stick with being considered a queer rather than this – after last night's episode as well."

Sam laughed aloud. "Peter, good man. Back from your panic attack!"

*

Cliff looked up to the crest of the track, which was about a hundred metres away. It was the one they had come over as they approached the crossing and he decided it was the best point to wait for the late arrival. On the pontoon Sam was already getting instructions from the operator, following which he would do a few crossings as a co-pilot to familiarise himself with the controls and the process.

Waving to them as he departed for the first time, Sam looked rather pleased with himself in his bright orange life vest and oversized gloves. By the time he brought the pontoon back for the final time, he considered himself a highly skilled operator. He appraised Cliff and Peter of this fact at length, boring them with anecdotes about which levers did what and all the steering technicalities before he finally drove them up to the crest of the hill and parked facing the pontoon.

*

It was already dark, and Peter had not moved since they arrived at their waiting point, adamant he was not getting out for anyone. On the seat beside him was an unopened box of small rounds ammunition that Cliff hoped was going to stay closed. Peter clenched his rifle between his legs, the barrel resting on the seat in front of him.

"You going to fire that thing through the windscreen or what?" Sam called from where he and Cliff were sitting with their backs against a tree.

"No. Now that you have taught me how to drive, I'll just drive us off to safety," Peter yelled back, his head out of the window.

"Then we will probably be safer out here with the SWAPO guys!"

Even with the rising moon, under the forest

canopy it was very dark. After half an hour of seeing nothing but hearing plenty – each time visualising either an enemy patrol or rogue elephant – Sam and Cliff joined Peter in the vehicle.

"Just cold, that's all," Sam said, as Peter wagged a finger at him. "Fuck off, Peter. And point that rifle away from me."

Below them the Kwando River glistened silver in the moonlight as it snaked away from them, threading its way through the black landscape. They could see the lights of the commanding officer's newly established camp on the other side of the river. Sam kept glancing into the rear-view mirror hoping to see the lights of the truck they were waiting for.

Suddenly the whole inside of the Land Rover was lit up by an intense search light piercing the rear windows.

"Oh, shit, this is it!" cried Sam, ducking down as Peter nearly took his eye out swinging his rifle around to point it in the direction of the light.

Craning their necks to look through the rear window, they watched the approaching light. It momentarily blinded them and they sat inert like the proverbial deer caught in headlights.

Finally it was sheer panic that forced Sam and Cliff to get out of the vehicle. Sam struggled with the bolt on his rifle and Cliff lost a second battle with his unyielding webbing holster.

"Fuck! Fuck this thing!" he said just before they heard someone call out from behind their searchlight.

"Whoa, take it easy guys. It's just us – from the convoy."

"You scared the shit out of us!" Sam shouted shielding his eyes from the light with a hand.

"Sorry. Our headlights failed so we've been using our searchlight, switching it on and off to conserve our battery," the voice explained. "I put it on every time we took a corner to see what was ahead and then off again. We let the ruts in the sand guide us until the next turn. That's why we surprised you."

"Can you switch it off now? You've arrived," Cliff called, taking his hands off his holster to protect his eyes.

"Oh yes, sorry sir."

The light died.

"Let's get going. After that they'll be lucky if we let them on the pontoon at all," Sam said, as he climbed into the driver's seat of their Land Rover.

"You didn't pee your pants again did you, Peter?"

"Fuck off, Sam." Peter spoke his first words since the search light had come on.

Then he laughed, and the others joined in, more out of a huge sense of relief than genuine humour.

*

Cresting a hill late in the afternoon of the following day, the lead Ratel and the commanding officer's Land Rover fell below their line of sight to reveal the mighty Zambezi in the far distance. Its wide dark waters curved across their panoramic view and beyond it lay Zambia. On this side of the river they could discern a small town with an airstrip on its outskirts.

"That must be where we are heading," Cliff said. "Katima Mulilo. At last! Oh for a shower and a cold beer."

"First bit of good news I've heard in days," Peter said, clapping with delight.

"A little to the right there – well, a few hours south – is where the Chobe River meets the Zambezi, and the four countries of Zambia, Zimbabwe, Botswana and Namibia meet too," Sam informed them.

"Yup, our driver's a geography major," Cliff said looking back at Peter. "Did you know that?"

Sam continued educating the other two. "Not far south of that point is the Victoria Falls we spoke about the other day. Gee, it seems like a year ago now."

The landscape soon flattened out again and that enabled their vehicle to pick up speed. There were camouflaged helicopters passing high above them that all seemed to be heading towards the same point, like bees returning to their hive.

"That must be the base," Cliff said. "Where those choppers seem to be congregating."

They were startled when all of a sudden, from seemingly out of nowhere, they heard a loud thudding and a dark shape appeared from behind and above them into their windscreen view.

It passed over the commanding officer's Land Rover and the Ratel leading the convoy before peeling off; gaining height at speed before veering off over the bush a few hundred metres in front of them.

"Think he was checking us out?" Sam shouted. "That felt a bit like *Star Wars*."

"A welcoming 'buzz' maybe? I hear our chopper pilots are a bit out there," Cliff responded.

*

Both helicopter pilots stared at him blankly. They had just landed their craft and were heading for the administration building for their regular post-flight debrief. Before they could reach their destination, however, they had found themselves accosted by a person who looked like he had been in a dust storm.

"So, I have to come all this way to see my old school mates, do I?" Cliff grinned.

The pilots' faces didn't register any sign of recognition.

Finally, Cliff realised he was disguised by the

accumulation of dust on his face. "It's me – Cliff Barkerfield. You guys are lucky you fly above the dust!"

"Oh wow! Cliffie boy! It's been years," one of the pilots, Billy, laughed.

"Good to see you Cliff," the other, Guy, said, pumping Cliff's hand.

After some jovial back-slapping and apt quotations from *Lawrence of Arabia*, they agreed to meet up later in the mess.

"Was that you who just buzzed us – back up the road?" Cliff asked, before the men parted company.

"Oh yeah. Was that you guys? Sorry about that Cliff. Camp standing orders are to check out any military vehicles we come across and don't recognise as being from this camp. Especially a large convoy like yours so close to the camp," Billy said.

"OK, we better get to our debriefing," Guy laughed as the pair hurried off.

*

Later, just before the officers' mess closed at seven p.m., Cliff's re-discovered friends insisted he go back to their tent with them and carry on with the merriment.

"Sam and Peter are welcome to join us as well," Billy said. Cliff had shared some anecdotes about his two 'staff' earlier.

"Yeah," Guy chimed in. "Go and give them a shout. We have plenty to drink. We've been here for over seven months and are getting sick of the same old faces and conversations – present company excluded of course," he chuckled. "See you at the tent."

The two pilots followed behind Cliff through the entrance flaps of the mess tent. Although he felt slightly tipsy, Cliff had remembered to seek out the camp commandant to excuse himself before he left the mess tent. He stepped gingerly over the guy ropes near the entrance, and after making a few twists and turns around the other tents, he spotted Sam and Peter walking up the main gravel path on their way back from the other ranks' mess.

"You two clean up well," Cliff said, putting his arms around both their shoulders as he came up behind them. "Come on, I'm taking you to a party with my pilot mates. Time to enjoy the high life – 'scuse... the... pun," Cliff said, as he hiccoughed and burped through his apology, leading them in search of his friends.

"Excuse *you*, General," Peter said, leaning forward to exchange a wry look with Sam on the other side of Cliff.

"Oh no, not you too," Cliff said.

Billy and Guy's tent was easy to find thanks to the loud music coming from within. They were both captains and so had the privilege of an orderly who had made sure their illicit bar was well-stocked, including a cooler box with ice.

Lolling on beds, Sam and Peter were soon chatting like they had known Billy and Guy all their lives. The strangers did not seem to notice nor care about Peter's effeminate demeanour. As the evening wore on, Cliff noticed how Peter was growing in confidence.

In Guy and Billy's company, he was full of self assurance; laughing out loud rather than just grinning quietly when one of the pilots made a joke. He was unreserved when he expressed astonishment, adding his own comments after their flying anecdotes were relayed.

Peter even shared the personal anecdote of his nightmare experience on the troop carrier that Cliff had saved him from (although he didn't mention the 'personal accident' part of the story). Sam added detail to Peter's tale, courtesy of his observations of the incident from his driver's seat in Cliff's Land Rover. He also added a few impersonations of Sergeant Swartberg.

Having been part of the anecdote and therefore knowing the story well, Cliff's thoughts turned to other things. He reflected upon how the interaction between he and Sam and Peter had changed; how his perception of both of them was changing again, even now.

He wondered how quickly one's judgmental attitude towards an individual might be re-aligned by peers. If Guy and Billy had not been accepting of Peter, would that have influenced how he felt? *Do we need our peers to re-affirm that someone is OK because we need the support of the 'pack'? Or is it the fear of being alienated by the 'pack'?*

"So the general's your hero, Peter?" Billy laughed.

Cliff tried not to appear awkward when he heard Peter confirm that he sure was. Cliff swiftly changed the course of the conversation.

"Sam can tell you about how an old antipersonnel mine got between him and the very same sergeant," he said, nodding at Sam to begin the tale.

It transpired that Sam's story was the first of many mine incident anecdotes relayed that night; the two pilots having been involved in several themselves. These featured casualty evacuation from isolated bush locations that called for some creative manoeuvring with fast landings and takeoffs. It was nearly midnight when Guy suggested they turn in as they were flying early in the morning.

"We have an interesting mission tomorrow," Guy said. "Top secret. It could affect the outcome of this border war."

The two pilots had had their audience captivated by their exploits all night but now it seemed there was to be a finale. Billy threw himself backwards onto his bed and stared up at the tent ceiling.

"I still can't believe this is going to happen," he said.

"Yes, tomorrow we are flying south to a farm our camp commandant knows. It is owned by his friend, a beef farmer," Guy confirmed.

"Really? Are there insurgents operating there or what?" asked Cliff.

"No, we're going to pick up the meat for this weekend's camp barbecue," Guy chortled.

*

It was past midnight when the three of them attempted to sneak back quietly to their allocated tents. Sam dawdled and tried to persuade Billy and Guy to take him up with them in the morning on their patrol at dawn – *braai vleis* patrol, as Billy had called it. The mandatory pre-flight non-alcohol policy for pilots did not seem to apply to these two especially, it seemed to Cliff, when given the task of doing a personal favour for the camp commandant.

"All I need is a blue overall with the wing insignia. No one will notice. Come on guys!" Sam begged, as the two pilots gently ushered him out of their tent, promising to take him up another time.

Sam was more inebriated than Cliff and Peter, so his friends supported him as they made their way through the darkness, stepping carefully over tent pegs and guy ropes. The trio laughed and joked, which resulted in the occasional, "Shut the fuck up!" from their fellow recruits who were trying to sleep inside the tents they passed.

Cliff veered off to his tent.

"Uh oh, lost a wing Sam. But no fear, I'll get us back to base," Peter said.

They are certainly the Odd Couple, thought Cliff, as he watched the slim-built Peter struggling with his large, unsteady charge into the night; Sam hanging on to Peter as the pair attempted to dodge errant tent stays. After a few moments observing the scene, Cliff sighed and slipped inside his own tent.

He was just dozing off when he heard Peter whispering at the tent flap. "Cliff, are you awake? Can I sleep in your tent? Sam could wake up the dead with his snoring!"

"Sure, go for it," he said, turning his back to avoid any awkwardness.

*

The sound of a helicopter above them was fading away as Peter slipped out of the tent, telling Cliff he had better get back to his own tent before sunup. Seconds after leaving his head poked back in through the opening.

"Thanks for saving me again – this time from Sam's snoring!" Although Peter's face was just a featureless silhouette in the dim dawn light, Cliff sensed he was grinning.

Relishing the thought of the two days off duty they had all been given before the return trip, Cliff had just dosed off again when the tent flap was thrown open and light poured in from a gas lamp.

Both Peter and a dishevelled Sam stood before him wearing blue flight fatigues. From behind them, Guy and Billy's orderly appeared and laid out a set of fatigues onto his bed.

"The captain says to get these on and meet them at their aircraft, quick time. I will show you where, sir."

As he stumbled into the overalls trying to keep his balance, Cliff noted Sam's grin was in complete contrast to Peter's look of trepidation. Within a minute they were trotting behind the orderly towards the airfield. There was a guard at the gate who did not seem that interested in their sudden arrival; waving them through when the orderly said they were the crew accompanying Captain Guy Todd. The orderly pointed at a helicopter positioned behind two others.

"Head for the chopper in position three. The flight engineer will set you up," the orderly said, saluting Cliff. "And keep your heads down," he shouted over his shoulder, as he disappeared back into the administration building they had just come through.

The noise from the *Allouette III* was deafening as they approached it; their hands on their heads in an attempt to hold their ill-fitting flight caps in place, their backs hunched over even though the helicopter's rotating blades were not close enough to pose a threat. *This is what arriving or departing passengers do in the movies isn't it?* Cliff thought.

The trio were seated by the engineer who leaned in through the doorway and fitted the men with headsets. It was a relief to climb inside the helicopter and away from the turbulent air outside.

"You chaps all set back there?" Guy's voice came through their headsets as he turned to look at them. Billy did not look back however as he was busy flicking switches; his eyes moving from one dial to the next. As Guy began *his* checks, Billy scanned the sky while addressing his passengers.

"OK, let me tell you what today's flight is about. It's not meat delivery after all. We will not be in communication a lot after this. Firstly we have to complete our pre-flight checks and thereafter this aircraft demands most of our attention, especially in a low altitude search mission. OK? We are allowed to take spotters on these search missions, so we decided to sneak you in. Enjoy, Sam," he said, but gave them all a thumbs-up.

"That doesn't mean total radio silence, but keep any questions short," Guy added.

Billy went on to tell them that their orders had changed overnight. There was apparently a major incident taking place in Rundu, and the helicopters that normally supported the police patrols out of the Divundu outpost were unavailable. They were standing in for them today, flying ahead of the patrols, to look for signs of the insurgents they had been struggling to capture or kill following several attacks on their camp.

When Billy mentioned the Divundu area was their destination Cliff exclaimed, "That's where we slept over, just two nights ago!"

"Well, you will be saying hello again. We will have to re-fuel at the camp before we return," Billy said.

*

In little over an hour, they were in radio contact with patrols on the ground. The three passengers listened, fascinated as the pilots interacted with the unmistakable raspy voice of Colonel van der Nel and other patrols. The colonel directed them to an area where he and his patrol were sure a group of insurgents were located. They had been tracking them for days but had still not made contact with them.

The police patrols had left their vehicles and were tracking on foot so the colonel now needed air reconnaissance back-up in case the insurgents outran the officers on the ground. He had also sent a second patrol team to approach from the rear of where they thought the insurgents were.

The next minute the passengers heard a different voice on the radio and their mouths gaped open in surprise.

"Airrec. This is patrol2. My signal strength. Over."

"Patrol2. This is Airrec. Good. Over."

"Airrec. This is patrol2. Leader standing by. Over."

Guy said, "What the hell? That sounded like a Zulu accent. Since when?"

Cliff confirmed Guy's suspicion. "It was. Zeb Hani. Major Zeb Hani, actually. He is a friend of mine, would you believe, since I was about twelve."

"Well, you learn something new every day in this bush war," Billy said. "I suspect there is a Koevoet connection there."

"My thought too – when Zeb and I met up a few days ago," Cliff responded.

"Patrol2. This is Airrec. Stand by for sitrep on bandits, as available. Over."

"Copy that Airrec. Over," came Zeb's voice.

*

The three passengers exchanged looks of disbelief and terror at times during the flight, as the helicopter skimmed over the tops of thorn trees, diving one way then the other looking for any sign of movement in the bush below.

Sitting in the backseat, it felt like riding an out-of-control roller coaster. Through a side window they watched the green canopy below them flash past one moment, before next seeing the static blue of the sky through the windshield as they swept upward, readying for another diving fly-by of the trees below.

"I see the colonel's gang but not much else," Guy said.

"And Patrol2, east of them, about two Ks," Cliff responded.

There was a sudden, sharp metallic smacking sound, like a stone hitting the windscreen of a car on a dirt road.

"Shit," Cliff exclaimed.

"Was that a bird or a ground contact?" Guy said.

"That was no bird. We took fire. AK47, probably," Billy said

Gaining height quickly and swerving away out of danger, they reported the position that the shot had come from to the patrols below.

"Copy Airrec. That's what we needed. Over," came the colonel's voice.

Cliff pictured the big frame of the red-headed colonel in the bush below, ivory-handled magnum in one hand, mic in the other.

Then Zeb's came in response. "Copy, Airrec."

*

Cliff, Sam and Peter were pale faced but excited, buoyed by adrenalin. The helicopter seemed to hang in the air as it settled gently to the ground – the exact parking area where they had previously laid while listening to a fire fight.

Standing outside while the helicopter was refuelled, the three men marvelled at the experience they had had that morning.

"Now we can definitely claim a war veteran's pension. We were shot at, man!" Sam said.

Guy and Billy were checking their aircraft with great care. Their head shakes and shrugs interspersed with relieved smiles suggested they were not finding any indication of damage other than a dent in one of the wheel supports.

"Yes, my father is going to be impressed with *that* anecdote," Peter said.

"I bet," said Cliff. "My God, what an experience. And just another day at the office for those two!"

*

A few days later, despite his lack of sleep and a slight hangover following the farewell party with Guy and Billy, Cliff found himself in good humour as their vehicle lurched from side to side in the thick sand behind the commanding officer and adjutant's Land Rover, which was hardly visible in the surrounding dust cloud. They and the armoured Ratel in front of them kept up a good pace, seemingly keen to get back.

Having dropped off its load of fuel drums, the convoy was able to pick up speed on the return journey and the lookouts in the turret of each truck had replaced their sunglasses with army-issue goggles discovered in the quartermaster's store back at camp Katima Mulilo. This gave them a look of First World War biplane pilots flying at low level in a desert dust storm.

Cliff, Sam and Peter were still talking about their flight with Guy and Billy, and how professionally the two pilots handled themselves when flying (despite their love of late socialising the night before a mission).

"After we got shot up, I was thinking of the film *Apocalypse Now* and the guys sitting on their helmets to protect their privates," Sam laughed.

"Yes," exclaimed Peter from the back seat. "While we were ducking and diving in *our* chopper I was remembering how, in the film, their colonel insisted on playing Wagner during an attack."

"*The ride of the Valkyries*," Sam called over the noise of the Land Rover, humming a few bars from the film's soundtrack.

"You never cease to amaze me, Groucho Marks," Cliff shouted back, giving his shoulder a shove.

"*Oscar* Marks," Peter laughed.

Thinking back over the last few months, Cliff felt the three of them had experienced a growing bond that had been cemented in the last few days;

living in each other's pockets and sharing some frightening experiences.

*

They arrived on the outskirts of Rundu in the late afternoon. The sun was only just beginning to set so the airfield's big security floodlights were not yet lit, making it harder to identify. The angle of the sunlight was now catching the surface of the Cubango on the far side so that the backdrop to the town was a glistening, winding image of the same river they had made a return crossing on earlier in the day.

Jazzman and Nuka had persuaded Sam to part with the whole pack of cigarettes this time. This earned him several hearty slaps on the back and a fond farewell in response, as they climbed back into their Land Rover with the pontoon's arrival at the jetty.

However, before they could discern the edge of the airfield and camp alongside it, the convoy was stopped at a roadblock manned by several military police. After a brief exchange with the commanding officer they were waved on.

As they approached the airfield, the sight of over twenty Hercules aircraft left them open-mouthed; the planes having increased in number substantially since their previous visit. Further along were helicopters and Mirage jets. Some of the helicopters were Puma troop carriers, Sam reliably informed them.

"Yes, something big *is* going down. Guy and Billy were correct," Sam continued.

The assembled aircraft looked like mini anthills as support personnel swarmed over each in order to attach hoses for fuel, cables for meters and other electrical devices, and load ammunition.

Some distance away, spilling out of a large aircraft-hanger, were what looked like a whole parachute battalion whose chin straps dangled from their helmets that had replaced their maroon berets; the latter now tucked under their shoulder epaulettes.

"Hey Sam, think any of those guys are paratroopers from our basic training days?" asked Cliff.

"If there are, I hope they're OK after this, General," Sam responded, shaking his head.

"Let's hope they *all* are," Peter added

There was a similar scene at the camp when they arrived at the parking area. Scores of armoured vehicles and troop carriers were being prepared for departure and, as a result, they were directed to another area to disembark.

When their commanding officer and adjutant later briefed them, they learnt that they were to remain in Rundu for the next few weeks as they were needed to provide base camp support for what was being called Operation Tracer. This was a search-and-destroy operation using a parachute battalion to destroy insurgent camps inside the Angolan border.

*

That evening, as they ate their evening meal, all three were quiet. Cliff thought they were probably each having similar thoughts. This army training business had got a lot more serious over the last few weeks than they could ever have guessed.

A month ago, Cliff had been sitting in a Land Rover with Sam watching Peter trying to find the courage to jump off the back of the troop carrier. Who would have thought they would now be supporting an attack on a neighbouring country? Just a week ago they had lain in the middle of a firefight that had resulted in body bags being loaded on a truck the following morning.

Cliff sighed. *It will be a relief to get home to a normal life.*

Chapter 9

Departures and Arrivals

Their vehicles rumbled back into the game-park base where they had first started their camp time two months ago. They had been away three weeks, including the convoy mission and the time spent in Rundu supporting the Operation Tracer.

It seemed much longer since they were last there at the camp, and the one-hinged door on Cliff's ramshackle office looked almost welcoming as it swung gently in the late evening breeze, as though waving a greeting.

There had been little time for sleep during that last week on account of the regular noisy landing and taking off of helicopters and jets as the mission in Angola proceeded.

Nobody seemed very knowledgeable about what was transpiring across the border. All they knew came from the odd anecdote overheard during mealtimes. Helicopters arrived with casualties and some even carried body bags. This was no training exercise.

Given the time since their departure, Cliff was not surprised the following afternoon when Peter and Sam arrived back from the nearby town with multiple boxes of post for the camp. What did surprise him were the three envelopes Peter handed to him.

"Three for you, popular boy," Peter smiled.

"Must be two from my mother," Cliff said, wondering to himself why he presumed there could not be two from his wife.

Upon looking at the address on the third envelope – to Combat General Sir Cliff Barkerfield OBE – he discovered that the sender was his cousin Josh whom he had not spoken to since his mother and sister's funeral. He slipped his pencil through the top of the envelope and unfolded the letter.

Hi Cliff,

As you know this last year did not start off well and since then it has continued to go downhill, what with my health, and my dad struggling to come to terms with things – not just the death of my mom and sister but...

Let me not get ahead of myself. Firstly, I wanted to give you this news first-hand so when you got back you did not hear from others before we caught up, buddy. It has all come about because of my condition and...

It seemed Josh's long-term problem with his kidneys had deteriorated to the point where he was having to go into hospital regularly. The initial indications were that he had some kind of chronic disease that was incurable. As time went by, his test results confirmed the seriousness of his condition, and it became apparent to his doctors that he would need a kidney transplant soon.

His specialist was convinced they should be guided by the positive outcomes of previous patients who had received a parent or sibling donor as opposed to considering a donor from a distant family member. The doctor had established that where patients were monitored for at least two years after a transplant, the absolute two-year patient survival rate was nearly ninety percent, while actuarial statistics for survival at four years were over eighty percent.

Josh's problem though was that his siblings were either too young to donate, or unlikely to be prepared to undertake such surgery. This left only his father Frank, who was more than willing to volunteer.

As Cliff read Josh's letter, his look of incredulity prompted Peter, who was sitting opposite him at his desk, to enquire, "You OK?" as Cliff continued to read.

So you see not only was it a mismatch from an organ donor point of view but it turns out, as a result of some of the test results, that Frank (as I think I may have to call him now) is not my biological father. Yeah OK, so now that you are back on your chair, imagine how I feel? I am going to have a go at tracking down my real father – after all I am an investigative journalist, well nearly anyway. What can be hard about it? OK, so now you know.

I would love to ask Aunty B if she knows who my real dad is. Your mother and mine were pretty close so she might know something, but I don't want to put her on the spot. Do you think you could talk to her about it? See if she's OK with talking to me?

Let me know about this when we meet up. Looking forward to seeing you soon, cousin.

Your trusted servant
Josh

As he read his other two letters, Cliff's mind kept reverting to Josh's and the double-whammy revelation he had been hit with. His mother's letter gave a watered-down version of Josh's condition as relayed to her by Frank.

Brenda's letter was her normal no-nonsense account of what was happening in their home; detailing the things that had to be fixed around the apartment once he returned. It did get a bit more light-hearted though when she said she was looking forward to getting some embellishment on the anecdotes he had sent her in his letters, but not on the unfortunate sergeant's incident!

She said although she had a lot more time to write now, without having to worry about cooking for him, she looked forward to not having to do everything herself. That was as close as she came to telling him she was looking forward to seeing him again. Cliff sighed. It was going to be an interesting few months.

In the morning the troops were due to be demobilised and driven to the town where they would board the first of two trains home. Their last few weeks had gone by at a snail's pace, which was often the case in the army once the end date had been set.

Sam had arranged a refund for the first-class plane ticket his mother had sent him for his return trip home. Her driver had been unavailable to collect him, and so now Sam was insisting the three of them share a private compartment on the train home once they were out of the border area and transferred to a main line passenger train. The upgrade would be his treat he insisted. Well, his mother's really.

*

The conversation on the train between the three

had skirted around the ultimate farewell that was getting closer, along with the exchange of contact details. It was early on the final morning, a few hours before Cliff's stop, when the thought came to him without hesitation.

Peter was sitting on the top bunk; his socked feet protruding from his dangling camouflage trousers. Sam's bunk was directly above Cliff's head. Cliff looked up at Peter while at the same time knocking on the underside of Sam's bunk to get his attention.

"So what about a reunion drink in Durban in a few weeks' time? See how we're coping, back in Civvy Street?"

"Highest rank buys the first three rounds, General," Sam yawned.

"Sounds like fun," Peter said.

Waiting for Cliff's train to arrive, Brenda stood below the old station clock, apart from the crowd. She was lost in thought as she stared down the track; the parallel silver rails narrowing until they disappeared from view at the end of a long gentle curve after the platform's end.

As was always the case when a train was about to arrive, there was an air of expectancy along the crowded platform. The regular glances down the track from the assembled onlookers punctuated the excited conversations being exchanged between waiting families. Brenda however was not feeling expectant, she was thinking how much the distant empty space represented her past life.

What is behind where the tracks are lost from view? she mused. *My lost time before the orphanage?* On either side of the rails stretching into the distance were her foster homes; each with an unhappy ending.

Where had she come from? What were her parents like? What had she got up to as a toddler? How old was she when she took her first step? She knew nothing of what happened before she was old enough to remember for herself. There was no lap to sit on while she was told about her early years or photographs to point at and laugh about.

Soon a giant locomotive, as yet unseen and unheard, would trundle into view, filling the void on the curve. Yet her life before would not appear just like that; she had to retrieve it. Or was the whole scenario the other way around? Was she staring at where her life was going, getting narrower and narrower like the tracks, until it disappeared altogether?

Suddenly the locomotive *was* there, moving slowly and irresistibly into view; the interval between the *clacks* from the carriage wheels rolling over the expansion gaps getting longer as the train slowed to a stop. Brenda could see a lone worker crouched on the track up ahead with an iron bar in his hand that he used to tap each wheel as it trundled past him. He was listening for cracks in the steel wheels. *Like the cracks in my life?* she thought.

"Gotcha!" Josh suddenly laughed over her shoulder. She felt his arms wrap around her from behind, making her jump at first and then giggle.

"Can I join your solitary welcoming party, Brenda?"

Part Two

Chapter 10
Changing Places

As he waited for the kettle to boil, Sam absentmindedly watched a squirrel clinging to the bird feeder swinging gently under a branch outside the kitchen window. As usual it had found a way to circumvent the preventative measures he took to stop them from stealing the birds' nuts.

The bird feeder had been Peter's idea. During his last visit, he had suggested to Grace, Sam's wife, that the robins and blue tits needed one. Sam's convoluted joke involving the latter bird's name and the cold weather in England had attracted a gentle punch on the arm from Peter and an exasperated shake of head from his wife.

In the empty room next door, the TV was playing an after-news 'stinger' before a presenter introduced the next program. Sam wondered why their *au pair* did not seem able to switch the TV off when she was finished watching a program or left the room, as she had now, having just been summoned to the nursery by his wife.

The boiling kettle was getting louder and the squirrel outside was joined by a friend who worked his way down the wire that attached the feeder to the branch above it. Like a novice firefighter about to descend a pole for the first time, the squirrel had probably been watching the other one to see how it was done.

By now, Sam and Grace had been in England for several years. Their move was prompted by his mother's response to the odd snippet that slipped through P. W. Botha's censorship laws, and what Sam had told her about his Caprivi experiences, which included Operation Tracer, when he returned from his last army camp on the border.

This last tour of duty had been enough for his mother. She decided that her son was not going to be called up regularly by the government's military to risk life and limb protecting their Apartheid regime (at least not if she had anything to do with it). At her insistence Sam's father, who was English by birth, had arranged for a British passport for his son. Before he knew it, Sam and his new wife were on their way to the misty isles.

Although they missed their home country terribly, they realised that England was a safer environment in which to raise children. They had found, however, that having a young family without a support network around them had proven challenging at times too. Enlisting the services of an *au pair* had helped the situation but it was not like having a full-time live-in maid. Rather, it was more like having a teenage daughter!

The reason for the *au pair*'s earlier departure to the nursery was the same reason Sam was busy in the kitchen making his own tea: both children had colds. In fact, they seemed to permanently have colds. *The children constantly being ill is not the only thing I haven't got used to*, he thought as he put his pot of baked beans on the stove plate. *Why do they call this tea?* he mused. *It's supper or dinner in the evening surely? Tea is what you have a cup of at any time of the day as the mood takes you or when a friend visits.*

The kettle's intense sound subsided as it came to the boil, and now it had quietened down, Sam could hear the TV presenter's voice coming from the room next door. Keeping an eye on his bread in the toaster, his baked beans heating on the stove and the squirrels outside the window, he glanced between each of them in turn as he poured hot water over his tea bag, listening to the sounds from the TV at the same time.

Over the noises in the kitchen, Sam had only picked up snippets from the TV programme.

"... the following documentary *No Easy Road*..."

Up to this point he had not really been taking much notice of what the speaker was saying.

However, when he heard the voice of British journalist Michael Buerk introducing the documentary, Sam's attention was suddenly caught.

"My Africa was just a memory. It might as well have been a dream..." Sam heard the broadcaster say as he moved to the open door to see the screen.

The narration was then followed by the sound of the beautiful yet sad voice of a woman singing in Zulu as a train, which Sam could now see from where he stood, moved slowly through the early morning Soweto smog.

Moving back, he switched off the stove and, with a last paranoid look at the squirrels, Sam grabbed his cup of tea and headed for the TV room.

"... living in South Africa with my family... reporting on that country as it went through one of its bloodiest convulsions of the time... I was gassed, shot at, beaten and reviled..." came the reporter's monologue.

Sitting on the edge of the sofa, Sam was mesmerized by the voice of Michael Buerk and the images played out on the screen. At this stage, Buerk had only been back in the UK for a month after being thrown out of South Africa unjustly for projecting what Prime Minister Botha had called 'an untrue bad image' of the South African situation. The prime minister had expressed his opinion on TV; his finger pointing skyward in emphasis as was his custom when speaking in front of an audience.

The documentary Sam was watching was compiled using previously unseen footage and reports. Such information had not been allowed to be revealed by any journalist or publisher in South Africa; the leaking of such punishable by deportation, which had been Buerk's situation, or for journalists working for a local newspaper, the closing down of the offending publisher.

On the back of a lorry with SAS number plates – the registration number for vehicles of the country's railway, Suid Afrikaanse Spoorweg – an innocuous load of large wooden crates passed by along a township road where there had been earlier reports of rioting.

Even though the plates indicated it was a government organisation, because it was not a police vehicle or armoured vehicle it did not pose a threat to the chanting 'toyi toyi-ing' groups of youths dancing on either side of the road. The toyi-toyi as a protest dance was considered a threat by the authorities.

The dancers ignored it the first time it passed by, even though it seemed to be traveling unnecessarily slowly. However, the second time it passed, in the opposite direction, some of the youths considered it to be provocative. The third time it trundled towards them, one of the youths could not resist retaliating. A rock hammered onto the cab's roof, followed swiftly by another until within moments a shower of rocks rained down.

The truck rolled to a standstill as the wooden lids were thrown off the boxes, and from crouching positions inside, men in camouflage fatigues rose to their full height with their pump action shot guns pointing at the youths.

A few minutes later, the crowd had scattered in panic before the hail of bullets; four young men lying dead in the aftermath.

"I had no idea this shit was going down in the suburbs of Johannesburg. Nobody does over there – in their own country," Sam murmured, his transfixed pale face over the lip of his teacup as he watched the documentary unfold; Sam's dinner turned cold in the kitchen while the squirrels ate theirs.

As the documentary ended, he felt horrified and slightly numb. He stared into nothingness for a long time then calculated the time in South Africa before reaching for the phone beside him.

Josh glanced up from his desk on the twelfth floor as a gust of wind threatened to tear out the floor-to-ceiling window facing his desk. The southerly which attacked the Durban coastline from time to time, was at its howling worst. At this height one really felt it, like being in an aircraft about to land on a windy day.

Through the glass panes, which were slowly misting up with sea salt borne on the wind, above the buildings in the foreground he could see the ocean. As always when a southerly wind whipped it up, the ocean became angry and green; the threatening big swells capped with white foam.

It reminded Josh of the many times this image of the sea had greeted them, seen at first from a distance, when he and his family arrived at the outskirts of Durban having driven down from their hometown of Pietermaritzburg for a day at the beach.

As her impatient passengers got ever closer to the coast, still far enough inland and high enough up to overlook the city when it appeared momentarily between hills, his mother would grasp the opportunity to distract the siblings from arguing and teasing each other on the back seat.

"I wonder who'll spot the sea first?" she would call out.

She always repeated her question from time to time as the topography changed and they all scanned the distant sugarcane-covered hills.

Occasionally there would be a break in the line of green and a patch of blue would appear for a moment. The sight always resulted in immediate yelling from the rear.

"There it is!"

"I saw it first."

"Stop pushing!"

When the sea was green and choppy (as it always seemed to be on their chosen day out) he and his siblings would give different responses.

"Oh no, white waves! It must be blowing a gale."

"*Sand*-wiches for lunch. Yuk!"

The memory made him think of his mother. He missed her a lot after the accident but less so now as time went by. And his sister, barely a teenager, killed in the same crash.

He pictured her, still very young then, on these outings, standing unsteadily on the back seat as a toddler, being held by her older sister so she could also 'spot the sea first'.

He wondered how his dad and the twins were. They were lucky Aunt Raechel was prepared to take them in. She had become like a mother to the twins, and she mothered his father for that matter too. He needed to visit them before he left.

*

"Maybe an enforced transfer to head office is not the worst thing," he muttered to his colleague, who sat at the desk next to him. "The wind never seems to stop in this place."

Josh was feeling particularly anti-wind today. Earlier that morning, climbing out of his car, he had made the mistake of not hanging on to his inside car door rest with the required grip of steel, thus allowing an unexpected gust to rip it out of his hand, snapping the door's retainer arm as the wind slammed the door against the car's side.

"Blows up there too," came the dry invisible response from the other side of his partition.

"And it's full of dumb vaalies dreaming of Durbs by the sea," came another from behind him.

The comment referred to the influx of people from the Transvaal highveld every school holiday who came in search of the beach while snarling up the Durban traffic, much to the irritation of the locals.

"You could always go back up the road to sleepy hollow, Josh," Brenda said, breaking into the conversation as she strode through their open plan office on her way to the conference room.

"Careful Brenda. Remember that's Cliff's hometown too," Josh shot back.

"Whoops, sorry yes!" she laughed.

Her teasing reminded Josh that he really should go up to his hometown to say goodbye to his family, before heading off to what his colleagues referred to as 'the Big Smoke'. It was basically a promotion as he would now be doing investigative projects on his own, but there were those around him that claimed it definitely *was* a banishment rather, mainly because of how few goals he had scored lately for the local branch's soccer team.

"Yup, go play for those 'vaalies' Josh. With you on their side maybe we will win the next game against head office for a change!"

The upside of the move was that he would be living in the same city as Cliff again. He missed their times together since Cliff had moved there. They had a long history together and shared the same family skeletons.

Cliff stood in the doorway of Muriel's small room in his mother's back garden. It had been empty since she left to join her husband in Durban where he had eventually found a job that could sustain the family without her needing to work. She had worked for Beryl as her live-in maid for four years.

He looked around the tiny room, with its faded whitewashed walls. The steel bed was still in the corner with its thin mattress that both Zeb and his mother had shared during the school holidays. It was hard to believe that the dashing, uniformed officer Cliff had met in the Caprivi was the same scrawny kid who used to sleep here with his mom.

Tacked to the wall was a torn and faded magazine picture of the Manchester United football team: Zeb's childhood heroes. The torn half hung downward and moved slightly in the draft Cliff had created by opening the door. The room reeked of cooking smells just as it had always done, even after all these years of being unused.

It had seemed bigger in his youth and not as desolate. Back then, as kids, it had not seemed bizarre when Zeb told them of how they had to use the kettle to heat some water to wash themselves while standing in a large plastic basin. It seemed strange and totally unacceptable now though.

He hadn't heard her car approaching up the drive and so Cliff jumped at the sound of her voice behind him.

"Well, well, well. Look who finally came to see his mother," Beryl said.

She instantly managed to make him feel guilty; even more than he had already been feeling after looking around this room.

"What are you doing in here?"

He knew she did not require an answer, her tone alone made him feel he shouldn't be snooping.

Cliff had only been back in his hometown twice since he and Brenda split up and he had moved to Johannesburg. The last visit was for his dad's funeral. He and his mother still spoke regularly on the phone though; at least regularly enough for him to learn what a fine husband his dad had become in his mother's eyes since his death. Cliff always smiled at the irony of it whenever she slipped it into their conversations. Sometimes she even combined it with one of the many guilt trips she liked to send him on.

"You should have invited your dad on your fishing weekends. He did so much for this family, worked so hard. It would have been a nice gesture to include him, Cliff. Not leave him sitting here all weekend. Now it's too late."

She seemed to forget that his father had shown little interest in anything he did. Had never once bothered to watch one of his soccer games, let alone go fishing with him. She also seemed to have forgotten that it had been her with the steady job, not him.

With another three-month long army camp looming, he had decided he should pay his mother a visit before it turned into a two-year interval. He hoped there weren't going to be any guilt trips.

"Come on then, your Auntie 'Chel will be here any minute. She said she wouldn't miss seeing you again for anything." His mother laughed as she eased past him and closed the door to the tiny room. "And don't forget she has banned *auntie* nowadays – it's just Raechel. She says the auntie thing ages her."

"Did you ever hear from Muriel?" Cliff asked. "Did I tell you I met up with her son, Zeb, at that camp I did in the Caprivi?" he continued, putting his arm around his mother as they moved away from the door.

Walking across the neatly cut lawn of the backyard and enjoying her son's rare demonstration of affection, Beryl shook her head.

"No, never a word from her. I didn't know they had blacks in the army," she added.

"Black *people*, Mom. And well, it's complicated," Cliff said. "Especially as far as Zeb's concerned. He's quite a big deal actually – a major," Cliff added, smiling at his mother's incredulous expression at this additional revelation.

Cliff was tolerant, yet always surprised at his mother's old-school conservative views, so typical of her generation in South Africa. She had inherited certain other old-fashioned beliefs from her parents as well, such as being adamant she would never go into a liquor store, declaring them not nice places for a woman to be seen in, and her astonishment whenever she saw a woman smoking in the street. Her outdated attitude always made Cliff smile.

As they entered the house through the back door, a bell chimed down the hallway from the front, followed by a few loud knocks and Raechel's somewhat impatient voice.

"Is anybody going to open this damn door?"

Hurrying down the hall to open it, Cliff was swallowed up in his aunt's hug before he even had a chance to try out her new form of address.

"It's been so long, my *other* favourite nephew!

What have you been up to? Have you heard from Josh lately? I haven't seen him in ages. Hi Beryl," Raechel said, without pausing for breath; punctuating each sentence with a kiss on Cliff's cheeks and forehead.

Cliff was disappointed Josh could not come to his dad's funeral, but Josh was in hospital at the time undergoing tests. Although they spoke regularly on the phone, the last time Cliff had seen Josh was at a reunion in Durban he had organised for himself, Peter and Sam before Sam left for England.

Despite his early departure from their initial basic training, Josh had insisted he qualified for the reunion as well, having at least done three days in the army even if they weren't at their border camp. Besides, he felt like he knew Sam and Peter well, what with all the anecdotes Cliff shared with him in his letters home.

"Fine," Sam had agreed during a phone call with Cliff who had mentioned Josh's request. "But I hope this is not going to blow out of proportion. Brenda isn't coming as well, right? We will be talking about the army and the old days; sharing anecdotes without inhibitions."

"Probably academic in Brenda's case anyway," Cliff replied. Despite Sam asking Cliff to elaborate, he refused to clarify any further, telling him it could wait until they met.

*

Having dropped off his overnight rucksack in his room, Cliff headed back down to the hotel's bar where their reunion was due to take place. Looking around as he entered, he noticed a woman sitting alone at a table near the door. With her head down, she seemed to be searching for something in her bag.

She looked up and smiled as he walked past her on his way to the bar. Cliff felt as though his heart had just skipped a beat. The fine features of her beautiful face were surrounded by curls of black hair, her eyes a striking cyan. The woman was indeed stunning. Her resemblance to Audrey Hepburn brought back memories of Cliff's pre-teen crush on the film star.

Upon reaching the bar counter, Cliff realised he had been so distracted by her beauty that he had not returned her smile. *She must think I'm rude.*

He almost turned back from the bar to go back to her table and apologise, but then deemed it inappropriate and felt silly for having even considered it. Instead, he slid onto a bar stool and ordered a drink. Glancing past the bartender to look at her image in the barroom mirror behind him, he saw she had returned to searching through her bag, her black curls falling forward as she did so.

Cliff only allowed himself the occasional furtive glance after that. Brenda had taught him that women know when they are being stared at without even having to look up. She reminded him of his mother telling him once that she had eyes in the back of her head.

The more times he glimpsed at the woman the more Cliff was convinced he knew her from somewhere. *Oh God, I hope she isn't someone I have met at a client meeting and now she thinks I am rude! No, I wouldn't forget a face like that. It must be my imagination. I bet she's not single*, he thought ruefully.

He shook his head slowly, asking himself what the point of such a thought was. Was he seriously considering approaching this woman? He had a wife (or at least as far as he knew he still did).

The next time he looked in the mirror he saw Peter's reflection, he was at that moment coming down the steps into the bar area. Slipping off his stool, Cliff turned to greet him. However, in the few moments it took him to do so, he discovered that Peter had done a detour to the table of the beautiful stranger and was currently bending over to kiss the top of her head!

Cliff was still trying to close his gaping mouth when, hand in hand, Peter led the young lady towards the bar.

"Hi Cliff. This is my twin sister, Jodie," Peter said, introducing her while shaking Cliff's hand. "I should have taken her seriously when she said she was going to gate-crash our reunion!"

"I thought it might be you, Cliff, but you looked like you were preoccupied with something, so I didn't say anything." Jodie smiled.

After an overly long pause, Cliff grabbed onto the crumbs of an excuse to explain his earlier rudeness.

"Oh yes, sorry. You looked so familiar I was distracted trying to think where I knew you from. Of course you two are not identical but the likeness is very close. So sorry for being rude." Cliff cringed inwardly at the sound of his own babbling.

Her knowing smile in response told him she knew the real reason he had been so distracted. He wondered if he looked like an idiot for having been found out? He considered taking a surreptitious look in the mirror behind the bar for signs of embarrassment. but that would have just confirmed he was.

"Do you mind me inviting myself and gate-crashing your reunion? I have heard so many anecdotes from this brother of mine I feel I know you all. Sometimes I feel as though I was actually there. I was dying to meet you all."

"Not at all. It's a pleasure to have such a charming lady present." As soon as he had said the words Cliff regretted them; worrying they sounded pretentious.

"Ah, General. You're *an officer and a gentleman*. I loved that film."

Sam's voice came from somewhere over his shoulder and much to Cliff's relief they all laughed. They then all started speaking at once introducing Sam to Jodie, repeating the process a final time when Josh came down the steps with a grin.

*

The evening slowly morphed from a reunion into a farewell party for Sam who took centre stage as he acted out anecdotes from his and Cliff's basic training days and the camp where they had first met Peter.

Cliff watched his friends laughing together and interjecting as each story unfolded. Josh and Peter seemed to share a natural affinity; Josh providing moral support for Peter with statements of empathy and an occasional pat on the arm throughout the anecdote about the recruits jumping from the back of the troop carrier.

"I was terrified," Peter said.

Cliff wondered if Sam would add something inappropriate about Peter wetting himself. He sincerely hoped not as in the final days of their camp together Cliff understood there to be a tacit agreement between them that Peter was a peer and a friend, which was confirmed during the trip home.

It had happened in a quiet moment when all three had been lost in their own thoughts on the train back from the camp on the border. They had each sat and stared out of the window into the dark countryside, the wine in their glasses on the table between them sliding gently from side to side with the movement of their carriage. It seemed like years ago now.

"You know what Peter?" Cliff said, breaking the silence. Reaching for his glass with a sideways glance at Sam he continued. "We would not be honest if we said we hadn't had some thoughts about you as an individual."

Peter looked back from the window with a smile. "Yes, I know what you're going to say, but so what? Everybody else does," Peter said.

"Well, our time with you taught us an invaluable lesson about being judgmental. Hey Sam?"

Sam had already been nodding as Cliff spoke. Now he smiled at Peter. "We are lucky to have you as our friend."

Peter leant over the fold-down table between them with tears in his eyes. "Grit your teeth guys.

Like it or not, incoming hug," he said, before taking Cliff's glass from him and putting it down.

Peter continued his anecdote; recounting how Cliff had put the sergeant in his place by telling him how it could end in serious injury if he did not stop. "Or shit – a nervous breakdown at least," Peter added with a wry smile.

"Well, I would never have been able to launch myself off the back of a moving truck," Josh said. "To be honest, I would have crapped myself right there and then. You did well Peter to jump, even if that dumb sergeant helped you along!" he laughed, as he slapped Peter on the leg.

Cliff waited for Sam to add the part about Peter peeing his pants but instead his friend just nodded in agreement with Josh.

"Peter, you never told me about that!" Jodie said. Her hands were open in disbelief. "My brother's guardian angel," she said, as she reached across to squeeze Cliff's hand. "So gallant."

Cliff could sense the glances being exchanged between his friends. Despite the conversation he had had with Brenda earlier in the week, Cliff still felt guilty about the warm glow he felt at Jodie's attention.

A few months after Cliff returned from camp, Brenda decided she needed to try some new things in life. At the same time, she wanted to try to satisfy the yearning she had always had to find out more about her birth parents.

Were all her values, likes and dislikes developed during her upbringing? Had she inherited any personality traits from her birth parents? What had her parents looked like?

She had waited for Cliff's return from the border to see how she felt about their relationship. Although she was very involved in her writing and her job she was still spending so much time agonising over why she was not feeling fulfilled. *Is it just because I am alone?* However, his return did little to distract her thoughts and so she decided the time had come.

Ultimately, the changes she sought would include a new job, moving cities and, for a while, living alone. This was something Brenda had to do until she had satisfied her obsession, which was what it had become, to find her birth parents.

The discussion Beryl suggested she have with Gerry had not yielded much in the way of finding a solution to how she felt, but he had mailed her details of organisations to contact regarding finding one's birth parents. She wrote to thank him although her letter had gone unanswered. Beryl later told her that Gerry had been transferred to the Transvaal and now had a parish of his own.

Josh had also offered to help in the search but from their combined efforts, all they had been able to establish was that her first orphanage had been in Johannesburg. This prompted her to move there as part of her new life-changing plan.

The newspaper she worked for were happy to grant her request of a transfer to their head office. They needed an additional editor there and she was highly regarded. Her boss had teased her when she had asked him about a transfer.

"Following your protégé Josh, are you Brenda? Be careful, people will talk," he laughed.

"Well it would be keeping it in the family at least. He's Cliff's cousin," she retorted, with a smile.

Brenda was slightly irritated by Cliff's lack of emotion when she told him of her plans. She had expected more of a reaction when she explained to him the rationale behind her decision one morning, as they took their regular walk on the golf course near their apartment. Beryl had been very upset when she had told her the previous day, but Cliff seemed more resigned than upset by her announcement.

Brenda tried to be positive by telling her husband that a separation might do their relationship the world of good. Give them both time to consider exactly what they might enjoy having in their lives that they currently did not have.

While she waited for him to respond, she watched the grounds men mowing the fairway in the distance. One stopped his mower to light a large zol. Clouds of smoke drifted across the pristine freshly cut grass. Even from this distance, Brenda imagined she could smell the marijuana. *The aroma of more than one type of cut grass in the air*, she thought wryly.

Alongside her, Cliff seemed lost in thought as he studied the golf ball in the palm of his hand. He had found it hidden in the rough while looking down and kicking at twigs as Brenda spoke. This conversation made him feel awkward.

"Hmmm, a Titleist," he said, putting it in his pocket for safekeeping.

Now, Cliff, what about our lives, Brenda thought trying not to show her impatience.

"I suppose so," he said, not looking at her as they continued their walk.

Sam stood up to regale his audience with the anecdote about the barracks' floorboard fire. His loud voice coupled with their laughter soon had others in the bar listening in to his story. His moustache added a touch of reality to his parody of Company Sergeant Major van Plettenhof. The laughter around him reached a crescendo when he delivered the sergeant major's final line: "... before the first birdie come down for a piss!"

As he was sitting so close to her, Cliff overheard a giggling Jodie say to Peter, "It was before a *canary* came down for that piss, wasn't it?"

*

During the evening, Josh had taken him aside to update him on his latest news. His health had improved dramatically as a result of some new medication his specialist had administered, but the need for a transplant was still inevitable. However, at least Josh was well enough to wait for a transplant for a year or two rather than a matter of months.

"It will give me some time to try to find my father – if he is even still alive. Damn, if only my mom had told me before she died. Anyway, under the circumstances she can't be blamed for being less than forthcoming, and on top of which she didn't know she was going to die before she had the chance to tell me."

Cliff told Josh he had broached the subject of his parenthood with his mother, as requested, but she said that she was unable to tell them anything. Cliff told Josh she was either not prepared to disclose what she knew for fear of breaking a confidence, or simply did not know. He was not sure which.

Josh had shrugged. "Thanks for trying buddy. So be it, hey? We'll chase that skeleton out one day," he said, patting his cousin on the shoulder.

"We'll see. What will be, will be. I heard you've gone up in the newspaper world – investigative journalist now?"

"Not quite, but I have been given a few stories to run with on my own," Josh replied.

Raechel finally let Cliff free from her embrace at the front door, and the three of them moved to his mother's lounge. As they sat, Cliff smiled at the faces of the two women he had known all his life. Despite this fact, however, sometimes he was not sure how well he knew them – even his own mother.

He and Josh had spent a great deal of time with their Auntie 'Chel, over the years and she had become almost like a second mother to them. Their weekends together on her smallholding were full of new experiences (some of which had their own mothers frowning!).

"Oh, he's doing great," Cliff said, in response to Raechel's enquiry about Josh. "His new meds appear to be keeping things functioning as they should. He seems to be enjoying Johannesburg but is very busy. Having him up there is great, but with all his deadlines I haven't seen him that often lately. His newspaper is trying to stay ahead of their competition covering all the political action going on at the moment."

His mother and Raechel listened intently as he relayed some of the things he and Josh had got up to recently, but except for the occasional gasp or exclamation, neither of them asked many questions. It felt to Cliff as though they were waiting to hear about something else; something specific they were not prepared to broach themselves.

"And of course, he is still intent on finding his birth father."

Cliff's casual comment appeared to cause some consternation as he saw the two women exchange glances. Yet still, neither commented.

"And what about *you* Cliff? What's your news?" Raechel asked

Quick change of subject, Cliff thought.

Cliff wondered if she was alluding to how he was feeling after his divorce. He and Brenda had moved to Johannesburg at different times and when being apart had not yielded anything towards their relationship, they had decided to make their separation permanent with a peaceable divorce.

"Well, I'm still enjoying the new role and I've made a lot of new friends – mostly through work. There are many after-work parties of course."

Then came the inevitable question from Raechel. "Any *lady* friends?" She smiled.

He supposed it was his own fault for making the comment about new friends.

"Oh, 'Chel, give the boy a break," Beryl said, forcing a laugh while slapping Raechel's knee gently.

Cliff had found that the worst thing about his break-up was the insatiable desire some friends and family seemed to have for finding him a new partner as fast as possible. The truth was, all he wanted to do was let the old memories fade away quietly and get used to this new way of life before moving on.

He had not been emotionally distraught when Brenda had brought down the final curtain on their marriage. In some ways, he and Brenda had become like brother and sister so he was never going to be broken-hearted by the split. In fact he felt sadder on his mother's behalf than he did for himself. Brenda had always been like a daughter to his mother – the daughter she had never had. Beryl's feeling towards Brenda had always seemed to him to have a maternal sense about it, and that just intensified once he and Brenda became a couple.

"Oh – and the army promoted me again," he said, trying to change the subject.

"Not a mistake this time, I hope!" his mother laughed, prompting a quizzical look from Raechel.

"An inside joke, 'Chel," Beryl smiled.

"No now it's a bit like falling dominoes," he laughed. Explaining that once you were an officer, instead of a normal camp, one could be called up to an officers' course which inevitably ended up in promotion. "That was the course I was on the last time."

"Oh, so you mean the time you were in Durban, barely an hour away, and you didn't come up to see us?" his mother said. "Yes Cliff, Jodie let it slip," she said, laughing at his surprised expression.

Cliff cringed as Raechel shook her finger at him, a look of mock anger on her face.

"Who's this Jodie?"

Chapter 11
Getting Promoted

To his surprise, Cliff felt every bit the officer as he stopped his car at the red and white chequered boom gate. It blocked the road through the colonial arch with its ornate letters of raised concrete that informed him he had arrived at Natal Command, one of the most historical buildings in Durban.

Cliff had never got round to resigning his commission as was his right after the camp. Inwardly he was slightly incredulous that he had started to feel proud about being an officer. Brenda had teased him.

"Getting old hey Cliff? More mature? Taking responsibility?" she had laughed.

He certainly did feel old when a young recruit raced out of the guard house and came smartly to attention next to Cliff's window with a salute. Cliff returned the salute. *My God he looks young! Where has the time gone? He must be delighted to be doing some of his basic training here in the middle of Durban*, he thought.

This was going to be Cliff's home for the next three weeks while he completed an officers' course for a promotion he had not requested. It would also be the first time he wore mess blues as there was to be a formal mess event to mark the end of the course. He wondered if they would fit him as he hadn't put them on once in the three years he had been commissioned. *Shit, I hope they don't have any moth holes. I should have checked*, he suddenly thought.

They had been fine the last time he had taken them off the hanger and out of their plastic cover a while ago. He had done so for Brenda, who had tried them on for a *Sergeant Pepper* fancy-dress party they were going to. She had said that the heavy silver epaulettes had made her feel like someone was standing on her shoulders.

"Smells like a musty cupboard. Do I look good?"

*

It would not be until he was called up for his next camp that Cliff would realise why, as part of their officer training, he and the other junior officers were being lectured on the topics they were. The lecturer was a senior officer – a major from some military academy who seemed to love his subject. The words 'Crowd and Riot Control' were emblazoned on a large freestanding screen behind him. His assistant kept adjusting the legs of the projector's stand and this made the heading dance.

Cliff was sitting in the back row, next to a man of a similar age and rank. What distinguished him from Cliff and the others in the room, however, was the maroon beret tucked under his shoulder epaulette. As the lecturer spoke about commonality of crowd behaviour in most countries, Cliff wondered what a paratrooper was doing in a group exclusively comprised of infantrymen. He was idly thinking through various possible reasons when the room lights were dimmed and the darkness was filled with the whirring sound of a 35mm projector. This was followed by a splash of white, random numbers rising vertically up the screen. Then a black and white film began; one that seemed to have been shot many years ago.

Having not paid much attention to the opening words, Cliff would now have to wait to find out the point of this projection. In it, a cameraman was panning across a crowd of people – probably in the Middle East somewhere by the looks of their robes and the desert like environment – who were chanting while waving all kinds of rudimentary weapons: sticks, rocks and what looked like old hunting rifles.

The crowd stretched back about one hundred metres, standing behind what must have been their leader. He in turn was positioned on a raised platform of some kind – a barrel or fuel drum – surrounded by yelling supporters responding to his loud rhetoric.

The way the camera was panning across the chanting mob suggested the operator was encircled by them. Suddenly the shoulders of a uniformed person momentarily blocked the camera's lens as he moved past and was followed by a succession of uniformed personnel. They moved forward, brandishing their weapons, and forced the crowd to make way as they moved towards the gesticulating leader.

One of the burly soldiers reached up and yanked the man down from his plinth, sending him crashing to the ground. The other two frog-marched him back to where the cameraman was filming and out of view, while more soldiers arrived to ensure none of the crowd intervened.

It wasn't long before the protestors showed signs of confusion and a lack of direction. At that point, the soldiers began to disperse them with an intimidating show of force, knocking some of them over with the butts of their rifles.

The film stopped suddenly and the assistant ran to turn on the light dimmer switch.

"The point is, this crowd of protestors lost effectiveness without direction," came the lecturer's voice, as he emerged from the darkness out into the light. "Just like any group – a football team, a platoon, a work gang or whatever –

without a leader its effectiveness drops off dramatically. Without direction, individuals begin to simply react involuntarily; in this case to the force shown by the army."

Much to Cliff's relief the lecture was nearing its conclusion. However, just before the end, the major's final words jerked him upright in his chair.

"There are of course cases where physical removal of a ringleader is not possible, and termination from a distance is necessary. This is known as Remote Disablement."

His assistant dimmed the lights again before starting a second film he had threaded through the cogs of the projector. This one was similar to the first except the individuals featured therein were very threatening, with scuffles taking place everywhere, from the start. The mob was armed with large machetes, and a homemade firebomb exploded near the film camera recording the scene. The ringleader himself had a weapon and he fired off a shot into the air from where he stood on a bench.

There was a second shot that sounded close to the camera. The ringleader's weapon fell from his hand as he toppled into the crowd. The lights came up and the major gave his closing remarks.

"In conclusion then gentlemen, the police control, disperse and manage a mob. When it's bad and the army is brought in, we bring it to an end with as much force as is necessary."

Cliff looked at the paratrooper officer next to him. "Did he just say we would be expected to give the order to kill a citizen if he or she was leading a mob, a riot?" he asked.

His neighbour had just opened his mouth to respond when someone in the audience asked a question.

"Sir, under what circumstances would we take such extreme action?"

"If you or your men's lives were threatened, or innocent bystanders' lives were threatened."

Cliff slumped back in his chair. *Oh, for the naive days of basic training*, he thought.

*

In the mess later that evening, Cliff slipped onto a bar stool next to the same paratrooper officer whom he had sat beside during the lecture.

"Evening. My name's Cliff. What brings a paratrooper to the lowly world of infantrymen?"

"Hi Cliff – Jimmy," the paratrooper smiled, offering his hand in greeting. "Buy you a drink?"

Cliff immediately returned to the aborted conversation he had started earlier on. He still felt revolted by the matter-of-fact way the lecturer had informed them that they would be expected to take someone's life in a non-war situation; potentially a fellow citizen on the street.

Jimmy, however, did not seem to share Cliff's sentiment. The paratrooper shrugged his shoulders and pointed out that what they were involved in was unlikely to ever be handled in a humanitarian way.

"We carry weapons. There's a reason for that, don't you think Cliff?"

"You sound resigned Jimmy. Why *are* you here by the way?"

"The army withdrew me from border duties after Operation Tracer, a few years ago. You may have heard of it, or maybe not – they keep things pretty quiet in our country."

"Oh my God! I was there, at Rundu, when that was starting. We had just got back from a convoy to Katima Mulilo and they kept us at the camp to provide ground-based support for the operation."

"Oh well, there's a coincidence," Jimmy said, but did not smile.

"We had just arrived back. We saw all you paratroopers on the apron about to board the C130s and guessed something big was going on. Maybe I saw you and didn't even know it?" Cliff continued.

"In that case you would have seen me *and* my two brothers," Jimmy observed, without humour.

With his back against the vibrating fuselage of the

C130, Jimmy watched the face of his older brother, Paul, in the seat opposite as the aircraft thundered through the clear morning sky. He appeared relaxed, and when he saw Jimmy looking at him he winked, although his facial expression remained deadpan. This was their third jump in a live operation so they were pretty sure they knew what to expect.

A few seats to the right of Paul the youngest of the three siblings, Martin, was staring straight ahead with a pale face. While maintaining eye contact with Paul, Jimmy moved his head surreptitiously in the direction of Martin; indicating he needed to reassure him on this, his first operational jump.

Jimmy smiled as his brother leaned forward and reached across two other paratroopers alongside him to squeeze his younger brother's arm. Their pale-faced sibling then gave both his brothers a reassuring thumbs-up.

*

Once they were out of the aircraft and away from its thundering engines it seemed so quiet, like riding a bicycle in the countryside. Hanging below parachutes ripped from the paratroopers' backpacks by the now parted static lines still attached to the aircraft; flapping together in the turbulence as the C130 disappeared into the distance.

"Hidee hay, hidee hay, here we come MK!"

Jimmy heard the informal battle cry over the whoosh of the wind. He swayed from side to side like a puppet on the end of its strings, turning his head to look around for his brothers.

Below him were the circular tops of greyish-white parachutes, like newly emerging mushrooms, blending with the dusty white earth of Angola far below. After a while Jimmy spotted them not too far away from him. He exchanged a wave with Paul but Martin was too focused on the ground rushing up to meet him to respond.

The family had been incredulous at the coincidence of the three siblings being called up for the same camp. His mother had said it was good as they could look out for each other, while his father had been stony-faced at the disclosure, trying not to consider the probability that such odds increased their opportunity for tragedy.

A rifle shot rang out from the ground below just as Jimmy waved at Martin who had finally looked upwards in his direction. There was no return wave, however. His brother's head seemed to slump forward and a suddenly horrified Jimmy could see the crimson patch spreading on the back of his fatigues and harness.

The firing, from what seemed to Jimmy like a single AK47 on the ground, was regular now and he cast around, looking to see if Paul was OK. A round whistled past him before he heard an explosion of automatic fire. Looking down as he closed with the ground, he saw Koevoet scouts deploying around a bushy knoll where he presumed the AK47 fire was coming from.

Jimmy looked around again for Paul but before he could find him, the ground raced up and he braced for impact. A few seconds later, after freeing himself from his parachute, he ran for the cover of a bunch of thorn trees. He had only gone a short way when he stumbled over the body of Paul.

"Jimmy, I am so sorry," Cliff groaned, feeling wretched for having initiated the conversation.

"No problem. It's a few years ago now and you could never have known. Another drink?"

"Yes sure, my round," Cliff managed to say, as he signalled to the mess orderly behind the bar.

Knowing Jimmy's parents had lost two of their three sons on the same day, army headquarters immediately withdrew him from duty on the border and sent him home. Subsequently, having turned down the offer of an honourable discharge, he was transferred to non-combat duties for the duration of his time.

Josh got out of the lift on the tenth floor of the austere government building in downtown Johannesburg. The sign on the door was large and comprehensive; designed by a civil servant, Josh surmised. It read:

Births, Deaths and Marriages Registry

He had to start somewhere with his search, so he reasoned it may as well be here as anywhere, and who knew what he might discover.

An efficient young lady led him to a desk with a microfiche reader and dumped a pile of folders in front of him.

"Everything we have on the name Barkerfield is here. Please don't remove anything from this office. If you want copies, you can order them from me," she said as she returned to her desk behind the reception counter.

After half an hour of nothing more than the sound of her own nails tapping on her keyboard and Josh rustling folders, her head came up in shock when Josh suddenly exclaimed from behind the microfiche reader:

"Oh, fuck!"

"*Excuse* me, sir."

"Sorry. Really sorry," Josh said, as he raised his hands in supplication before falling back in his chair in shock.

*

Josh was disappointed when there was no response to his knock on Cliff's apartment door. However, he hadn't phoned his friend to tell him he had actually already arrived in Johannesburg as he wanted his visit to be a surprise. The following morning, after receiving no answer to his phone call, or the one the previous evening either, he called Cliff's office number. It was only then he learnt that his cousin was away for a few weeks on an army camp in Durban.

Sods law, thought Josh. *I should have called him earlier. We could have met up in Durban before I left. Could have even come to my farewell party – maybe?*

Cliff's absence did conveniently put off making a decision he knew he had to make: whether or not to tell Cliff about the discovery he had made while trying to find out his birth father's identity. They had spoken about skeletons in the past but he was still agonising over whether it would be right to disclose this one. He was pretty sure this was the confidence Auntie Beryl had wanted to keep to herself and wondered if anyone else in the family knew about it.

He looked around at his new office surroundings. It was much the same as his previous office – open plan in a high-rise building

– but this time there was no sea view, just mine dumps in the distance. *Oh well, as long as the pay packet I get at the end of the month is better, that's all that matters*, Josh thought.

Gazing out at the brown, flat topped, manmade hills in the distance, Josh mused how it was funny that after all the years of moaning from the public about mine dumps being an eyesore, there was now a clamour from locals to preserve their flat-topped rectangular pyramids. The residents had even formed a special preservation society in order to fight for the slowly disappearing mines that had become victims of technology.

New processes had yielded significant gold from the discarded soil that had been originally brought up from the depths of the earth over many years. Black miners had come from all over the country to work on the mines; separated from their families for long periods of time and paid poorly for their efforts.

Josh smiled to himself as one of the editors waved him over. *I hope that won't be my first journalistic assignment here: 'The Disappearing Mine Dumps of Johannesburg'*, he thought.

The formal mess event that would mark the end of their time at Natal Command included wives and girlfriends. This left Cliff scratching his head as to whom he could ask to join him. Brenda had long ago informed him their relationship was over, and although she looked forward to catching up from time to time, she was now in Johannesburg and hardly likely to come down for the event.

Then he thought of asking Peter if he might know someone he could invite. Cliff wondered if he had the courage to ask Peter if Jodie might be interested in going with him, as he dialled his number.

The answering machine intoned: 'no one is available, leave a message', which he had just started to do when a voice broke in.

"Cliff is that you? Oh my God, what a surprise!" said Jodie. "What are you doing in Durban? Can you come round? Peter is just at the gym. We have one around the corner from our apartment."

"Oh... I... hi Jodie, good to hear you... your voice," Cliff stammered, trying to get over the surprise of hearing her as well as processing the revelation that she appeared to live with Peter. "Yes, I am on a course at Natal Command that will finish in the next few days and was hoping to meet up with the guys."

"Ah, that's great, but Josh moved to Joburg last week – Peter tells me – so it would be just him and I. Am I inviting myself again?" she laughed, and so did Cliff, although he wondered why she had automatically included Josh in 'the guys'.

"Typical Josh, he never told me his promotion

had come through already."

Cliff explained a bit about the officers' course and then about the formal mess event he had to attend. He told Jodie he was going to ask Peter if he might know of someone he could invite.

This sounds so contrived, Cliff thought. *She'll see right through me, there's no way she won't.* Cliff thanked the gods that at least she could not see him blushing.

"*I* would love to go – if you want me to? Love dressing up and have the perfect little number just waiting to escape from my cupboard."

"Jodie that's fantastic! Thank you. And in case you're wondering, Brenda and I have split up."

"Oh, I know Cliff, Josh told us. Otherwise I wouldn't have offered. Sorry it didn't work out for you both."

"It's OK, I'm glad Josh told you. One thing I should mention about this event – for some strange security reason the officers on the course can't leave the camp until they've completed it, so can Peter drop you off and pick you up?

"No problem. I'm going to get him a chauffeur's cap for the evening, complete the image, hey?" she laughed.

*

One by one the officers who had been waiting along with Cliff, all resplendent in their mess blues, moved inside to the ballroom as their partners arrived until he was the only one left in the expansive hallway.

He paced up and down the ornate marble floor; the spurs on his boots clinking as he walked. Finally he stopped, and stared anxiously through the glass doors, hoping to see a car pull up.

To Cliff's surprise, when a chauffeured car did drive up it was occupied by Colonel Roverstone and his wife. He clearly did not remember Cliff from their time on the border, informing him enthusiastically that he was the guest of honour.

Only you not your wife? thought Cliff.

He had made the assumption that Cliff was the officer designated to formally receive him and his wife at the entrance.

The couple hesitated when Cliff did not lead the way. Being ignorant of the colonel's expectation, Cliff just stood there smiling at him while continuing to glance anxiously towards the large glass doors.

The colonel, beginning to feel awkward, finally gave a hearty British officer style laugh.

"Don't worry young man. We've been here enough times to know the way," he said, and moved off slowly with his wife on his arm.

Cliff turned his attention back to the doors. Through the reflected image of himself in his mess blues Cliff saw a car with Peter at the wheel come to a stop in front of building. By the time Cliff got through the heavy doors to the car, Jodie was already climbing out gingerly; taking care with the close-fitting long dress she was wearing.

As she straightened up, Cliff was once again taken aback by the sight of her, just like he had been the first time he had seen her.

"Sorry we're a bit late." Jodie smiled as she turned to him.

"Thanks Peter, see you later," he managed to say, before they headed for the doors and escaped the gusty Durban wind.

"Have fun," Peter called back before driving off.

Cliff had forgotten just how beautiful she was. Tonight, in a scarlet dress with her hair worn up, black curls piled above her amazing eyes, Jodie looked captivating. Cliff thought she was sure to turn heads, and that was exactly the response she attracted when they entered arm in arm.

The chatter quietened and the heads of several officers turned to see what had caused the person they were in conversation with to suddenly stare, open-mouthed, past them over their shoulders.

Halfway through the evening, Jodie found herself cornered by yet another aging officer attempting to impress her with his war stories. Looking over the silver epaulets on his shoulder, she saw Cliff and Colonel Roverstone's wife stood back to back, both engrossed in their respective conversations. Jodie realised the colonel's wife had got the hem of her long white dress snared on one of Cliff's spurs, and neither appeared aware.

Jodie was about to excuse herself to warn Cliff of an impending incident (a convenient escape from her unwanted admirer) when the colonel's wife attempted a wine-induced pirouette to show off her dress that had just been complimented by someone.

Raising both hands dramatically – one still clutching a glass of red wine – she rotated with a giggle. Her laughter swiftly faded however as her dress, which was firmly held by Cliff's spur, tightened around her legs.

In the same instant, Cliff felt his boot being pulled and tried to turn around to see what he was snagged on. However, the direction he chose to move his leg in exacerbated the situation, tightening the dress even further. The involuntary movement of his shoulder in addition provided the colonel's wife with a little nudge she did not need.

Colonel Roverstone tried to save his good lady, but all he managed to achieve by spontaneously grabbing her was to bump her glass. This resulted in a splash of red wine down the front of her pristine white dress as, with legs locked together, she collapsed gently to the floor like an imploding building; her wine-stained dress crumpling into the spreading pool on the floor.

Cliff's instinct was to try to free her dress as fast as he could; the only way being by bending over and reaching between his legs to grab at the material hooked onto his spur.

What onlookers saw, when they turned to see the source of the commotion, was a woman kneeling on the floor in a pool of red wine and a crazy man, bent over, looking at her from between his legs like a character in a slapstick comedy sketch!

Chapter 12

A Township like Alex

In the kitchen of his new apartment, Cliff jumped as the buzzer connected to the ground floor entrance door sounded.

"Don't know if I'll ever get used to that thing," he said to the empty lounge, as he walked from the kitchen, soup ladle still in hand. He pressed the button on the control panel next to his apartment door.

"Who is it?" There was no answer and squinting at the buttons again he saw that he had pressed the one that opened the door – *not* the button with the answer icon. *Oh well*, he sighed to himself returning to the kitchen.

He was back a few minutes later in response to a gentle tapping. After fiddling with multiple locks, he finally swung the door open. Standing there was Jodie, at her feet a carry-all. She smiled in greeting.

"Hi, it's *that* woman again – the one who invites herself all the time!" she cried, in mock exasperation.

"What a surprise! Come on in. Welcome to my humble abode," Cliff said, beckoning her into the sparse room with a grin, aware of the increase in his heart rate.

"Love what you've done with the place Cliff." She smiled as she put her bag down and looked around the empty room.

"I know, I know. I only bought the basics. I am hopeless at buying furniture. I will buy the wrong stuff. So, I am procrastinating – a lot!" he laughed.

"And what brings you to the Big Smoke?"

"Well, Peter wanted to come up to see Josh. Something to do with a call he had from Sam the other day? Sounded more like a good excuse to me, but anyway, I thought what the hell, I'll go along for the ride – surprise you."

"You're in luck. The things I felt confident enough to buy were beds and the assistant helped me with linen for them, so you have a bed to sleep in. Unless you are staying with the boys? Mind you, Joshie only has one bedroom and one sofa bed thing in the lounge room as far as I remember."

"Exactly! So please *let me stay at your inn, sir*." Jodie clenched her hands together in exaggerated supplication. "I'll tell you what I can offer in return," she went on, with a smile. "I am good at furniture and decorating stuff. I could go shopping with you if you like?"

"Deal," Cliff grinned. "I'll organise a few days' leave."

"Tell them it's an unexpected visit from an old aunt," she winked.

*

"Are you and your husband being looked after?" the shop assistant smiled.

Without missing a beat Jodie said, "Actually, no. Do you have this lounge suite in a lighter shade and a coarser weave?"

"Let me show you what we have over here." The assistant smiled as she beckoned for them to follow.

The two women moved off together, already discussing colours and textures. Cliff smiled as he picked up the heavy fabric swatch Jodie had pointed at with a smile before she had turned to follow the shop assistant.

Walking behind the assistant and his beautiful interior designer, Cliff felt like he was in a dream.

During the week following the completion of the Natal Command course, before he returned to Johannesburg, Cliff and Peter had met up. Much to Cliff's relief, the subject of the mess evening had not been raised. It transpired that Jodie had saved the story of the spur incident until all three of them were together.

It was one night while they were sitting in a Chinese restaurant waiting for their menus that Jodie finally brought it up. The way she began describing the incident made Cliff laugh, despite himself (he had had a few days since the incident for his embarrassment to subside). He had consoled himself with the fact that at least it had not been Jodie in Mrs Roverstone's place.

Peter had begun laughing halfway through his sister's anecdote, and when she finally reached the climax tears were running down his face as well as hers. It had taken her some time to finish her story as she kept being interrupted by uncontrollable giggles. They were sitting in bench seats at a diner-style table, Peter opposite Jodie and Cliff. The harder he laughed, the funnier it seemed to get. Peter held onto his stomach as he gasped and laughed at the same time. He slowly slid down in his red leather seat and onto his side until he was almost hidden by the table.

Most of the restaurant were either staring at them totally bemused or laughing along with Peter. Jodie and Cliff dabbed their own eyes with napkins as they watched him lying there, shoulders shaking.

Slowly he began to roll over and slid completely under the table. As he disappeared from view, he took the tablecloth, bowls, glasses, chopsticks and water jug with him.

Cliff had to give the two young waiters who rushed to their assistance credit for the way they had mostly kept straight faces as they helped Peter up from under the table. Jodie's snorts appeared to help her suppress another giggling fit while she dabbed at her brother's wet shirt.

"It wasn't that funny at the time," Cliff said with a serious expression, moving his head to look at Peter between the waiters who were re-laying the tableware.

"Oh no! You've started her off again!" Peter said, as Jodie tried to disguise a snort behind a fresh table napkin.

The brown envelope with the South African Defence Force's logo leant against the empty flower vase in the centre of the coffee table. *I can open you if I want to*, Cliff thought, *just not yet*.

It was the second SADF envelope he had received in as many weeks, and after getting lucky with the first, he was expecting the worst this time.

He had regarded the first with a similar feeling of dread; certain it would be a call-up for a second three-month stint on the border. Given that his last camp had only been a three-week officers' course at Natal Command (which had ended memorably) he reasoned that it had to be. It had taken him an entire week before he had slit it open one evening, and then only after several glasses of wine. Had Brenda been there she would have encouraged him to have opened it much sooner no doubt. He could hear her voice now. "Open the damn thing for God's sake Cliff. You're like a child!"

After quickly scanning the letter and establishing it didn't contain the dreaded sentence 'required to attend a three month...' Cliff had read with relief that it was not a call up to another camp but an official confirmation, telling him that as a result of completing the course at Natal Command, he had been promoted to the rank of captain.

He hadn't really cared about the promotion, but the fact he was not being called up to the border again deserved a celebratory glass of wine. With a happy sigh, he had sunk back into his chair, enjoying the chill of the wine glass in his hand and the ambience of the room. Looking around, Cliff had once again been amazed at the change Jodie's styling had brought to his previously drab apartment.

Bringing himself to the present, he reached forward and snatched the second brown envelope from where it leant against the vase. Ripping it open, he scanned it quickly and sure enough, there was the dreaded 'three-months' sentence.

"Damn, damn! And so soon after the officers' course too. Not even a year apart," he said aloud.

Since the Natal Command course, Cliff had become paranoid about brown envelopes, thinking that he should expect Colonel Roverstone to find a way to avenge himself and his wife for the officers' mess debacle. *Is this it?* he wondered, as he re-read the letter, paying closer attention to the details.

Halfway through he sat bolt upright. *So that's what the officers' course was really all about then – all those lectures on crowd control and riots... that's the reason this call-up is so soon after it*, Cliff concluded.

Cliff stood on the tarmac looking up at what would be his office for the next three months. Unlike his previous Angola border camp office with its one window, this one was mobile and had multiple small windows with glass that looked to be an inch thick. He would find that the inside was open-plan and there was space for twelve workers (fourteen if you counted Cliff's seat and the driver beside him).

For this camp his 'office' would be a Casspir armoured troop carrier; the gun ports below the small windows confirming what might be expected of it. It was a vehicle that had already become synonymous with the bush war Cliff had erroneously presumed he would be going to again for his next three-month camp.

Now it seemed like the Casspir's capabilities had been re-assigned from the bush to a suburban township; quelling the increasing unrest amongst the peoples forced to live there. He felt somewhat bemused that, for the next three months, each day he and his men would drive a short distance in the Casspir along pristine suburban tarmac streets to the township of Alexandra and its narrow dusty roads.

The township was only ten kilometres away from where they were encamped at Brigade headquarters in the upmarket suburb of Sandton, just outside downtown Johannesburg. In fact he could have *walked* to Brigade headquarters from his Sandton apartment.

'Alex', as it was known to most, was the second biggest high-density township in Johannesburg. It was also home to some of the worst violence of the era, and it was where he and his squad would be operating for the next three months. Their orders were to escort the local and international press corps on their daily travels around Alexandra.

From what Cliff had read in his briefing notes, it was as much about ensuring they did not go to any of the places listed therein, as it was about protecting the journalists and camera crews from any threat.

*

Alexandra, like other townships, had become extremely violent. This was a result of numerous factors that characterised the intensification of the freedom struggle against the apartheid regime in the 1980s as the bush war moved into the cities. The Eighties witnessed an increase in the armed struggle, combined with mass politicisation of the oppressed peoples of South Africa.

The ANC called on residents to, 'make townships ungovernable' by destroying the local authorities formed by township dwellers under the so-called guidance of the government. These councillors and the council 'police' they recruited from the township were under intense intimidation and told to resign their positions or face the consequences. Municipal buildings and homes of councillors and collaborators were attacked.

As this apartheid government-sponsored administrative system broke down, people established their own democratic structures by forming street committees and peoples' courts to administer their communities; an informal infrastructure with rival groups that saw, amongst other violence, the emergence of the horrific 'necklacing', involving putting a petrol-soaked tyre over a person and setting it alight.

Troops and police who moved into the townships to maintain order were engaged in running battles with youths in an effort to re-establish control.

*

From his lofty position in the passenger seat of the Casspir, Cliff looked down on the early morning traffic passing through the Sandton suburb. It was only six thirty a.m., and the affluent white people of the northern suburbs were already on their way, dropping off kids at school before heading to work. *They need to make money to pay for the flash house and the private schools the kids go to*, he thought to himself.

Just as incredulous to Cliff that his three-months' army stint was taking place in his recently adopted home suburb, was the fact that the people in the cars below him probably had no idea (just as he hadn't before reading his briefing documents) why a large armoured vehicle came to be parked alongside them at a traffic light in the middle of suburbia, in rush hour.

Little was being reported in the newspapers about just how serious the violence was in the townships, and certainly nothing like the information in his briefing papers about what was taking place in the likes of Alexandra.

Down below, in a car beside the Casspir, a young white boy was looking up at him through the window of the rear passenger seat. He gave Cliff a smile and a thumbs-up as they waited for dozens of black people to hurry across the intersection in front of their stationary vehicles. Cliff looked back to the faces passing by. *They must have walked all the way from Alex to get to work*, he thought.

What's this boy communicating with his thumbs-up signal? Cliff wondered. *Is he thanking us for protecting him so he can go to his expensive private school in peace, without being threatened by marauding gangs from Alexandra?*

Cliff chided himself for being cynical and waved back at the youngster, forcing himself to return his smile. For some reason the exchange made him think of Sam and the way he had pre-judged Peter that day on the troop carrier. Glancing at his driver, he regretted he was not instead seeing the big burly man with a large handlebar moustache and dark sense of humour.

Alexandra police station was a small yet heavily fortified new building that marked the entrance to the township. Already parked outside were several press vehicles adorned with various TV station and newspaper logos, some with antennas and some with satellite dishes on their roofs.

Beyond them Cliff could see the vast, seemingly never-ending spread, of what the government referred to as 'high density housing' for approximately four hundred thousand people. In reality, this was just a vast hodgepodge of little shanties that were continually expanding under a haze of smoke caused by the countless cooking fires (electricity being in scant supply).

They were built from whatever substantial materials people could find, including discarded corrugated iron sheets, black plastic sheeting and timber stolen from building sites. The roofs had boulders placed on them to stop loose metal sheets from blowing off during the violent Highveld storms that occurred regularly in the summer months.

There were a few formal small homes constructed from brick but even those had shanty buildings attached as the families within grew. Cliff grimaced. He had no idea an environment could look so poor and derelict – so *hopeless*. He could see some bigger multi-storey buildings as well. These were the hostels – single-gender accommodation for workers from distant parts of the country. They reminded Cliff of prisons with their plain brick work and small windows.

Split up from their homes for upwards of a year, they came to earn money to send back to their homes. The hostels were the place where, according to his brief, most of the trouble started. Clashes were common between the migrant workers and local groups or between Inkatha and ANC dominated hostels.

The streets that ran between the houses were

mainly dirt roads. The few tarmac roads he saw carried formal grid electricity cables on poles. This was mainly for commercial buildings that required electrical equipment and the churches and hostels. Cliff saw that some people had illegally hot-wired the overhead cables to supply power to their own homes too.

He climbed down from the Casspir and strode into the police station where he exchanged salutes with the sergeant seated at the desk in the charge office.

"Captain Barkerfield, reporting for press corps security patrol." Cliff smiled as he introduced himself.

Picking up the mic of the two-way radio on the desk, the young sergeant said he would call his station commander who he thought was just on the way back from an incident in the township.

"Major Hani. This is the gatehouse sergeant, sir. The army's press corps escort unit is here. Yes, I will sir. Over."

The desk sergeant looked up to tell Cliff the station commander would be back in fifteen minutes but was a little taken aback by the gaping mouth that had replaced the smile on the face of the army captain.

Wondering whether Zeb had changed much since in the intervening years, Cliff left the station and walked across to the journalists who were standing around looking bored. They were not allowed to roam the township at will; only to attend a particular event, incident or situation they had agreed, as a group, they wanted to report upon. They all had contacts in the township who tipped them off about situations whenever they arose, so they could request an escort to them.

Cliff gathered the journalists around him so he could address the group. "You guys all know the drill so tell me if I am telling you anything you already know. My briefing notes inform me *you* decide when you want to chase after something – only one thing at a time that is – that you have all agreed on?"

They all nodded.

"I decide whether or not that something is off limits or not, understood?"

Cliff's instruction was again greeted with nods of agreement.

"The appointed Alex guide will take all of you to the location. We follow behind and make sure you are all safe, and don't do anything dumb, right?"

"The dumb things have already been done by our prime minister and his buddies, Captain. We're just reporting on the consequences," said one of the journalists.

Cliff shrugged. "I'm just your bodyguard. I don't have an opinion – unless you're buying me a beer!"

They all laughed.

"By the way, where *is* the guide?"

At that moment, a young, casually dressed man

stepped forward. Despite the absence of a uniform, he still came to attention with an exaggerated stamp of his foot and preposterously exaggerated salute.

"Zeb's man reporting, sir. I am Sifo," he said.

"You mean Major Hani's man, don't you?"

"No, Zeb's my cousin," he replied with a huge grin.

The journalists all laughed.

"So be it, Sifo," Cliff smiled, already taking a liking to the young man.

A hundred metres away, two sergeants from the armed response unit of the SAP (South African Police) glowered in their direction. The two naturally burly men seemed to Cliff to be even larger in their battle fatigues and bullet proof vests as they exchanged a remark. Walking over to introduce himself, he presumed that their remark was about him and would have been fairly derogatory. Cliff smiled to himself at the thought.

"Good luck with that, Captain," one of the journalists said quietly at Cliff's departing back.

Some of their colleagues chuckled while another added, "Tweedle dum and Tweedle dim are not very cooperative, Captain!"

The two sergeants moved their pump-action shot guns to their left hands as they saluted Cliff with their right. Behind them stood two Casspirs and several Land Rovers equipped with water cannons and tear gas guns.

"Good morning, sergeants. I just wanted to introduce myself. My men and I are assigned to look after the press over there. I'm Captain Barkerfield."

Cliff examined their faces. They both had coarse features and pale blue eyes. The bigger of the two introduced himself as Sergeant Smitswart. He appeared to be in charge.

"Just keep those vultures away from the township as much as you can please, Captain. *They* start all the bloody trouble. The blacks play up to them, then it gets out of hand and we have to clean up the shit," he snarled.

Cliff decided it would be a waste of time getting into an ethical debate about their derogatory reference to the very people for whom they were supposed to uphold the law. He knew this particular response unit had a reputation for being overzealous (to put it mildly) and that they reported to a very high level in the security chain of command within the SAP who allowed them a lot of latitude and authority to go with it.

It now seemed to Cliff that what he had been told about this rapid response unit was true: they *were* racist, and basically a law unto themselves.

I wonder how they get on with the Alex station commander, thought Cliff.

Zeb had been delighted when his commanding officer informed him that they required a Koevoet officer to take command of Alexandra police station. His superior insisted in Alex it was more about understanding the people and their motivations than actual policing methods.

Zeb had been in the bush for a long time and a chance to get back to suburbia was attractive. It meant he could be in contact with his parents regularly again by phone, and even visit one of his relatives who lived in Alexandra, if he could track her down.

The police station was manned by white officers but there had been little resistance to having a black commander, Zeb's reputation as an operational leader in the bush war having preceded him. In fact, they felt more secure having a Koevoet man to guide them in the unconventional policing situation they found themselves facing in a high-density township where many of the residents were hell-bent on disruption.

Alexandra's warring parties did not play by the rules. The police were there to try to keep them apart – to keep the peace – but they could turn against the peacekeepers just as quickly as they could on each other.

Being a member of the police did not command respect; rather it seemed to promote hostility. However, Major Hani had already started building a network of support within the township where he could go for information and guidance. He preferred to know potential threats so he could try preventative action rather than having to find the cure.

Zeb had always worried that his father would hear about his defection to a South African police undercover unit; even more so now that he was based back in the country. His fears were finally dispelled, however, the day he summoned the courage to have the conversation with his father.

Over the telephone, father and son had exchanged greetings and Zeb told his father he was now based in Alexandra. Zeb was worried he would inquire about his time on the border, which Zeb wanted to avoid reference to. To his relief, all his father wanted to talk about was how happy he was to hear his son was back in the country, and how he and Zeb's mother would enjoy being able to talk to him more often.

"Zeb, you must find where your granny lives in Alex. We do not know the address – only a post box where I send money for her."

Zeb remembered that his father's sister had been killed in the Soweto riots and his grandma now looked after his aunt's son.

"Ngizozama baba (I will try father)," Zeb said.

They had not spoken for over a year but his father's enthusiastic appreciation for the monthly transfer of funds from Zeb's bank account (into which his wages were paid by the SAP) confirmed his father was not aware of the source of the money. This was a relief to Zeb.

"We have saved up the money you send us and have been able to fix up our old car. Your mother is very happy we can now travel to visit her relatives. And we are adding on another room – for you of course one day, when you return," he laughed.

After replacing the receiver Zeb leant back in his chair, contemplating the bittersweet position he was in. He wondered if he would still be welcome if it was discovered he was a defector. *Well at least now I have repaid those wasted university fees*, he thought to himself.

Chapter 13
The Little General

Sitting at an outside table, thirteen-year-old Midgy Batwana raised his eyes from the café's three-day old newspaper to stare down Alexandra's Seventh Avenue; the street on which in the early 1940s Nelson Mandela had lived when he moved to Johannesburg from his homeland in Transkei. His gaze flicked across the faces on the dusty street but he saw no threat.

Midgy commanded an army of over five hundred young dissidents who were feared by both the Alexandra municipal police and right-wing vigilantes. Ten of them were now lounging close by. A few were playing cards, one of whom was playfully threatening another in mock anger with a large rock held in his fingers that were already gnarled, despite his youth. Innocent they may have looked, but they hid their knives and remained vigilant knowing their little general was under constant threat.

There were some who called their leader a snitch. They believed he played one side against the other and should be killed. Yet his soldiers didn't believe it. Being in the Under Fourteens – the name of their army – had given them dignity in this barren landscape.

For many of these boys, being in this army was about belonging and getting back a little of what they had lost. Some had been forced to leave their homes when their families were torn apart by alcohol; their fathers finding solace from the hopelessness of Apartheid by spending a week's wages on drink over a single weekend, leaving no money for food. And beating their mothers too.

Like many of these young boys, leaving home meant Midgy also did not have anywhere permanent to go. When there was no relative or charity to give them shelter, they spent months living in storm water drains in Alexandra and the affluent nearby suburbs occupied by white people. Yet it was a home, and a hideout.

The young couple seated at a table on the pavement of one of Sandton's upmarket cafés was involved in an argument. The women stabbed her finger into the tabletop to emphasise her point, spilling her coffee in the process. She slid her bag to the edge of the table out of the way of the spreading splash as the man she was with laughed dismissively.

The young boys, hidden amongst the cars parked along the street, appeared suddenly at the table of the distracted couple. They had been watching intently to gauge the suitability of their target. While the couple continued to argue, two held out their small black hands and begged for money.

"Please, please master. Money for food."

Approaching from behind the woman, another boy leant over, and before she could react, he snatched her bag and ran off, swiftly followed by the other two. Chased by her partner, the boys raced down the street and across a small park. By the time the man crested the slight rise they had just disappeared over they were nowhere to be seen. It was like they had simply vaporised.

Baffled, the only thing the young man could identify as a possible escape route was a storm water drain in an embankment nearby. Its circular dark entrance gaped at him as he thought, *Surely not? Well, I'm not crawling into that!*

Shrugging in defeat, he turned and walked back across the park. In the darkness, head jammed against the top of the damp pipe, the gang's leader rifled through the bag as another held a lit match over his shoulder.

"Is there money, Midgy?"

Midgy sipped his free mug of tea the café owner always gave him whenever he dropped in and looked back to his newspaper. He read everything he could to keep abreast of the political situation in the country. Under the table, his dangling, broken old takkies did not reach the ground. Midgy was only thirteen and less than a metre and a half tall.

"Midgy. Midgy. Bheka casspir uyeza!" he heard one of his soldiers shout to him. He looked up and saw the Casspir; the approach of which always meant trouble.

"Linda kube ngabantu bephephandaba!" Midgy called back, as he gazed up Seventh Avenue. "The newspaper people want to talk, comrades. They want to know about our struggle. Amandla!" he called out loudly.

"Amandla!" his soldiers echoed, with their fists in the air.

The Casspir crunched to a stop on a gravel side-road at the start of Seventh Avenue, at the top of a slight rise. Cliff decided he should keep his distance. He knew the people found the Casspir threatening as it represented the Regime. He could just as easily keep a watchful eye on the press corps from up here.

A corporal at Brigade headquarters had arrived

at Cliff's room earlier that morning to say the press corps had arranged an interview with one of the activist leaders, and were requesting permission to proceed. Cliff was slightly thankful that there was something to relieve the monotony of the last four days and presumed the press felt the same.

The vehicles carrying the press proceeded slowly down Seventh Avenue and parked off the road in a dusty, gravelly clearing that was used as a soccer field by the local children. Cliff wondered what the township's children thought when they saw the lush green sports fields at the schools of their white counterparts. The only thing green on theirs was the odd clump of weeds resilient enough to withstand the Highveld dryness and cold.

With the cameramen in tow, the journalists approached the café that Sifo had pointed out to them before making a hasty retreat, having previously seen the consequences of being on the wrong side of the 'Under Fourteens' army.

From his position, seated in the Casspir, the scene looked surreal to Cliff. A dozen grownups surrounded a mere child who was holding a mug of tea. The adults appeared to be listening to his every word as he answered their questions about his followers – his soldiers – all of whom were under fourteen. One of his foot soldiers was only eight years old.

"We came together to protect the people. The

Under Fourteens army is braver than the adults. The municipal police and the vigilantes don't scare us. This is what they get," he laughed, drawing his knife from behind his back and waving it in front of the journalists' faces. "Amandla!" he shouted.

His soldiers nearby echoed the chant, clenched fists in the air.

If the journalists had previously been sceptical and disbelieving, then their cynicism was fading fast as they listened to the little general quote long passages from the ANC Freedom Charter, like it was a bible he read every night.

"What is the direction, comrade?"

They would hear that catchphrase from Midgy Batwana many times.

"Can you tell me, what is..."

In mid-sentence, Midgy's grin faded and was replaced by a glare as he spotted a large group of young men appear from a side-road and proceed towards them. ANC colours in various forms seemed prevalent in their dress – shirts and beanies as well as bracelets and flags. He whistled loudly; the sound immediately repeated by his nearby followers and on, to those beyond, until it slowly faded into the distance.

The leader of the approaching group, drawing closer, yelled out. "Press people, why are you talking to this umfaan?"

"I am not your *boy*. Maybe this is your *boy*?" Midgy yelled back, holding his knife up at the approaching young man. Midgy's group were behind him now and more were appearing from between the shacks in response to the spreading whistles.

Of course, thought Cliff. *The whistling is a rallying call. The drums have sent out the call to arms*, Cliff realised, feeling decidedly apprehensive. *It's a horror film in the making*, he thought, as he watched over twenty young adults with machetes and homemade spears become surrounded by a crowd of fifty or more children, armed with knives and machetes that seemed as big as them.

The journalists were backing away, trying to put distance between themselves and the impending confrontation yet determined to watch the outcome. Cameras were clicking. Cliff was trying to decide what his next move should be when two rapid response unit SAP Land Rovers raced down the street and skidded to a halt alongside the now scattering crowd. This action knocked some of them to the ground and one casualty appeared to have a broken leg.

They fired off several rounds over the heads of the running people as they retreated down the street, not caring who was on whose side. As the crowd dissipated the police sergeant rounded on the journalists.

"You fucking people, causing shit again!"

One of the journalists was about to protest that

they were not responsible for the confrontation between the rival armies when the sergeant interjected.

"Vok af hier uit. You have five minutes to disappear or we will arrest you all."

"If anybody is going to do any arresting then it will be us," came Zeb's voice, seemingly from out of nowhere.

He was flanked by several white police officers striding alongside him.

They had parked their vehicle in the next street and had been observing developments from a distance. They were hidden behind the other township's dwellers who had gathered to witness what appeared to be another violent township confrontation. Zeb had held back, gauging whether this confrontation between the two township factions was nothing more than professional jealousy – a slanging match that would turn into a stand-off and dignified mutual back down in front of the press – or a pre-meditated confrontation that would have a bloody outcome. Zeb's informant had told him the latter was unlikely today.

The two sergeants grudgingly saluted Zeb as he approached, and one launched into a diatribe about all the trouble journalists caused in the township. After allowing him to finish, Zeb pointed out that whether they liked it or not the press *were* allowed to report on incidents in the township, provided they were escorted and stayed together as a group. Furthermore, the sergeants and their men were a response unit and were there to quell serious outbreaks of violence. They had no policing jurisdiction in Alexandra's township.

They were clearly irritated by the fact that this black officer was overruling them, and even more so by the respect shown for Zeb on the faces of their own men. His reputation as a Koevoet operative was well-known throughout the police force, and his appearance commanded instant respect.

"OK, gentlemen, let's call it a day," Zeb said to the journalists.

Gesturing towards the Casspir nearby where Cliff sat watching, he grinned at the two sergeants. "And I will make sure Captain Barkerfield hiding in the Casspir over there keeps a close eye on things in future Sergeant. OK? In fact I will talk to him now," Zeb said, as he ushered the journalists back to their vehicles and headed towards Cliff's vehicle.

Cliff climbed down from the Casspir as Zeb approached.

"Hell Zeb it's been a while," he said, as they exchanged salutes.

"Yes, and look at you – a captain now. And I thought you considered this army stuff all nonsense? Sorry I have not made contact since you arrived," Zeb said, shaking Cliff's hand. "Let's go back to the station, there is something I want to share with you."

Like his soldiers before him, the little general also disappeared amongst the shanties. He moved quickly without pausing to chat to the occasional adult who recognised him and called out a greeting.

"Hamba ngokucophelela okuncane (go carefully Little General)."

In response, Midgy raised his clenched fist in the air and heard them call out, "Amandla!"

"*What is the direction, comrade?*" he responded.

He was soon at the church. He stopped to slip his knife into its hiding place behind the fuse box attached to the wall of the church as the priest did not allow knives in God's house. Walking across to the manse and in through the open front door, Midgy was relieved to see that the priest was not home. He did not go to the room he shared with three others, instead walking directly towards the priest's room where the phone was located.

Midgy knew this was risky. He was lucky to have been given a home with the Father so the last thing he wanted to do was jeopardise his shelter by breaking the rule of entering the priest's bedroom. As he lifted the receiver, he kept a watch on the bedroom door, and the church entrance through the window. He knew the telephone number as he dialled it frequently. He waited impatiently as one ring after another sounded in his ear.

In his office at the police station, Major Hani finally put down his pen and responded to the insistent ringing of the phone connected to his private line.

Cliff towered above the Sandton traffic in the Casspir, now on his way back to Brigade headquarters after the aborted press conference with the little general. He was still trying to reconcile what Zeb had told him during their conversation at the police station afterwards. The presumptions he had made about Zeb's role in the border war, when they met on the border a few years before, were very wrong.

Chapter 14

Weekend Funerals

Weekend funerals were often the background to some of the worst outbreaks of violence in the townships and the press, knowing this, were inexorably drawn to them. Funerals could bring together rival factions, either gang related or politically aligned, and in a highly emotive environment they were ticking bombs.

Cliff made sure his driver kept their vehicle far away from proceedings as the crowd gathered for this weekend's funeral; that of a government sponsored councillor, Walter Botsween, who had been shot and killed the week before when he was accosted outside his house late at night by four killers.

Three young boys on their way home had witnessed the attack but had not recognised Walter's assassins. They had seen him park his car in the dim alley alongside his house and walk to the front door. Out of the darkness four balaclava-wearing figures had appeared. Without a word they began firing repeatedly, continuing even after the councillor's body had slumped to the ground.

Walter Botsween had grown to become well respected by the constituents in his small part of Alexandra. Unlike the other councillors, when appointed to the post he had not immediately raised the rent for the small brick dwellings in his constituency as others had done, pocketing the proceeds with little embarrassment or questioning from the government. They had even demanded a fee for the attachment of shanties to the said dwellings; in effect taking the food out of people's mouths.

To the contrary, Walter had petitioned for lower rents, and began harassing the officials he reported to in the government to extend the electricity grid to their area. When they refused, he arranged a boycott by withholding rent payments.

He led three attempted marches into the upmarket centre of the Sandton business district. However, as they slowly departed Alexandra, all of them had been curtailed by heavily armed police response units who destroyed their placards and banners while the toyi-toyi chanting procession was chased away by sjambok-wielding police officers.

Government officials were increasingly frustrated with Walter – their puppet councillor had become a bit of a 'Frankenstein's monster', playing into the hands of the ANC and their 'make the townships ungovernable' message.

In his pocket, the leader of the hit squad could feel the still warm bulb he had pulled from the vanity light above the rear-view mirror. This was so they could leave the car doors ajar for a fast escape when they returned from their mission. The bulb's warmth accentuated the icy Highveld air as they crept towards the house.

Taking up their positions near the front gate, they were invisible in the darkness of a moonless sky, stars dimmed by the smoky haze that hung in the cold night air polluted by Alexandra's countless wood fires. All they had to do was wait for the arrival of their unsuspecting target who they knew arrived home around the same time each night. When he left his car, they would seize their opportunity.

*

Coming across the killer's car in the darkness, the three street urchin soldiers had already seized *their* opportunity. Seeing the open doors, they had lit a match to check the number plate in case the registration number was personalised – maybe the car of one of Alexandra's popular soccer players – before rifling through it in the hope of finding something of value. It was difficult in the dark interior, and after a few minutes when nothing more than a security ID card attached to a lanyard lying on the back seat came to hand, they gave up.

Moving on, they were forced to get out of the way as a car's light beams came around a corner, lighting up the black plastic walls of a group of shacks before entering a lane between two small brick dwellings. The vehicle came to a stop. The driver switched off the engine and got out, slamming the door shut before walking to the house he had parked next to.

In the dim light coming from the torch in his hand, the onlookers saw him reach for the small rickety gate and then stop. It seemed to the boys he thought he had heard something. He half turned to look back and the three of them instinctively crouched down in case he shone the torch in their direction. In that instant, his face and body were lit by the beams of powerful torches and multiple shots rang out, deafening the boys.

They watched his expression turn from fear to horror and then blankness as he collapsed to the ground. One of the gunmen bent and turned over the prostrate body of Walter Botsween. After firing several more times, the killer seemed satisfied their victim was dead and nodded at the others in confirmation.

There was screaming coming from the house now as the four figures moved quickly from the scene, one muttering under his breath. What he said was not clear to the boys but they recognised the dialect as the killers ran towards the car the boys had been searching just a few minutes earlier.

Watching the killers disappear into the darkness, the three boys agreed that if asked by anyone, even the priest, they would say it was impossible to recognise anything about them.

This was not what they told their general later though.

To the mourners, the Casspir represented the government no matter who was in it. In an emotionally charged atmosphere, anything seen to be an official intervention in any way breached the sanctity of a funeral of a loved one. This could be a catalyst for a violent confrontation with a resentful crowd – hence Cliff and his squad's distant position.

Even though they were far away, the height of

their vehicle and its raised seating allowed them an adequate view of the journalists and cameramen as they recorded proceedings. Although the press had been given permission from the family to attend the ceremony, they did so from a respectful distance. The press was generally tolerated in the townships, as they were thought to be showing the world the plight of black people. Things could go wrong very quickly though, and that was why Cliff and his squad were there.

Watching the crowds gather Cliff felt his *own* anger towards the government; that he should be in this position, potentially in a situation where he might have to threaten these people with force if they did not maintain a reasonable level of order. *This is not a damn battlefield, even though many of these people are deeply resentful as a result of their treatment over the years, today they're still just a bunch of people going to a funeral.*

The toyi-toyi-ing crowd had formed itself into a procession behind the pall bearers and was moving slowly towards the burial ground. As they moved by, Cliff noticed that many of the youngsters were carrying knives. Although some were little more than thirteen or fourteen they considered themselves to be soldiers, and shook their clenched fists while calling out, "Amandla!" over and over again. He wondered if they were part of the little general's army.

He turned to the men in the back of the troop carrier who were pale-faced and anxious. Despite having been in Alexandra for a month, they had still not got used to the almost continuous violence, or threat thereof. They were not much older than some of the black youths they were watching and whom they might be forced to point their weapons at.

"A lot of those young guys are carrying knives. I think there is a vengeance thing that might be going down here this Sunday. Keep all eyes on our press corps. They will have picked up on that as well and will go for a front row seat which is very risky, OK?"

"Yes, Captain," came the collective response.

So far, they had barely had to leave the safety of their armoured movable office, but they all knew it was only a matter of time before that changed.

Josh looked at the laughing faces gathered around the barbecue that Sunday afternoon with incredulity. Beers and glasses of wine in hand, Josh's workmates and their friends seemed oblivious to what real life was like for the majority of the population, some of whom lived only ten minutes away by car from where they now stood.

He had had no idea how dire the township situation was either, even as a journalist who was supposedly part of the 'inner circle of news'. He had only become aware of the situation when Peter had told him about his telephone call from Sam. Sam had relayed in graphic detail what he had seen in a documentary on UK television.

"How's it going Josh? 'Nother beer?" his host Cody called across the smoky charcoal barbeque he tended. "Have you been introduced to everybody hey Joshie?"

"Sure have," laughed Josh, taking the beer from the hand reaching over the coals before it disappeared to replace the lid of the cooler box beside the barbecue.

Better take it a bit easy, he thought to himself taking a sip, *if you want to start feeling better than you have. These Joburg people know how to party all right.*

Later on Josh found himself in a conversation with two other journalists. Emboldened by the beers he had drunk, he asked them what they thought about the incidents happening in the townships around the country.

They both agreed it was going to spiral out of control. On the one hand there was the ANC calling on the people to make the townships ungovernable, and on the other the government, promoting conflict between black opposition political parties.

"Imagine you have a hostel full of migrant Zulu workers who support a particular political party, and in the hostel down the road a whole bunch of locals that support the ANC. With the government stirring the pot it doesn't take much to achieve ignition," one of the journalists said.

"But isn't the government shooting itself in the foot?" Josh asked. "The more unrest, the more nervous the white people get and the more pressure they put on *their* government to negotiate change, surely?"

"Ever heard of P.W. Botha's version of freedom of the press?" the journalist said, by way of an answer. "You can publish anything you like, as long as it shows South Africa in a positive light. Everything else is simply censored so nobody sees what is reported or knows what's going on."

"Except the people in the suburbs close enough to Alex to hear the gunfire and smell the smoke from burning tyres," commented the other journalist. "Anyway, even if it is reported, some might say the government is creating a situation where they can say to their critics '*see what happens when you give these black people free reign*'," he concluded.

Later, sitting at an ornate cast-iron table on the deck surrounding the large sparkling swimming pool, Josh observed the faces of the laughing, joking people and wondered if they actually preferred not to know.

He heard Cody call out to their maid from behind the smoking fillet steaks.

"Sunrise! Sunrise, please bring more meat from the fridge. And more beers, maybe? Honey, does Sunrise know which meat is for the braai?" Cody called to his wife, who ignored him as she was in a conversation with two women about a mutual friend who had just purchased a handgun.

Josh was fairly sure Sunrise knew what was going on in Alexandra.

Cliff watched the throng of mourners as they made their way slowly down the dusty road towards the cemetery. The singing mass of people reminded him of the surface of a dark, slow-moving river.

Unlike most, Cliff did not see beauty in *all* rivers – certainly not the muddy ones he could not see down to the bottom of. They always seemed ominous to him. *What dark shapes were moving about unseen down there?* Much like in this human river before him. Disturbing the procession's flow were various small groups of people doing the toyi-toyi protest dance. They were like the swirls one sees appear suddenly on a river's dark surface; a reminder of the dangerous currents that exist.

Most of the press contingent were grouped together, following alongside the procession of people to remain close to a particular point in the procession. *What do they know that we don't?* Cliff thought.

The tail of the human procession had now moved past them so Cliff asked his driver to move the Casspir to a new position. They drove through Alexandra's irregular road layout before reaching a position where they could still observe the scene but without being too intrusive. Cliff wondered why there was no police presence. *Are we all there is, if any trouble breaks out?* he wondered.

The thought had barely crossed his mind when Cliff noticed him. Like a salmon swimming against the current, working its way upstream through the rapids, a young man was elbowing his way back through the people moving towards him, looking back over his shoulder from time to time.

Cliff could not see what had frightened him but with the aid of binoculars, his driver could.

"Ten o'clock sir. There's about ten of them. They're on the other side of the procession. Ducking down. There. See them?"

"Yeah, I have them. Of course, they have knives, right?"

"Affirmative, Captain."

"Stand by to deploy." Cliff gave the command to his squad in the Casspir behind him as they moved the vehicle closer in, attracting angry stares from some in the procession.

The person the knife carrying youths were after could not see exactly where his pursuers were as they moved towards him but he knew they were there in the crowd.

They crouched over, on the edge of the throng, using the people as their shield. Cliff thought that the safest option for the man was to stay in the midst of the procession and maybe even hide and move with the flow instead of against it, until the armed gang lost sight of him.

Cliff wondered if what was unfolding had anything to do with the killing of the person being buried. The one who had been attacked the previous week. *Is this a case of the criminal returning to see his job completed? Surely they wouldn't turn up to the funeral of a person they've just killed, would they?* Cliff thought.

The journalists and cameramen were not far behind the pursuers.

"Damn, they *are* like fucking vultures," Cliff groaned. "Prepare to deploy. Safety catches off," he commanded.

"Where is he? He must be trying to duck out without them spotting him," one of the squad said.

"There he is! He's making a break for those shacks."

"They've seen him."

Leaving the driver in the Casspir, Cliff and his squad moved on foot into an opening between the shanties. They saw the pursuers had gathered around a small house and were smashing the windows.

"We did not let him in. Our son is not here. Please!" pleaded the voice calling loudly from within.

Yet the persecutors did not care. If they could not have the boy then they would take the boy's parents instead. The gang was so enraged by this time that an attack on anything associated with their wrath was good enough for them.

"Ukahona, ukahona (you are there)," cried the pursuers as they spotted their target.

As he appeared running from the back of the house where he had hidden, he tried to change direction to evade capture, tripping and falling before his knife wielding attackers.

"Move in. One round over their heads," Cliff shouted.

The crack of the rifle shots stopped the attackers just as they had begun lunging at the victim with knives. They looked back momentarily before running for cover. Township residents had long since learnt that when weapons were fired at them, it was to cause injury, not just to frighten. The gang did not expect any more warning shots and had no intention of waiting around to find out.

Cliff stepped forward and grabbed the boy by the wrist. Yanking him to his feet, he saw a look of resignation in his eyes rather than fear. He had a few knife wounds but nothing life-threatening as far as Cliff could see. He dragged him back towards the Casspir.

Pointing their weapons in the direction the gang had run, Cliff's squad backed their way towards the vehicle to provide cover for him.

"OK, you men stay with the journo's while I deal with this guy. You two stay with me," Cliff panted.

He looked into the faces of the two as they turned towards him. They looked to be barely out of school; this stint in the townships their first after six months in basic training. More experienced army personnel were either being deployed to the border war or, as in Cliff's case here, leading men deployed from the training battalion in the townships.

They looked slightly shocked. They had just fired live rounds over the heads of young people the same age as them; boys that on any other day they could have been playing soccer with. Cliff wondered about the consequences for their mental health should they be required to actually shoot someone in the next few weeks. Given their reaction to this incident, the effects would no doubt be devastating.

It was only after he had loaded the injured boy into the Casspir and instructed his driver to leave that Cliff noticed the cameras had been filming them the whole time.

"We're going to be in the news I think sir," laughed his driver.

*

Cliff's hurried conversation with their bloody

passenger who was now huddled in the back between two of his armed squad, revealed that he was not one of the killers from the previous week. It would appear that someone had told the gang lies about him.

Five minutes after they had left the funeral, the driver stopped the Casspir as per the captain's instructions. Over the tops of the spreading shacks, in the distance they could see cars travelling along one of Johannesburg's busy freeways.

Cliff considered what the occupants of the speeding vehicles were thinking as they looked across the narrow strip of veld towards the smoky township. Were they concerned about what was going on in the troubled township? Or just focused on getting to their friend's home and the Sunday lunchtime barbecue they were about to enjoy on a patio, sitting beside a sparkling swimming pool of a luxury home in the northern suburbs? Alexandra seemed so close and yet so far away.

The driver's voice penetrated his thoughts. "I thought we were going to the police station, sir?"

Glancing down at his hands to see if they had stopped trembling now that his heart had stopped pounding, Cliff said, "It's not for us to decide whether he has committed a crime or not. Who the hell would know? Anyway, we aren't the police here. He's not necessarily going to be safe at the station either." His driver gave him a puzzled look that Cliff ignored while he turned to look at their prisoner. "Do you want to get out here? We can take you to the police station if you want to go there for help?"

"No. No. I don't want to go to the amaphoyisa."

"Thought so," chuckled Cliff, looking at his driver with a shrug of his shoulders.

After a few seconds, the young man spoke again. "Can you take me to the umpristi ukulunywa (priest who itches) at the church? I will be safe with the white father."

The church was only five minutes' drive away. The boy directed them to a simple brick structure with an A-framed corrugated iron roof, a wooden cross at its apex.

There was a manse alongside, and in the vegetable garden in front of it knelt the priest. He looked up in surprise as the large Casspir halted in front of his church. Their passenger jumped down to the gravel and raced past the church and through the front door of the manse. The priest swiftly followed.

Who itches? wondered Cliff.

*

Driving back to the funeral and the press corps, Cliff kept thinking about the look of resignation on the young boy's face as he lay on the ground. *He was like an animal that knew it was prey, facing an inevitable outcome. Pointed out to the gang, he became like a buck pursued by a pack of wild dogs, safely hidden, standing on a dry branch by mistake, giving its hiding place away.*

Chapter 15

New Awakenings

Jodie could see the ocean from where she sat at the table in their kitchen. The water was being ravaged by the strong southerly wind that ripped off the wave's teetering blue tops, throwing foam upward like the manes of white horses.

"If the southerly's howling, it must be Saturday morning in Durban," she said to herself over her coffee cup that was poised half an inch from her lips.

The level they occupied in the building was not high enough to see the beach itself, but it would obviously be deserted today just as it had been for the last nineteen weekends.

"One more and I win that dinner," she had said to Peter over breakfast that morning.

Ever the optimist though, at the end of every wind-blown Sunday, Peter always insisted that the next weekend would be a beach weekend. They had agreed that if he was proven wrong after twenty weekends, he would buy her dinner.

She felt suddenly miserable. Her life was going nowhere. *Is it time for something new?* she thought with a sigh. She knew this mood was only because it was the weekend and she was not occupied by her job. She needed the distraction of the beach at the weekend. *Roll on Monday*, she thought slapping her hand on the table.

The last time Cliff and Josh had visited them they had spoken about what there was to do in Johannesburg at the weekends with no beach to go to. It seemed to be all about barbecues and restaurants on Sundays up there, sport on Saturdays. *Sounds like you need to be in a relationship if you live in Joburg, or have lots of friends*, Jodie had thought.

"Ouch, damn!" Peter exclaimed, as his knee caught a chair. "Guess who is on page two of the weekend paper?" he said from behind the newspaper he carried, reading as he negotiated his way into the kitchen. He lowered the newspaper dramatically to reveal a mischievous grin. "Your 'boyfriend'!" he announced. "Whoa," he exclaimed, as Jodie sprang up and snatched the paper from her brother.

"What?" exclaimed Jodie. "Oh my God," she said, as she moved her cup with one hand and laid the newspaper on the table with the other.

There were two pictures buried in the copy

under the headline: 'Army captain saves life of black dissident in funeral attack'.

Jodie's eyes darted between the pictures, captions and the report quickly as she tried to absorb the information. The first picture was printed in colour to better convey the drama of the young man's blood-soaked shirt as Cliff hauled him up by the wrist to a standing position. The second image showed Cliff pushing him up the steps of the Casspir with the soldiers of his squad surrounding him, pointing their rifles down the street.

Jodie looked up at Peter and he was surprised to see she had tears in her eyes.

"I thought it was just another silly army camp thing you guys do. This looks awful! Gangs with knives... Cliff and a few soldiers amongst hundreds of rampaging protestors. He could be killed!" she cried.

"Well, Cliff's lot have guns (or rifles if you like) to fight against their knives, and the entire population of Alex is not trying to attack them Jodie, they're just trying to survive as best they can," Peter said, his back to Jodie as he searched the top shelf for his jar of decaffeinated coffee.

"I didn't realise what this camp was about. This is terrible! What am I going to do?" she said, ignoring his last comment. "I will try to contact his mother for a phone number. There can't be many Barkerfields in a small place like Maritzburg, surely?"

Peter smiled as he turned from the cupboard with the jar of coffee in one hand and cup in the other. "Are you in love with him?"

"Are *you* in love with him?" Jodie retorted, her face crimson. "Oh no sorry, of course it's not with him," she smiled evilly.

Now it was Peter's turn to be red-faced. The siblings stared for a few seconds before they smiled and then laughed.

"You're such a bastard!"

"And you're such a bitch!"

They hugged briefly as Jodie passed her brother to find a tissue in her bedroom.

Brenda had begun devoting her lunch break to making calls to orphanages and childcare organisations. It was tiresome work but being alone in one of the meeting rooms was preferable to the conversations she regularly heard between her peers in the office canteen.

All anybody debated nowadays was whether one should have razor wire on top of their walls or electric fencing, buy a gun or emigrate.

Brenda replaced the receiver with a feeling of hopelessness; yet another place that no longer existed. She had lost count of the number of lunch hours she had spent calling the numbers on her list. As she put a line through the latest dead-end, she estimated she was about halfway through.

She clapped her hands together lightly to motivate herself. *Come on Brenda, the next one could be that positive response you're looking for*, she thought.

Josh had been a great help; searching through the classified records in their newspaper's archives to give her an extensive list of orphanages that had used the paper's classifieds pages to post job advertisements, deaths and legal notices, searches for foster parents and so on. He had tried to increase the relevancy of the results by limiting the search to three years before and a few years after the date of her first orphanage placement.

One lunchtime when they were considering a strategy for progressing with the search, Josh had concluded she had no option other than to phone each company on the list and ask if they had any record of someone by the name of Brenda Tarrant.

"You at least have a reasonably precise timeframe. That should help. You have to start somewhere," he said, pushing the list across the table towards her. "There were no computers of course in those days and I bet their records are pretty basic so you'll need a bit of luck." He reached across and took her hand. "Sorry Brenda Tarrant, but I guess you're just going to have to start at the top and work your way down."

Well, she had the time to go through such a

laborious task given that her writing had been stop start lately.

The book was a parody on military training, it was intended to support the cause of the anti-conscription lobby. However, her scenes were very dependent on what Cliff relayed to her from his personal experiences. The long gaps between the periods he was actually involved with the army, coupled with separation, meant she had not heard much from him at all recently.

Despite that, she was not that far from completion and even had a publisher interested. Unlike most aspiring writers, she had been spared the agony of getting a publisher interested in her debut work, she already had an introduction to a publishing house through her editorial boss. The publishers thought it was perfect timing for such a novel in South Africa and were keen to see her manuscript, if only she could just get it done. She resolved to call Beryl to ask her for Cliff's contact details.

Investigating the suppression of information being practiced by the government had become Josh's new-found passion. This had distracted him from his own quest to find out who his birth father might be. Sam's disclosure about what he had seen in the documentary in England, which was later relayed to him by Peter, had piqued his interest in the story and prompted him to propose an exposé to his editor.

"We all know censorship like this is unethical Josh, but there's nothing to find out about. It's not a story. It's just what it is – suppression of information – the prerogative of a government with an overwhelming majority in a whites-only electorate that can do what it likes in the name of so-called internal security."

"But the extent of it!" Josh exclaimed. "Surely the voters should be allowed to make an informed assessment of how their government is handling their wellbeing? Notwithstanding the fact that they are already in good shape compared to the majority of people – the ones that can't vote and are experiencing the government's brutality."

"I know where you are coming from son and I agree, but to be honest I'm not sure the majority of the white population gives a damn about what is going on, so long as it does not spill over into their neighbourhood and spoil their good times," the editor said.

"But that's the whole point – it *will* spill over, eventually. What the government is doing is positioning itself to be in the best negotiating position by sacrificing the lives of innocent people; pitting political groups against each other simply to promote violence!" Josh said, palms upward in incredulity.

He stared out of the window while the editor drummed his fingers on the desk.

Josh turned back to look at his boss. "What if the government had lost control of the people they initially gave free rein to in order to promote this situation? What if actions were being taken by rogue individuals without the government even knowing? What if it even included assassinations?"

"Now that *is* a story," his editor interjected. "I'll give you a week Josh to convince me *that* might be going on."

Jodie and Peter looked like a couple in love, as they clung to each other for support on the gusty Durban beachfront promenade the following day.

"Are you thinking what I'm thinking?" Peter said, as they lurched forward, once again propelled by a gust of wind hitting them from behind.

"That this wind is a pain in the butt, and we should try living on the Highveld?" Jodie laughed.

"No, that we should turn around and walk backwards," he laughed. "Actually, as it happens, I have been thinking about a change," Peter said.

"Of course it's the weather, and nothing else, that would make you give up your job and move to a place you have always claimed you would hate to live in?" Jodie teased.

Then she decided to let him off the hook, mainly

because it suited her just fine given her thoughts lately about her future. She had surprised herself at her fearful reaction to the newspaper report about Cliff. Maybe it was time for a new job in a new city. A move to Johannesburg would facilitate that and at the same time she could test what her feelings for Cliff really were.

"Yeah maybe. I don't mind trying something new, if that's what you want," she smiled, as she turned to look at her twin.

"We're not married. You don't have to move just because I do," Peter said with a wink, putting her on the spot now. "You should stay here. You have a great job."

She gave him a shove with her hip, the result of which made them both stumble, attracting stares from the other walkers nearby.

Beryl thought the young girl at her front door must be some kind of cosmetics salesperson as she had a large bag slung from her shoulder over which Beryl could see Mrs Levy across the road watering her pot plants. She was very business-like, notwithstanding the smile on her beautiful face.

"Mrs Barkerfield, is it?" Jodie inquired.

"Yes dear, but I don't want to buy anything today. Sorry."

"Oh, no that's not why I am here." Jodie chuckled, and Beryl was immediately charmed by the way her laughter lines transformed her face into one of mischievousness. "I'm a friend of Cliff's."

*

Such was her slight frame, that she was almost swallowed up by the large soft cushions of the sofa upon which she sat. Jodie looked around Beryl's lounge and tried to imagine Cliff as a young boy in this house. Beryl made tea and spoke to her from the kitchen as she did so. *So, this is where he grew up*, Jodie thought.

"Have you and Cliff been friends for long?" Beryl called over the clatter of cups. "And please call me Beryl, dear."

Struggling up from the sofa and walking to the kitchen door, Jodie told Beryl how she and Cliff had first met, and that he had later invited her to the officers' mess function.

Beryl was maddened with Cliff for not visiting her when he was so close by, or even telling her he was in Durban. However, she directed her frown of annoyance at the kettle she was pouring the hot water from rather than uttering her feelings out loud.

"Oh, you're Peter's twin sister. That's interesting."

Jodie explained that she had read an article about Cliff in the newspaper and was now very keen to make contact with him. However, she did not have a number for where he was based. All she knew was that it was an army camp somewhere in Johannesburg.

Jodie had decided to visit Beryl in person to ask for her son's number as she thought it more likely his mother would provide it this way rather than over the telephone, given she was a stranger. She neglected to say she had driven an hour just to ask for it though!

"All I have is a number for something to do with the headquarters in Sandton," Beryl replied. "Brigade HQ, I think he said," Beryl murmured, while leafing through her little pocket address book. "I know it's here somewhere, I found it for Brenda just the other day. Ah, here it is. You have to leave a message and he will call back when he can. I know which news piece you mean. It worries me terribly all this business, and now Cliff is involved too."

"I agree Beryl, it is so worrying. That's why I would like to call him."

Beryl decided she would take it at face value; Jodie was just a friend wanting reassurance that her son was safe. *Well, she could have just got that reassurance from me on the phone*, Beryl thought.

*

Beryl stood waving from her veranda as Jodie drove off with a beep of her car's horn. Beryl said to herself, "Well my son – when one door closes, another door opens I suppose."

Brenda had been on hold for ages. Her mind wandered as she waited for the woman she had spoken to ten minutes ago to return to their call. She seemed to have disappeared entirely. Brenda pictured her bent over a filing cabinet, flicking through folders in search of the information she sought.

Even if I do eventually find the right orphanage, will they have any worthwhile information to give me? And if I can find a possible birth parent's name, how will I ever find them? Hire a private detective maybe or place an advertisement in a newspaper? Would anybody see it and, if they did, why would they respond to it? What if they don't want to meet me? All these questions ran through Brenda's mind as she waited

"With an 'a' or an 'e'?" a voice asked, interrupting her thoughts.

"What?" Brenda said, startled. She had expected the inevitable response of 'sorry, we have no record'."

"Tarrant – spelt with an 'a' or an 'e'?" the

woman repeated patiently.

"An 'a'."

"Well, we had a baby brought to us for adoption on the fifth of April, 1946," she said. "Brown eyes," she continued with a murmur.

Brenda imagined her at the other end of the line, scanning a document for relevant details.

"It's noted here that the name on the birth certificate was Brenda Tarrant. Sorry, are you all right dear?" the woman asked after several seconds when she had not received a reply.

There was no one to hear the query as Brenda, sobbing uncontrollably, had dropped the receiver, and now it swung gently at the end of its chord beside her chair.

They had parked the Casspir beside the dusty field surrounded by shacks whereon two young teams were playing soccer, watched by the entire press corps. Cliff did not immediately give the order to disembark from the troop carrier, instead deciding to just observe their surroundings from an elevated position in the vehicle.

"First time they've had spectators watching from a 'grandstand' I bet," said his driver, referring to the height of the Casspir and its side-on position near the touchline; its passengers staring through the thick glass windows.

The young players had only old boots or tattered trainers in which to play. Some were even barefoot. Cliff marvelled at how they still seemed oblivious to the stony, dusty surface they played on. He wondered if they avoided certain tackles to ensure they did not sprawl painfully in the stony dirt. *I bet there are no slide tackles*, he mused.

"Shit, some of these guys have got great skills!" The praise came from one of the squad seated at the rear of the Casspir.

"I'll say. That big chap would make a great centre back – big timber in a set piece," the driver responded.

"See how he is instructing his back line to move up?" observed another.

The boys were cautious at first, perhaps slightly intimidated by the Casspir and its occupants. However, as the game progressed, they appeared to love having the journalists as spectators, as well as the clicking cameras and roaming TV camera. Their energy levels as they played matched their frustrated yells at any teammate who made a wrong move.

*

The reason the press corps were on the side lines that morning was due to the publication of a government press release that had featured in all the newspapers the previous evening. The sports minister had suggested that providing sports facilities would stop the unrest in the township. He was quoted as saying:

"These boys need something to use up their energy on." In support of this, he added, "The government is thus busy upgrading all the sports fields to accommodate more sporting events, especially soccer – the first love of black people."

The press corps had not moved from the police building at Alexandra's entrance for several days and they were growing restless. When the press release came out there was an immediate response – a slightly cynical one at that – but they were keen to see how the big upgrade was going to look.

*

Peering over the heads of the journalists gathered on the side line below them, Cliff could not identify any signs of an upgrade to the sports field currently in progress. However, he did have to admit the last time he drove past this square of dirt he could not remember seeing the white goal posts that were now at either end. *Better than goalposts formed with dead tree branches as they used to have here*, he supposed. *At least it's a start.*

He decided to give the order to disembark to just half of his squad. He did not want to spoil the enthusiastic atmosphere of the boys' game so he decided the troops should leave their weapons in the Casspir.

"Rotate as you see fit. Just make sure half of you are in here with the weapons at all times," he ordered, as he climbed down. "Those outside need to have eyes on the surrounding terrain for any unfriendly approaches. Just in case."

He sauntered along behind the line of press watching the game between them, occasionally looking away to scan the shacks surrounding the soccer field. Most of the journalists had pulled up their coat collars or wore hoods to protect them against the cold Highveld morning air. Cliff did not immediately recognise anyone from where he walked behind them. He stopped halfway down the touchline before addressing their anonymous backs.

"Good morning gentlemen," he said.

Some of them just waved a hand but without turning as they were too intent on watching the game, while others did do him the courtesy of turning to greet him face-on, one of these faces left him open-mouthed in surprise.

"Josh! What the hell? What are you doing here, buddy?"

"Am I allowed to give you a hug, *Captain*? Being in uniform and all?" Josh asked.

"Just come here!" Cliff said.

Several of Josh's fellow journalists laughed at their public display of affection.

"That's not going to get you any special

treatment, Joshie!" one of them called out. "Unless there's something we don't know?"

"Told you I had friends in high places," Josh called back in response, giving him the finger at the same time.

Josh took Cliff to one side to tell him about the opportunity his editor had given him: to investigate whether there were rogue government individuals at work in the townships, and whether these individuals had taken it upon themselves to solve the unrest problem in their own way.

As he spoke, Cliff noticed Josh had lost weight since he had last seen him. In spite of his handsome features, his face still appeared to be a little drawn, and even though he spoke with conviction, his eyes did not sparkle as brightly as they usually did.

"There is so little visibility allowed, who knows what is going on?" Josh was saying.

"Jodie told me Sam had let you know, through Peter, about a documentary he saw on TV in the UK. She said he had phoned Peter in some distress. Is that what this is about?"

"Partly," Josh answered, as he looked across to where the game was being played. "These kids are no angels but they have a cause – one you and I know is justified. If the government is treating this township disruption thing as some kind of Umkhonto we Sizwe-inspired 'war in the towns', then there should at least be some rules – the ones you have in a war. I mean, no coldblooded assassinations allowed at least."

"I know the situation has really got dark," Cliff responded.

Josh nodded in confirmation. "I just need to find out how I can get a look behind the scenes. I need a source – an ally – someone within the government, police force or even MK who want to see this clandestine stuff out in the open."

Cliff thought of his conversation with Zeb and wondered if he would be breaking a confidence by talking to Josh. However, Zeb had asked him to let him know of any avenues Cliff thought he might pursue to achieve his goal. "OK, let me tell you what I found out from Zeb the other day. You two might have some common ground."

Josh's head jerked back from the action on the dusty field at the mention of Zeb's name. However, once again Cliff noticed his cousin's expression seemed to have lost the hint of humour normally so integral to his demeanour.

"Oh, you didn't know? He's the station commander at the police station where you joined up with this lot earlier," Cliff said, nodding at the journalists who were still lining the side of the pitch.

Josh shook his head slowly in fascination, as Cliff told him the true story of Zeb; how he had found out that Zeb in fact had never 'defected' from MK to the South African police as he had originally suspected in a letter to Josh from the Caprivi camp.

Instead, right through the bush war, the entire time, since being recruited by Koevoet, Zeb had been an underground MK operative, passing information back to his MK superiors while establishing himself as a high performer in the police force.

*

When he was transferred to his position as station commander in Alexandra, his MK bosses seized the opportunity to use him undercover. Zeb was immediately tasked with exposing the executions of black activists in the township, and further afield on white activists. Some had been lost to an assassination-style gunning down, while others had been abducted and some killed with parcel bombs. It was also being alleged that premeditated shootings of dissidents and demonstrators in the townships during protest activities was also being concealed.

The ANC believed there were individuals in the government security forces who were exceeding their authority, doing as they pleased. The government emphatically denied the allegation, however, accusing the ANC's military wing, MK, of using their accusations as a disguise to eradicate political rivals while blaming the government for the killings.

*

"Zeb told me the other night he had identified one such group and was ready to expose them. He needs a way of making sure it is fully covered in the news though; in a way it can't be rubbished or covered up by the authorities." Nodding at the spectators on the edge of the playing area in front of them, Cliff continued talking. "He asked me if I knew if any of the journalists were the type of person he could confide in – involve in the exposé, as it were. In return for exclusivity on the story, he wants their commitment that they will provide detailed coverage in their newspaper."

"Let me talk to him!" Josh said excitedly.

However, Cliff was not giving Josh his full attention now as he suddenly realised the enthusiastic yelling from the soccer pitch had subsided. The players had gathered together in the middle of the pitch with some appearing to be arguing while pointing at the journalists.

Cliff felt tense as he glanced across at the Casspir. The men in the vehicle were attentively watching what was developing in front of them.

Suddenly, one team began to approach the journalists and cameramen while the other straggled off the pitch looking disgruntled, arguing amongst themselves and yelling insults at those players left on the field. Cliff's men were standing behind the journalists. Some of the troops were glancing back at the Casspir; calculating how long it would take to get back to retrieve their weapons.

Standing behind everyone, Cliff said quietly, "Don't move anyone. Not until I say so."

He looked towards the driver in the troop carrier who had the mic for the two-way radio already in his hand, but Cliff signalled him to hold off for the moment; the rest of the squad starting to disembark slowly. *These young men are smart enough, even after only a few months in the township, to know the likely negative result of looking too reactive*, Cliff thought.

As the boys approached, the player in charge was the big centre back whom one of his men had pointed out earlier. The followers looked less intimidating. The leader stopped the group just short of the row of newspapermen and smirked as he looked up and down the line of apprehensive faces.

"Hhhawu, is this your team? Come, you play us winners," he laughed, as they trotted back to the pitch.

With Cliff's blessing, a few of his squad, who were regular soccer players, joined the hastily assembled press corps team, and together they participated in what turned out to be a fiercely contested game.

"How come you two aren't playing?" Zeb asked,

from behind them.

"Speak of the devil!" Cliff laughed.

"Well, you called him – or at least your driver did," Zeb smiled. "He called in and said there looked like a situation developing, but then he changed it to an all clear. On your instruction, he said. I thought I would pop down anyway, and I'm glad I did." Zeb turned to Josh. "Josh! It's been a long, long time. And that was also a soccer game – in Cliff's backyard."

The two men shook hands warmly.

"Yes, it was. Good to see you again Zeb. What a career you have had since those days! Cliff has always kept me up to date whenever he has heard from you and your escapades."

Zeb laughed at that, but then his expression turned to one of apprehension as Josh continued.

"He has also just told me about your last conversation. I think I'm your man – the journalist you need." Josh noticed Zeb frowning, as well as the glance he had just given Cliff. "Don't worry," he said, hastily. "I am on the same mission as you – just maybe coming from a different point of view. I am sure we can help each other, and you're secure with me. Remember, us journalists never reveal our sources."

Zeb finally smiled. "Fair enough, Josh, let's talk. Not here though – later. Can we meet for a beer tonight? Look, I do trust you guys but understand if this got out about me I would be a goner."

"Goal!"

The cry from the spectating journalists on the side line came through the cloud of dust the two teams were raising in the warming Alexandra morning.

Chapter 16
The Hit and Miss

In the cramped room he occasionally shared with several other homeless children, the little general smiled to himself as the three small boys described what they had seen; speaking over each other in their hurry to relay it all. As they spoke, one of them swung the security card's lanyard in a circular motion; letting it wind itself around his wrist before swinging it in the opposite direction for the cord to unwind again.

This is what Major Hani is after, Midgy thought. *This will make me important. He will see I know how a soldier can find what his officer asks for.*

No one knew that Zeb had made contact with Midgy Batwana. Having heard of the young activist's prowess, Zeb had enlisted his help as an informant, which had delighted Midgy. Zeb Hani's reputation was well-known to him, as it was to many others in Alexandra, even if he was in the notorious Koevoet fighting against MK before coming to the township he was still proud to be enlisted by the major.

The information Major Hani had asked Midgy to procure already showed him that even though he was a policeman of the government, he was looking out for his people. The information the boys had given their general was exactly what the major wanted.

"What's this?" an irritated Midgy snapped, grabbing the constantly swinging lanyard in mid-air to stop it. "Hhhawu, you talk to your general and play games at the same time, umfana oyisiphukuphuku (stupid boy)?"

"Hhhawu, General I am not stupid. This is the card of one of the three we tell you about," the reprimanded boy protested, pointing at the security card now in Midgy's hand. "I found it in their car. We have the number as well."

Their general could not suppress his grin at this. Major Hani was going to be very pleased. "You boys have done good work. I tell you what – I will ask the father if you can watch soccer on his TV one night."

Delighted at this, the boys stood up together and executed a toyi-toyi while whistling loudly.

"Shhh!" Midgy said, while waving at them to sit back down. Midgy leant forward on the bed to look through his door and down the hallway of the manse in the direction of the priest's room. "Father will get cross."

"Speak in English so the priest can understand," Zeb said to his young informant. "Tell him what you told me on the phone."

In the lounge room of the church manse, Midgy looked uneasy sitting with the priest and Major Hani. The major had insisted they share with the priest what the three boys had witnessed. He told Midgy he thought that the priest might offer to help with his plan, while Midgy hoped Father would not make the three boys leave their sanctuary for not having gone directly to the police.

Midgy relayed what the three latest inhabitants of the manse had told him. He was glad they were not there chattering like birds in a tree as he wanted to demonstrate his calm approach in situations such as this.

When Midgy finished his story, the priest turned to Zeb and simply shrugged his shoulders. "Why don't you just arrest them, Major? Lay a charge against them for murder?"

Zeb smiled. "There is nothing more I would like to do, but I don't want to miss this opportunity. I am worried about the evidence. The boys did not actually see their faces; they just heard one of them speaking and even then, not what he actually said. We have traced the owner of the car so we know it's not the killers' although we know why they have regular access to it. We know where it's located – even now." Zeb held out the lanyard to the priest. "You and I know who this is, but it could be claimed the card was stolen – by the same people who, theoretically, could have stolen the car that night. I know what the truth is but proving it in court will be tough. I need to get these guys to show their hand and catch them at it. I think there is enough here to make them do that."

"How?" the priest asked with open arms, the draping sleeves of his robe rustling as he did so.

"If we could find a way of letting them know what these boys saw and where they could be found, they are sure to come after them; show themselves in an attempt to get at the boys."

"That would be dangerous for the boys though, surely?"

"No Father," Midgy piped up. "Major is a Koevoet man. He knows what to do."

The priest closed his eyes and remained silent for some time. Zeb wondered if he was praying. He looked at Midgy and shook his head slightly to indicate he should stay quiet. He wanted to give the priest time to think. This was the response Zeb had been hoping for.

"Maybe I could help you," the priest said, finally. "That person," he said, pointing at the ID card Zeb held, "and another man sometimes park under those gum trees out there." He nodded towards the playground-side of the church grounds. "They eat their lunch there."

The priest went on to explain why people parked their vehicles under the trees near the church to have their takeaways. The church was one of the few buildings that did not have small dwellings and shanties built right up close to it. There was a small barren playground for the Sunday School children on one side of it, and on the other a football field with makeshift goal posts installed by the priest himself in the hope of attracting youngsters to his flock.

The tall shade-providing gum trees rising from the long veld grass surrounding the rest of the church buildings were the only ones in the whole township that had not been felled for firewood. It appeared that the sanctity of the church grounds had saved them from this fate.

"Next time I see him, I could go across for a chat? I do this when I see people stopped there. I could mention that the boys who are staying in the church sanctuary at the moment had let slip they had witnessed the shooting of Walter Botsween, and saw the killers drive off afterwards."

*

Having parked the car in the shade near the

church, Walter Botsween's killers settled back for a relaxing half an hour. In their opinion, the curry sandwiches from the little café on Alexandra's Seventh Avenue were the best in Johannesburg.

Midway through eating their takeaway, they saw the priest come out of his church doors and look towards where they were parked. He waved before he started to walk in their direction.

"We are going to be told about God again my friends. Is the shade here worth the sermon each time?" However, in spite of the priest's unwanted attention, they said, "Hello Father," as he appeared at their window.

"Greetings, my sons. God bless you."

The killers used the same car as before, but this time there was no vanity light to worry about when they opened the doors in the darkness because their leader had forgotten to take the bulb out of his pocket before disposing of his bloodstained trousers that night.

Irrespective, the doors were not going to be left open this time; not after what had transpired in the last few days. In fact this was the reason they were here tonight: to repair the damage arising from their decision to leave the doors open and the car unlocked last time. The problem they had unwittingly created for themselves was only revealed during a chance conversation with the priest one lunchtime, parked in the shade beside his church.

Closing the car doors quietly, the four slipped balaclavas over their heads. As they began pulling on protective gloves, their whispered conversations began.

"*Must* we kill these boys? I feel very bad about this," one of the men complained. "It's not right."

"Not as bad as you will feel being in jail for life," the leader hissed at him.

"But a priest as well?" whispered another gang member.

Their leader growled quietly. "We have had this talk before and we all agreed. It's this or jail. They will tell others and probably go to the police. Do you want Hani on your backs?"

He opened the trunk and handed two of the three a length of wire and a set of pliers each. Then he took a small plastic bag from where it had been propped up in the corner before gently closing the trunk lid shut.

Their target was the little house alongside the church that served as the manse, but before they moved off in the dark towards it, the leader asked his men an important question.

"You are sure about the security doors having latches on the outside?"

"Yes," came the collective whispers. "It's for security when the priest goes away."

They moved silently across the children's playground like shadows, before positioning themselves near the manse. They huddled together in the darkness as the leader gave his orders.

"You two wire the latches on the doors."

Touching the third dark figure on the shoulder he whispered, "You come with me. We'll check the windows to make sure they are all in there."

*

Sliding the last plate into the drainer next to the sink, the priest inspected the rolled-up edges of his sleeves for dampness. When he had people staying with him in the manse he seldom removed his robes and washing the dishes was no exception. The robes only came off when he went to bed or when he was alone, tending the little vegetable garden.

While washing the dishes, the priest had smiled at the sounds of cheering and groaning coming from the small lounge behind him where a re-play of Saturday's Manchester United versus Arsenal game was being watched by the boys.

He knew Midgy was an Arsenal fan and it would appear that the three other boys staying with him were fans of the opposition. It seemed to the priest that, respecting their leader, they refrained from boasting about Manchester

United's one goal lead.

"They know about politics, even at their young age," he had laughed quietly to himself.

He pretended not to notice what his temporary lodgers did during the day; instead preferring to focus his efforts to give them sanctuary when they needed it. Keeping them safe took precedence over everything else although he did give them as much moral guidance as he could, teaching them about right and wrong and quoting the Ten Commandments. However, he was not sure how many of his teachings resonated with them.

'Amandla' seemed to be the only rallying call to which they responded. In this township, Nelson Mandela (affectionately known as Madiba) took precedence over God, it seemed to the priest. For the people of South Africa who had suffered so much, he represented the light at the end of the dark tunnel of Apartheid.

The priest sighed as he looked up from the dishes. He peered through the misty glass of the window above the sink into the darkness beyond, just as he had every other night that week.

He cleared an area of fog from the glass with the back of his hand but could see no movement outside, just a blurred reflection of his own face. *I wonder if tonight's the night?* he thought.

*

In the silent darkness of the church, the quiet voice of one of Zeb's officers came from where he was stationed near one of the small windows of the simple building.

"Four on the move, sir."

In order to see over the nearest windowsill, Zeb raised himself slowly on to his knees. Through his night vision goggles, he saw two green images on one side of the manse and two on the other. As he watched, one of the figures disappeared from view.

Putting his radio to his lips, Zeb spoke into the mouthpiece quietly. "All patrols. Begin approach. Spotlights off until I give the order."

He was giving the order to the drivers of the four patrol cars stationed on roads nearby. At that moment, it was only the beams of the powerful spotlights clamped onto the roof of each vehicle that he required from them; the arresting officers were already in the church with him.

Crouched beside Zeb, Josh's heart was pounding ; the adrenalin pushing aside the tiredness he felt. This was the fifth night they had been staked out in the freezing cold church since Zeb had called him. His cameraman had started moaning after the first night, but now he was equally as wound up and raring to go as Josh was tonight.

"What the hell are they doing? Can anybody see them? Are they trying to enter at any point?" Zeb whispered.

One of his officers said, "They appear to be

securing the steel frame door latches sir."

As Josh tried to see what was going on outside, beside him in the dark he could hear the cameraman's night vision camera clicking as it made internal adjustments every time he changed target. Judging by his positive murmurs, Josh presumed the cameraman was having considerable success capturing the images he wanted.

Suddenly Zeb exclaimed in an incredulous whisper. "What the? They're supposed to be breaking *in* through the door!"

One of his officers called in confirmation. "Appears the rear door is being secured as well. One target at each window sir."

"They look like they're using lighters. Maybe petrol bombs sir," observed another.

"Shit, of course! The bastards are going to torch the building!" Zeb cried, as they heard glass shattering in the darkness. "Go, go!" Zeb yelled his order to the men in front of him before issuing another order to the patrol drivers via his radio. "Patrols. Lights on. Lights on!"

Ten officers carrying weapons fitted with powerful torches thundered out of the church, followed by Josh's cameraman. Zeb grabbed one of the fire extinguishers from the wall at the entrance.

"Josh, grab the other one and follow me," he called over his shoulder.

The four attackers were frozen like statues, hands raised above their heads, in the light of the officers' powerful torches and the bright beams of arriving patrol cars. Through the windows, flames were already visible inside the rooms as the secured doors were smashed open by Zeb's men.

Dodging four young boys who were leaving in a panic, like mice fleeing when a pantry door is unexpectedly opened, Zeb burst through the doorway, swiftly followed by Josh. He began dousing the burning carpet in the lounge room, the flames already licking at the furniture. Meanwhile Josh, who was overdosing on adrenalin at this point, continued down the hallway to the kitchen where the other petrol bomb had been thrown.

It was there that he found the priest. He was yelling and jumping up and down on a burning mat as the flames began their erratic ascent from where they had caught hold on the hem and sleeves of his dark robe. Josh thumped the top of the extinguisher and doused everything with fire retardant, including the priest.

He was busy ripping his robe over his head as Josh concentrated on shutting off the extinguisher. When he looked up, he saw what he presumed to be a burnt upper body before him. Lifting his eyes to the face above, he discovered he was looking at his Uncle Gerry.

Outside, Josh's cameraman had re-set his camera to combat the bright lights and was now busy photographing a pale-faced Sergeant Smitswart and his three officers who were being handcuffed. Zeb was calmly informing the armed response unit officers of their rights.

Chapter 17

Finding Fathers

Brenda could feel her heart beating, faster and faster it seemed, as she listened to the director of St John's orphanage read from the file in front of her.

Brenda's birth mother had handed her baby over to the orphanage for adoption. Her adoptive parents had been on a waiting list and the orphanage immediately allocated this baby girl to them. The process of adoption was then initiated. Following normal procedure, the court 'sealed' her original birth certificate to protect her privacy, and issued an amended certificate with the names of her adoptive parents.

Unfortunately for Brenda, after only a few days into the placement, her adoptive parents had had a change of heart and returned the baby to the orphanage.

Upon application to the courts, her original

birth certificate was now available for Brenda to see. No one else was permitted to see it, however.

The director looked up and removed her reading glasses.

"Both your birth certificates have unusual anomalies, Brenda. Firstly, the fact that you have been able to use the second one issued for you all these years without anyone querying it is most unusual. I don't know why my predecessors here did not ask the appropriate government department to revoke it after the adoptive parents withdrew."

Brenda had never really thought about it before. She was only young when she had first discovered she had a birth certificate. She had established later that the people named on it were her adoptive parents, and that for some unknown reason she had ended up back in the orphanage.

"The second anomaly in the notes is that the only name on your original, and now sealed birth certificate, is your father's. The absence of a mother's name is most unusual. Despite your father's name being recorded on the certificate, the notes also indicate that he did not sign it as by then he had already enlisted to fight in World War II and was therefore unavailable.

"Gee, my mother, or her parents, really must not have wanted me to ever know who they were, so I would never get the chance to know them," Brenda said, dabbing at a falling tear with a tissue from the box the director held out to her.

Sitting in his uncomfortable hospital visitor's chair beside the bed, Cliff flinched when the alarm on Josh's dialysis machine sounded. With his eyes firmly closed, Josh hardly stirred at the noise. *He must have been given drugs to relax him or something*, Cliff thought, as he peered through the glass observation panel behind him to see if a nurse was coming. He was just beginning to panic when a nurse burst through the door with a look of exasperation on her face.

"Damn thing. That's the third time today," she said, as she muted the alarm with the flick of a switch. She studied the screen and began turning knobs and pushing buttons.

Cliff looked back at his friend with concern. He had never seen him so pale-faced. In fact, this was the first time he had actually ever seen him unwell, let alone visited him in a hospital. Cliff had received a message from his mother via Brigade headquarters last night. In such an urgent situation as this, she had managed to find someone to talk to in the SADF and ensure the message was relayed to him.

Her message was that Josh's boss at the newspaper had called Frank to tell him that his 'son' had collapsed at the office and been rushed to hospital that afternoon. He was in intensive care but in a stable condition.

He looked up at the nurse as he leant forward to lay his hand on Josh's wrist gently, being careful to avoid the IV drip.

"Is he OK? Why isn't he waking up with all this noise going on?"

"I gave him a mild sedative earlier. He didn't sleep very well last night. He needed some more rest poor guy. I hear he is quite famous?" she smiled.

Cliff frowned, unsure what that had to do with anything, but went along with her train of thought regardless.

"Yes, from zero to hero, our boy Josh here – in the world of journalism that is."

*

Josh had been given as much credit as Zeb for his part in exposing the story of the rogue elements within the police rapid response unit. Much to the anger of the Botha Government, Josh's report was syndicated globally; Sam sending them copies of the UK versions of the account as he came across them. It appeared there was a growing global demand for an explanation from the South African government.

It was a busy time for Josh; his editor pushing him to dig ever deeper into what was happening behind the scenes of the government's attempts to suppress political unrest, and to keep the white minority feeling secure in their comfortable homes.

One of Josh's follow-up stories was his interview with the chief-of-police who did his utmost to convince the young reporter the SAP were delighted with Major Hani's arrest of the rogue unit.

"We need to weed out these elements," he said. "There are always a few bad fish in a small barrel."

Amused by the mixed metaphor, Josh switched off his recorder before thanking the brigadier with a smile. "Would it be all right to contact you again for comment if we have any further questions, Brigadier?" Josh asked, as he was shown to the large oak-panelled door.

"Sekerlik, sekerlik. For sure," the brigadier smiled.

For sure? Josh was not so *sure* about anything the high-ranking policeman had just told him.

*

Josh's eyes fluttered and then opened fully.

"Well speak of the devil and there he is – our Josh," the nurse said, laying her hand on his shoulder. "Are you feeling OK?"

Josh nodded and smiled.

"Cliff! What are you doing here? Generals are

supposed to be in the field with their men, aren't they?" he murmured slowly.

"OK, that's enough high-rankers on my shift for now!" the nurse said, as she backed out of the room with a wave and a mock salute.

"She's a perky one, isn't she?" Cliff smiled. "How're you feeling buddy? You look pretty shit."

"Thank you sir, nothing like an honest appraisal," Josh grinned at his friend. He was quiet for a few seconds then he sighed. "Well Cliff, as I told you a long time ago, they always said there might come a time when the meds would not be enough – that I would need a transplant. Well, here we are."

"Oh shit! Not a very funny comment. Sorry," Cliff said, looking downcast at the news.

"It's OK. To make it up to me, you can give me one of your kidneys," Josh said, with a deadpan expression. Then he laughed out loud, making the tubes attached to him rattle as his body shook. "You should see your face!" he said with a mischievous grin, patting Cliff's hand that was still resting on Josh's wrist.

*

Initially Josh had thought it was just the job – the adrenalin rushes and lack of sleep that made him feel permanently tired. However, when he lost his appetite and started to feel unwell most of the time, he decided to visit the specialist he had been seeing since arriving in Johannesburg. Within days of his visit to the consultant, Josh was hospitalised; the diagnosis kidney failure.

The twins, Ryan and Simon, Josh's older brother Mike and his remaining younger sister Janet had been contacted about their thoughts on being a possible donor. Mike's partner was adamantly against him being considered, while his sister and the twins simply did not return the telephone messages left by Josh's specialist.

Josh thought that the memory of their mother's accident and the loss of their sister were still too distressing for them to contemplate surgery. It seemed they were not prepared to even have the conversation although they did send get well cards and the nurse reported she had calls from his family to enquire about him when he was still asleep.

He had run out of time to find his birth father as well. This meant that the opportunity to maximise a two-year patient survival rate of ninety percent provided by a sibling or parental donor was out of the question. As much as his local specialist agreed with Josh's previous Durban specialist about the benefit of a family donor, he believed time was of the essence and delaying was no longer an option.

The donor would have to be non-family. For this, he would be put on a waiting list for who knew how long.

The young woman behind the reception desk of the births, deaths and marriages registry office remarked that Brenda was the second Barkerfield she had dealt with in recent weeks.

That's because I'm treading the same path as Josh, so that's no coincidence, Brenda thought, as she considered asking the receptionist whether she should be keeping that sort of information confidential.

"Barkerfield is my husband's name. You must have got that from the application form I sent in when I requested an appointment. My surname is Tarrant."

Well, ex-husband, she thought, as she placed her birth certificate in front of the woman. Brenda explained that this was her current birth certificate but that she had also been told she had a second, original certificate, which had been sealed by the courts after she had been adopted. Now she wished to submit an application to the court to see it.

"You'll have to make a formal application to the court," the woman said officiously.

"Absolutely," Brenda said. She realised she would have to appear cooperative if she was to get the information she sought.

*

Brenda stuffed her copy of the submitted application form into her bag as she carefully negotiated the old stone steps of the large government building in her high heels, descending to the busy street below. She sighed. *Oh well, at least I nearly know my real name at last*, she thought.

Josh stared out of the window of his hospital window on the sixteenth floor and thought about where his life might take him over the next few months. It was getting darker and the lights of downtown Johannesburg were visible in the distance. *Will there be some bright lights for me in this dark time in my life*? he wondered.

The door opened and his nurse entered. "Your general's back to see you," she said.

She laughed as Josh said, "Twice in one day Cliff! What? Are you expecting me to go at any minute?"

"No, no. I did have a revelation though," Cliff said. Smiling in her direction, he waited for the nurse to close the door behind her. "I know you were joking earlier, but I *am* happy to be considered as a donor. Well, they could do the test to see if I am compatible, or whatever the terminology is. Hey, I'm a relative so maybe that's better than no family relationship at all? I don't know."

Filled with a sudden wave of emotion, Josh struggled to speak as tears filled his eyes. Finally he controlled his voice.

"Cliff that's amazing, thank you! I am really touched. Let's see how we go. It's nice to know you have my back. I will talk to the doc. Thanks, buddy."

With all the tubes attached to him, a hug would have been difficult so the two men shook hands instead; Josh forced to use his left one awkwardly, a needle in his right.

"OK Cliff. Whilst we are doing the emotional thing here, there is something I have been wanting to tell you. I am tired of the burden of knowing and not telling you."

"Oh no! Don't tell me you and Brenda are having an affair!" Cliff grinned.

"Very funny, very funny. No, in my search for my birth father I did some investigating at the births and deaths registry place, and by chance came across the fact that one of our close relatives changed their name."

"Not exactly shocking! But OK, who became who Josh?"

"Get ready for this buddy," Josh said, a twinkle in his eye betraying his serious facial expression.

"Yeah, yeah. Come on, spit it out!" Cliff laughed.

"Remember we had an uncle who moved on somewhere, never to be seen again? That photograph at Auntie 'Chel's place we found years ago? The three guys next to a ship?"

"Yeah, Uncle Raymond, I remember," Cliff said. "My mom was telling me about him a while back."

"Well..." Josh paused a moment for maximum dramatic effect. "Uncle Raymond didn't just wander off, he in fact became Auntie Raechel." Josh grinned. "For the second time today, Cliff, you should see your face."

The nurse opened the door with a flourish, grinning at them both. "Would you believe it? she announced. "*Three* famous people here in one day!"

Behind her, Zeb was smiling. He waved at them over the nurse's shoulder as she led him through the door.

"How're you doing Josh?" Zeb asked. "You may be the one in bed with tubes sticking out of him but you don't look as pale as your friend here. Are you all right Cliff?"

The young man stood to let the woman reach the window seat beside him. He was always relieved when his fellow passenger on a flight was a woman. It typically meant he had more room, and if there was any conversation to be had, it tended to be more interesting than the one he had with fellow male passengers.

"Would you mind if I held your hand during take-off? I am terrified of flying," she asked, raising her voice slightly over the noise of the revving jet engines.

He was initially taken aback but then felt rather gallant, as his sister would say, to be of assistance. Her hand felt rather big in his but then he conceded he did have especially small hands. Hers was soft and warm, and he suddenly thought that maybe he was getting as much comfort as he was giving.

*

The woman marvelled at the coincidence when she discovered her fellow passenger was also going to Johannesburg to visit someone in hospital there. *He is sweet*, she thought; he was so understanding of her fear of flying that it was almost as though he enjoyed the opportunity to support her.

They chatted for ages; she, mainly, about her one-time hobby that had since grown into a thriving small business. For his part, he told her all about his sister and the things they got up to, which he insisted were mostly initiated by her being full of mischief. He remarked they always got away with things though because she was so beautiful.

Sounds like she would be perfect for my abandoned nephew, thought his travel companion.

After a while, their conversation naturally petered out and each became lost in their own thoughts. She wondered how she would handle her visit to the hospital tomorrow morning. What would the reaction be?

Suddenly the aircraft was making its descent, ready for landing. The journey had passed by so fast.

Touching his hand, she said, "Do you mind? Again?"

"Of course not. And before I forget to introduce myself, I'm Peter by the way."

"Hi Peter, I'm Raechel."

"Hi Raechel."

Brenda's father stared at the classified advertisement he had cut out from the newspaper nearly a week ago. He had a lot more time on his hands nowadays so the newspapers delivered were well read. The personal columns – the hatches, matches and dispatches – were particular favourites of his that he enjoyed reading during his morning coffee. Not having a family of his own, he liked to find out news of old school friends; the arrival of their new grandchildren, their own children getting married, or indeed the death of one of his friends.

As he had done several times a day since first noticing the advertisement, he re-read the cutting again that morning. The piece stated that a woman named Brenda was searching for the father listed on her birth certificate. It not only gave his name, but also his date of birth.

There had been days in the past week when tears had filled his eyes, tears of pure joy. At times, he felt the burden of years of resentment and loss lifting from his shoulders yet on other days, the fear and guilt remained. Some days he questioned that it could be true, but the birth date was surely conclusive proof that it was him? Unless it was some kind of cruel joke? Yet who would bother with such an elaborate hoax, and he had no enemies he could think of with a motive to deceive. Besides, they would not know his date of birth.

Today he found his hand was drawn to the phone beside him whenever he lifted his eyes from the flimsy cutting. The cat on his lap *meowed* and made himself more comfortable.

"Don't worry," he said, stroking it gently. "No one could take your place old friend."

*

Brenda was startled when the phone rang. She had just removed her make-up and was staring at her reflection without really seeing herself, her attention miles away. Slipping on a bathrobe, she walked to the hallway where the phone was ringing in her apartment.

"Hello, Brenda here," she said, trying to sound chirpy but feeling exhausted.

"Hello. The notice in the paper. Am I calling too late? Sorry," the voice said.

Her heart pounded in her chest. She had given up hope. Was this another prankster? She had encountered one of those on the very first day the advertisement had been published, but her intuition told her that this caller was genuine. Brenda thought that the deep voice even sounded 'fatherly' as he continued.

"I am sorry I didn't call earlier. I couldn't believe it – that it could be possible. Such a wonderful surprise after so long. I have longed for this day."

"That's the nicest thing anybody has said to me in years," Brenda managed to say, as the tears streamed down her face.

"Auntie 'Chel! Oh my God, it's so good to see you!" Josh exclaimed, as Raechel's face appeared in the doorway of his room. "I mean Raechel. Sorry, Cliff did tell me it was not auntie anymore. I'll get it in time!"

Raechel waved away his apology as she sat down next to his bed and placed her hand in his. "'A rose by any other name'... more importantly, Beryl and Frank told me about you being in hospital but have there been any further developments?"

Josh laughed. "Well, you coming all this way to see me is a bit worrying! I hope there isn't something I haven't been told?"

"Josh of course not," Raechel said, as what she had to tell Josh came to the forefront of her mind once again.

Josh went over what the specialists had concluded about the advantages of a sibling or parental donor, based upon the evidence of previous outcomes for kidney transplant patients. However, this was no longer an option as neither his brother nor sister were able to assist. He went on to tell her that he had had no success even finding out the name of his birth father, let alone an address. "I've just been too busy on the story to do any more digging," he said, with a frown on his face.

"I heard," Raechel exclaimed, squeezing his hand gently. "I am so proud of you Josh."

"Oh thanks... 'Raechel'. There you are, I've said it!" Josh grinned.

She patted his hand and smiled. "For the moment, I am glad you are lying down, actually. I have something to tell you that is going to come as a bit of a shock I think."

His dialysis machine beeped once and they both looked up.

"Right on cue," Raechel laughed.

"It's OK, it's not an alarm. Just a re-boot apparently. Don't asked me why or what for, but I'm told it's normal," Josh smiled reassuringly.

"OK. So as I was saying... this news will be unexpected... but do you remember me talking to you about your Uncle Raymond?"

Josh grinned at Raechel's self-conscious expression.

"What?" she asked.

"Well, I am pretty sure I know what you are going to say so let me spare you the awkwardness. While looking for my birth father, I dug through old family birth certificates. I discovered that 'Uncle Raymond' did not disappear at all; rather he just *changed*. I am totally OK with it by the way, really I am."

He saw the tears forming in his aunt's eyes.

"I told Cliff what I had discovered, and both he and I are adamant you are still our auntie. You always have been, always, and you always will be. That's all there is to it."

Raechel looked downwards momentarily.

"I'm not sure whether that will help or not with what else I have to tell you – something you definitely don't already know."

Josh frowned slightly, his interest piqued.

Raechel was silent. She looked intently into Josh's eyes, for what to him seemed like minutes but was probably only seconds, before she spoke again.

"Josh, your mom and I were very close. Madge and I were kindred spirits, in many ways. Before I became Raechel, had the circumstances been different – the timing different – Madge and I may well have married all those years ago." Raechel took a sip from the glass of water Josh had poured her before continuing. "The day I left home for the last time... it was impulsive. I was devastated about being chucked out of the army, and totally confused about my sexuality. I was ready to do something drastic. I had nowhere to go. So I fled to your mom. Madge's love for me that night saved me. The comfort she gave me also provided me with the strength to move on with my life."

Josh watched Raechel's face as she fell silent; her eyes never leaving his as she told her story. He watched her expression change several times throughout and considered she was re-playing old memories in her mind.

Finally, she came to the nub of her story, tears now running freely down her cheeks.

"Josh, I am your real father. I am telling you now because I am going to be your donor. I understand if you don't ever want to speak to me again, but at least let me do this for you." Raechel blew her nose loudly, chuckling slightly with embarrassment. "We should have told you sooner, but it should have come from your mom – ideally after she had told Frank. Or maybe we thought we should let sleeping dogs lie? We didn't want to hurt him. Oh God, I don't know!" She was crying again. "But I do want to be your donor."

Neither were aware of the door opening but when the nurse said, "Visitor for you," they both looked around.

"Peter?" They exclaimed at the same time.

A very surprised Peter looked from Raechel's tearful face to the distracted expression on his friend's. "Have I come at a bad time?"

Chapter 18

More Discoveries

It seemed just like any other day; passing the time outside Alexandra's police station with the press corps, waiting for them to chase another story. A few of them sat on folding chairs under a beach umbrella playing a game of cards while others sat in their cars reading newspapers.

Cliff's squad were passing a soccer ball between them without it touching the ground, as one man counted aloud the number of successful passes. His driver busied himself with an oily cloth; wiping mindlessly at the vehicle's exterior, which reminded Cliff of his basic training.

On their long walk to Sandton, Alexandra's local residents paused momentarily to watch the impromptu ballgame. They were curious that these intimidating-looking soldiers in their camouflage fatigues whom they had only ever seen staring down at them from a big armoured vehicle or standing in formation pointing guns at them, would do something so ordinary as kicking a football, just like them.

When the ball went astray and bounced toward the road, one of the onlookers took a few quick steps towards it before striking it back with a deft flick of his foot. This engagement caused Cliff's men to applaud with amusement.

Sitting in the front seat of the Casspir absentmindedly watching their game, Cliff was still trying to absorb what Peter had told him the previous night over the telephone. Peter had started the conversation by informing Cliff of the melodrama he had unwittingly walked into at the hospital.

*

Cliff was using the phone in the hall of Brigade headquarters officers' quarters. As Peter spoke, Cliff wished he could reach one of the chairs nearby to drag it over and sit down but he was limited by the cord and did not want to interrupt what Peter was saying.

To ensure the patient was calm and relaxed for his impending operation the following morning, Josh had been sedated and therefore unable to tell Cliff his news in person, as Peter assured Cliff he had wanted to. So it had been left to Peter to share the facts with Cliff. Josh had been moved into a bigger room after he had requested to be put in the same room as his organ donor.

"Oh wow, a donor! That's great news! Who is it?" Cliff exclaimed.

"Bear with me," Peter said. "All will be revealed!"

Peter told him that Raechel was sitting with Josh when he walked in on their conversation. Although he had been surprised she was the same woman he had sat next to on the plane, he had nonetheless picked up the gist of their conversation; that she wanted to be his donor. Upon hearing Peter's account, Cliff began to suspect he knew the reason why.

"Don't tell me – you're going to say that Raechel is Josh's birth father, aren't you?"

Peter laughed. "Got it in one, General."

"I'm blown away. Who would have guessed it?" Cliff said, letting out a deep breath.

"Well, apparently *you* would," Peter said.

At that moment the line broke up with a high-pitched hum. Cliff put down the receiver and waited for Peter to call back. He was just replaying in his mind everything he had been told when the phone rang again. He snatched it up from its hook.

"Hello Peter, there was one thing I—"

A woman's voice suddenly interrupted him. "Sorry, do we have a crossed line? I was hoping to leave a message for Captain Barkerfield?"

"Jodie? Is that you?" he said, recognising her voice.

"Oh, Cliff, great. Your mom said I would have to leave a message. How come you're there?"

"I was just on the phone talking to Peter. What a coincidence," he laughed.

"I have been so worried after reading that report in the paper. What have they got you doing? It sounds like rioting in the township is terrible. Will you be all right?" Jodie went quiet suddenly, and Cliff could hear her softly blowing her nose. "Nobody can tell anyone anything. It's terrible! Your mother is worried too. She gave me this number."

Cliff spent the next ten minutes reassuring Jodie that he was fine and that his responsibilities did not really expose him to any real danger. He told her he was just there to look after the press and that the journalists had even had time for a game of soccer. He reassured her that the incident at the funeral was just a one-off; that he had just been in the wrong place (or the right place for the young victim) when the gang gave chase. "I've had my fifteen minutes of fame now," he laughed.

"I'm still not convinced but I had better go as I'm phoning from the office. Can you phone me occasionally please? Just to let me know how you are. Peter has my number."

"Sure I will. Sorry I didn't call before. I didn't realise that you..." He started to feel awkward.

"Call Peter," he said casually. "He has lots of news!"

He ended the call without even saying goodbye and then instantly regretted it. He wanted to call her back to apologise for being so abrupt but he did not have her work number. *What must she think of me after that? God, I'm hopeless at this*, he thought.

*

His eyes followed the trajectory of his squad's ball as it rose and fell in the air and he thought about his telephone conversation with Jodie. Notwithstanding its awkward and rather abrupt termination, sitting in the Casspir he recalled the elation he had felt after Jodie and he had spoken.

Just then, he was wrenched from his thoughts as the first of several rapid response unit vehicles rumbled past him and his squad at high speed.

They were on their way into the township, and the journalists ran to their cars in hot pursuit of a story. Meanwhile, Cliff was joined by his squad who clambered up into their big transporter. The Casspir began crunching across the gravel parking area to follow the convoy. They weren't far from the police station when Zeb's Land Rover, and several other police vehicles with lights flashing, forced them to pull to the side of the road so they could speed past.

They could see the smoke now; the black acrid smoke that is given off by burning rubber. Cliff knew what was coming. The smoke was rising into the already polluted Alexandra sky from an open area near one of the hostels. Upon arrival, they had discovered it was the scene of a violent confrontation.

By the time the press corps got there, several people were lying inert and covered in blood in the open area in front of the hostel. Many others were lying in the blood-spattered dirt but were still alive, groaning in pain. Cliff had no idea whether they had been injured in the battle or had been shot by the rapid response police, the latter still shooting at small groups who had stopped in mid escape to throw rocks at the police.

It was a single-sex hostel inhabited by men working on one of the mines in the area. These men were all Inkatha supporters, and about fifty of them had been doing battle with an ANC vigilante group that were responding to an attack on houses surrounding the hostel. The latter were aided and abetted by many very young boys whom Cliff presumed were part of the little general's Under Fourteens army.

Cliff saw Zeb talking to an animated Midgy, who was pointing rapidly in as many directions as was possible and talking just as fast. "They just came, those Inkatha men, and stole mattresses and clothes and food from all the houses here," he was saying. "They said it was their right. They are Inkatha, they can do that. So we showed them. We had to help the ANC men this time."

"Is anybody in those burning tyres?" Zeb asked, pointing to mounds of smouldering rubber.

"No, we just had the burning necklace ready when you people came and shot at everyone. I was running too until I saw you. I know you are not like those other police, Major Hani," he smiled. "The ones we had necklaces ready for ran too when you came. The other police shot one that was running. We were happy when we saw that!" he laughed.

He is just a kid. What have we done to these people? Cliff thought, feeling himself shudder as he turned away to see what his press corps were doing.

A few kilometres away, at the Sandton Hospital, Josh's nurse, Mary, was staring out of the window. She sighed as she watched the black smoke rising from Alexandra township. "Alex is burning again. What's happening today in my home?" she sighed.

"My God Mary! You live there?" he asked, incredulous.

"No Josh, I have a nice house here in Sandton," she smiled and he felt awkward. "Are black people allowed to live in white areas in Durban where you come from?" Mary laughed as she left the room, shaking her head.

Josh squirmed when he realised just how ludicrous his question had been. He decided to put his insensitivity down to the sedative they had given him. At least Raechel, who was lying in the bed across from his, had kept her eyes closed to spare him further embarrassment.

Although his mind was still reeling from Raechel's disclosure, Josh felt immense relief at her insistence on volunteering to be a donor. He had made sure they shared the same room throughout the procedure.

He had no idea what he should be feeling. He made a futile attempt to conjure up feelings for her as his father but the image of Frank just kept coming to mind. It would take a long time to adjust to this dramatic change but although it was complex and confusing, at least it was not a negative thing. Josh felt sure it would all work out eventually.

He had to share the unique circumstances with his specialist but the rest of the staff believed his donor was his aunt. To his mind she still was, and the secret would remain so except for the few people who knew the truth. Raymond was his birth father, and although this would remain in the past, in his heart, the reality was very present.

Brenda had decided to meet her birth father for the first time in a place neutral to them both. It was going to be emotional enough, without adding personal elements into the mix; those things like possessions that could be over-analysed and the wrong conclusions drawn from.

She had chosen a café in Rosebank not far from where Josh and Raechel lay in hospital. It was the same venue where she had persuaded Cliff to meet her a month ago after she had told him she needed an update for her book.

*

"You've lost weight Cliff. Stress of this township business?" Brenda said, as they sat down at a table.

Brenda had to admit to herself that her slimmer ex-husband looked rather desirable in his uniform, resplendent with the three silver stars denoting his captain's rank on either shoulder.

"Probably the crap army food. Although seeing what is going on in Alex behind the government's façade is quite something."

"Yes, tell me about it," Brenda said.

"Firstly, tell me what this book of yours is all about. I have not heard much about it lately. Is there a protagonist in it who has a suspiciously similar resemblance to me – after all the anecdotes

I've told you?" Cliff smiled.

As was her custom, Brenda gave a no-nonsense response. "The conscription of young men into the army to defend an illegal regime is unacceptable Cliff, but I don't think the average person cares. If the light-hearted side of my book persuades people that it's worth reading, then I get the chance to show them the other side too. Over the years you have educated me by sharing your experiences. There is a sinister side to what you have told me and my book will tell the full story. Don't worry, you are a well disguised protagonist. Anyway, I promise you will get to see the final draft before it goes to my publisher."

*

Taking a seat at a table next to the window, she glanced around. Most of the tables were empty at this time of the morning, except for a talkative group of young ladies who kept adding extra chairs to accommodate their growing number.

Brenda noted they were all immaculately coiffed and wearing make-up, their fingers sparkled with expensive diamond rings; their wrists festooned in gold bracelets. The preferred greeting as each arrived through the café entrance appeared to be superficial and repetitive.

"Hello doll, howzit?" and, "You look gorgeous, doll!"

Brenda cringed each time another exchange of greetings rang out and they all stood up to air kiss the latest arrival. She wondered if she had made a bad choice with the venue, and whether the scraping of chair legs on the floor would ever stop.

She glanced at her reflection in the window beside her. As she pushed her hair back over her shoulder, she considered she probably looked dowdy in comparison to those glamorous northern-suburb housewives. At that moment, he appeared on the pavement outside the entrance to the café and reached out to turn the handle on the glass door.

She instantly knew it was her father; she just *knew*. As he entered, he looked around briefly before seeing her sitting there. He grinned broadly and walked directly over to her table. Her heart was thumping as he approached; she noticed he walked with a slight limp.

"Brenda? It *is* you, isn't it? You look so much like your mother when she was younger."

"Yes, I'm Brenda. Should I call you Dad?" she laughed.

"That sounds wonderful," he smiled.

Brenda had detected an Afrikaans accent on the telephone but in person it was less so, his tone softer and gentler.

He took a photograph from his pocket and held it out to her. "This is of your mother when she and I were together – just before you were born."

Brenda eagerly took the photograph from his hands with a desperate need to finally see her mother's face.

"You see what I mean?" he laughed. "There is an age difference of course but you could be sisters. She was only sixteen then."

They paused while the waiter put down their tea, and Brenda used the time to gaze at the photograph.

"Tell me about her," she said. Then she felt awkward for asking the question, for there she was, sitting with her father for the first time, while seemingly more interested in her absent mother than her now present father. "Sorry, it's just that I feel so hurt that she gave me up. I need to understand," she said, dabbing at her eyes with a table napkin.

"I understand my girl. Can I call you that? I have dreamt for many years of having the opportunity to say 'my girl', like only a dad is allowed to."

"Of course," she said, briefly patting his hand; a gesture he appeared not to notice as his mind raced to construct a scene in his distant past.

Her father's eyes filled with tears as he began relating the circumstances surrounding her birth and the start of her life as an orphan. He insisted that the decision to adopt her was not her mother's. She was only sixteen and it had been her dominant father who had been adamant he would not endure the shame of an unmarried pregnant daughter.

He had wanted his daughter to continue her education, even if it meant giving up the child. They had sent her away to another town to give birth; her father forbade him to visit her. Eventually after many unanswered letters and threats of legal action against him from her father, he and her mother had lost touch.

Like many other young boys at that time, he had also enlisted to fight in World War II. When he returned from his training and before leaving for war, her father would not even speak to him, let alone give him any information about where the baby had been taken.

"Does Dad know?" Josh asked. "I suppose I will have to start calling him Frank now?"

"Why? He is still your father," Raechel said, raising herself on one elbow to look across at him as he stared up at the ceiling. "He gave as much of himself to raising you as he gave to any of your siblings. He loves you, as I am sure you do him. You and I have something different but it's just as precious, if not more so." Still, Josh did not look at her. "Follow your heart, my son," she said and smiled. "And yes, I told Frank before I left to come up here."

"And?"

"He was stunned, obviously, but to my amazement quite calm too. He poured himself a drink, knowing in the circumstances I couldn't admonish him for drinking too early in the day as I normally would. It was a really difficult conversation for a while. When I least expected it, he asked me if your mom had been in love with me? Before I could even gather my composure, he asked if she had said she did not love him when we were together? Then he really had me flabbergasted when he asked me if that was why I became a woman? Because I felt guilty? He did not seem to expect answers or even want them. He seemed to just be vocalizing thoughts in his mind until he said, 'tell Josh I will always love him, he will always be my son, I don't care about the past'. I thought he was going to cry then but he didn't. Not like I am."

Raechel choked, tearing tissues from the box next to her. She gulped some air and went on.

"Suddenly he said, 'we have to accept the cards life deals us, hey 'Chel. I would never have known had you not had the courage to give Josh his best chance at a successful transplant. Go and help fix our son'. That was it, more or less," Raechel concluded.

"Wow!" Josh gulped as tears ran down the side of his face and onto his pillow.

At that moment, Peter came through their door.

Scanning their faces, he said, "Oh no, I've not done it again have I? Bad time?"

"No, no. Raechel and I are all emotioned out. We can handle anything now, hey 'Chel?"

Raechel nodded, smiling to herself as Peter patted Josh on the shoulder, his hand remaining in place long after he had stopped patting.

Mary came in to collect Josh. "It's time to go mister," she said. "You ready Raechel? I'll be back."

"I wonder where she is nowadays?" Brenda said, glancing up at her father's face from the photograph she held.

Her father reached into his inside jacket pocket to retrieve a second photograph that he proceeded to lay face-down on the table.

"As a matter of fact I spoke to her this week."

"What? How?"

Her father told how her mother had contacted him a few years ago completely unexpectedly having seen an article about him in the newspaper. He had taken part in a charity walk for disabled World War II veterans and had made headlines by covering a greater distance than anyone with a prosthetic foot and ankle had ever done before.

"Oh, so that's the cause of your limp? It's very

slight though," Brenda added hurriedly.

"Yes, I am very lucky, considering what happened to me," he replied.

He continued with the outcome of her mother's contact: they had resolved to put the past behind them. Over the last few years, he visited her and her family quite often.

"She has two lovely daughters who are both in their twenties now, but she has told me many times she keeps the memory of her firstborn daughter close to her heart."

Her father paused while Brenda wiped at the tears on her cheeks and blew her nose. The housewives had quietened down and begun whispering amongst themselves. Brenda ignored their glances.

"The thing is, I felt compelled to let her know we had made contact. She was beside herself and wanted to come with me. But I said no as I thought it was too much in one go for you. She is desperate to meet you though – if you don't hold what happened against her? Would you like to meet your stepsisters?"

Brenda laughed. "Oh my God! I started out the day thinking I had found a father and was more than happy just with that. Now I have a mother and siblings! Of course I want to meet them!"

Her father turned the photograph over to reveal Brenda's mother with her two stepsisters.

When Beryl had first arrived at Raechel's smallholding, she thought Frank had looked a bit shell-shocked. Raechel had asked Beryl to keep an eye on him while she was away in Jo'burg, given her recent disclosure. Raechel was worried it might start one of the drinking binges she knew he was prone to, but Beryl was pleased to say it had not appeared to.

Raechel had confided her secret to Beryl before, then telling Frank. Her admission confirmed what Beryl had always suspected when Madge first told Frank she was pregnant. Beryl had done the calculations and worked out that Josh may have been conceived much closer to the day Raymond left their home for good than the day they had all watched Frank depart up the gangway for war.

Chapter 19

Getting Lost

His mind was busy re-playing the events of the last few days so Cliff did not immediately recognise the young boy waving to them. It was the same boy he had waved down to from the Casspir two months earlier.

"You've got a fan sir," his driver said. "He must read the papers."

"A misguided fan," Cliff grunted, waving back to the boy before returning to his thoughts.

Your aunt is really your uncle, who it turns out is your cousin's father. So how does Frank feel about that, and how is that handled within the family? Did my mother know about this all along? Knowing her, she must have had a pretty good idea – at least about her brother becoming her sister. I wonder if Gerry knows all this stuff?

He smiled to himself as the light changed and the Casspir lurched forward before turning onto the road to Alexandra a few kilometres further on. "Don't stop at the police station. Carry on down to the church we dropped that kid at a while back. It turns out the priest there is my uncle so I would like to pay him a visit," Cliff said to the driver.

"Sure Captain," he nodded, as he negotiated the Casspir along the ruts in Alexandra's dusty access road.

*

Gerry was bent over, busy working in his vegetable garden, when the troop carrier crunched across the gravel of the church's parking area. He looked up with a puzzled expression but waved anyway. *I suppose priests wave at everyone*, Cliff thought, as he climbed down from the Casspir.

"Don't wait for me," he said to the driver. "Go back to the station. Doubt he wants an armoured vehicle full of soldiers parked outside his church. Not a good look around here. I'll walk back when I'm finished. If the press guys move off anywhere, pick me up on the way."

Walking towards the manse Cliff recalled Josh's description of their uncle hastily pulling off his burning robes as he now observed Gerry rolling down the sleeves of his shirt. He did not recognise his nephew, who at that moment was entering though the small garden gate.

"Morning Captain," he called raising a hand in

greeting.

Of course, having been in the navy himself he would recognise rank insignia, Cliff said to himself.

"Hi Uncle Gerry. You don't recognise me, do you? It's Cliff, Beryl's son. It's been a while."

"Oh my! Of course, Cliff. Good to see you." Holding Cliff's shoulders in a strong grip, he gave him a gentle shake of welcome.

"What brings you to the township from your safe haven down south? Walk with me, I'll show you the garden and you can tell me your news," Gerry said, as he bent slightly to avoid the long overhanging leaves of a mielie stalk adorned with a large cob.

Cliff told him how he came to be in Alexandra and that he, like Gerry, lived up on the Highveld now. As Cliff spoke Gerry occasionally bent to pick some insect off a vegetable, flicking it away but never killing it. The act reminded Cliff of how, as children, he and Josh had chased their auntie 'Chel with live beetles. He asked Gerry if he had any news of the family, thinking his answer might give an indication as to whether or not he knew the truth about Raymond.

"I had a call from Frank just last week to tell me Josh was in hospital up here. He said Raechel was on her way up to visit him. He couldn't come because of the twins, he said. Apparently, Josh may need a kidney transplant?"

"He does. I believe they have found a donor too," Cliff ventured, in an attempt to lure out any more information Gerry may have learnt from Frank.

Cliff agonised over what, or how much, he should tell Gerry as he was not sure if Josh wanted to tell the family himself. He was just wondering why Frank hadn't told his brother, when Gerry stopped and turned to him.

"I have a favourite place down the road I go to for tea. Should we do that? You'll be quite safe with me. The benefit of being a priest. You, and those with you, have immunity from township violence. The church is their sanctuary, and they expect you to remember it's the priest's job to pick up the pieces sometimes," he laughed. "I'll be back in a minute. I'll just get my robe," he said, as he headed for the manse.

*

They strolled together between the shanties. Their path took them down narrow lanes where they dodged snotty-nosed children and shooed away countless malnourished barking mongrel dogs.

Some of the black plastic walls were adorned with paint-splashed slogans; many bearing the words 'ANC' or 'Freedom'. Some were daubed with 'IFP' – the opposition party in black politics based in Natal whom many considered sympathetic to the Apartheid government for economic reasons.

As they walked along, Gerry was immediately recognised. People waved and called a greeting to him from their doorways and tiny front gardens. Cliff was relieved to discover that no one seemed to acknowledge he was wearing a uniform

"Hello. Hello umpristi olindayo," the people called out as they waved a greeting. More often they called "Uhambl kahle, our white father."

"I know 'uhambl kahle' means 'go well' but what is the other thing they keep saying?" asked Cliff, as Gerry found himself surrounded by a group of children.

With smiling faces, the youngsters called up to him. "Bless me Father, bless me Father."

He patted each of them on the head in turn. "Bless you my child, in the name of God." He smiled at Cliff and answered his question. "Oh, it's just a nickname some of my flock have for me. It's nothing interesting."

"Well, you're certainly popular around here Uncle Gerry."

"Yes, I love the people here. What you see is what you get. Not like many white folk. The tea place is just around that corner. I could kill for a 'cuppa' as they say," he laughed.

They were greeted enthusiastically upon arrival and offered a table in the warm morning sun on a patio of well-swept gravel. Cliff watched people come and go with their purchases. Scanning their faces, he smiled to himself as he remembered Zeb's teasing words when they met up in the Caprivi years ago: "All black faces look the same to you guys, hey."

Opposite him, Gerry was also reminiscing; recalling when he had last heard anything regarding Cliff.

Gerry smiled and said, "I think it was when I met up with Brenda that I last heard any news of you Cliff. Your mother asked me to talk to her. Did you two resolve your differences?"

Cliff was slightly taken aback by his uncle's comment but didn't bother to ask for more detail. It was somewhat academic, really.

"Sorry to say Uncle Gerry, but Brenda and I did not. We split up a while back."

Glancing over Gerry's shoulder as he spoke, Cliff thought he saw a face he recognised. It was that of a young person, who was looking directly at him and Gerry without smiling. Then just as suddenly he turned and walked on. *Someone from the press corps soccer game morning?* Cliff wondered to himself. He soon forgot about it as two steel mugs and a huge pot of tea banged down on the table, with an equally huge laugh from their host.

"Kujabulela itiye lakho (enjoy your tea)."

"Ngiyabonga," Gerry thanked her.

The little tearoom was a humble one, with very old tables and chairs that had undergone countless makeshift repairs. Despite this, it had a friendly atmosphere and was spotlessly clean. Cliff leaned back and relaxed in his chair as he invited his uncle to tell him about life in Alexandra and the work he was doing for the church.

Gerry described how he initially struggled with the dramatic change in environment, getting to grips with the regular violence between the ANC and Inkatha, but more so the abject poverty of the place.

Returning to the present Gerry described how he had successfully attracted more people to his congregation, and in addition offered some of the rooms of the manse as a sanctuary for homeless children. This brought him to his version of events as they had transpired on the night the manse had been attacked.

"I think Josh must have been quite astounded to be reunited with his uncle in that way – dancing around pulling my robes off like a mad man, as he sprayed them with a fire extinguisher."

Cliff shook his head in wonderment at Gerry's account while remembering Josh's version as well.

Gerry was suddenly very serious. "When you have the little general staying with you, all kinds of scary things pop out of the woodwork," Gerry whispered, with a glance over his shoulder.

Deciding to try another attempt at finding out information, Cliff continued in as innocent a way as he could.

"I heard about Uncle Frank from Josh but have

you ever heard anything about Uncle Raymond?"

"No, I haven't," Gerry replied. "But I am sure he is OK. I just feel it is so."

Cliff smiled to himself. "Well, that's good to know, although of course it's not really important to me as I've never even met him." Cliff cringed at the lie. "OK, I better get back. It was so good to meet up after such a long time, Uncle Gerry."

Standing up, Gerry gave Cliff a brief hug before pointing in the general direction of the township entrance and the police station.

"If you're going to walk back to the police station, I better go some of the way with you – just in case. Anyway, best if we make sure you know the way. This place can be a maze when you are not sitting high up in a vehicle like that thing of yours," he laughed.

As they started walking up the road, something made Cliff glance back in search of the young person he had seen earlier. There was no one around. He and Gerry walked and chatted until finally they reached a point where they could see the high security lights in the distance that looked down on the police station, although the building itself was still out of sight.

"There's your guiding star – all four of them," Gerry smiled. "Go down this alley, left at the end, immediate right after about fifty metres and you will come out on Seventh Avenue. That will take you up to the station," he said, pointing between two shacks.

They shook hands and agreed to meet up again in a few weeks. Cliff waved as he moved down between the humble homes and dodged a squawking chicken being chased by a young boy. As he turned left at the end of the alley, he was confronted by a group of a dozen young men blocking his path.

He recognised one of the youths as the one he had seen earlier outside the tearoom. He seemed to be the leader. He demanded loudly, "Soldier, why did you take our time for revenge away? You put that boy in your Casspir before we could finish him. He was ours. He killed Walter!"

Cliff suddenly realised why some of their faces were familiar: they were the same gang from the day of the funeral.

"It was not him who killed Walter. We have found the murderers. It was in the papers. Did you not see it?" he said, as reasonably as he could.

"All lies!" the leader said.

"All lies, all lies!" the others repeated in unison.

"You all know Major Hani? Well, he caught them," Cliff tried in an attempt to defuse the situation.

The thought crossed his mind that if they knew Zeb was still an MK man working undercover in the police, then he might just be believed. However, that would expose Zeb and who knows what the outcome of that would be?

"All police lie to save the Inkatha boy you saved. Nothing will happen to those police. You will see."

Cliff knew that anyone seen as a sympathiser for the allegedly government-supported Inkatha movement would be in trouble with this gang who at that very moment were holding knives. Cliff started to panic.

He thought about his weapon in its holster but they were too close. If he reached for it, there was every chance it would provoke an attack on him; possibly even before he had had the chance to fully withdraw it. His record for getting his handgun out its web holster was not great. *Anyway, am I really going to shoot a young person like this? But what if I am about to be stabbed with a knife? Fuck this government and its army for putting me in this situation. Fuck, fuck*, he thought.

If he turned and ran, would he make it back to Gerry? Maybe if he could, he would be safe with him. The leader was still glaring at him and was holding his knife in his hand. *That came from out of nowhere*, Cliff thought, as he tried to surreptitiously unclip the cover of his holster. The leader switched his glare from Cliff to the holster and smiled. It seemed as though he was almost willing Cliff to just try it and see what happened.

The seconds passed although Cliff felt like he was frozen in time. There was the odd quiet murmur between some of the gang during this time. Cliff tried another tactic: if nothing else, it might buy him a head-start. If he couldn't get back to Gerry, he might at least be able to lose them in the maze of shanties.

By now he was struggling to suppress his panic but with as much authority as he could muster, he said, "OK, I am not going to arrest you for obstructing an officer, but I want you to disperse immediately when I leave. If I return and you are still here there will be trouble."

Their faces were impassive as they stared back at him.

"Is that clear?"

Without waiting for an answer, he turned on his heel and strode off back down the alley; pretending he had no fear of any of them. For a few seconds it seemed to have worked as the gang stood silently unmoving.

Cliff was just breaking into a trot when the first rock hit him. It landed just above his kidneys, and he felt like he had been punched by Mike Tyson in a round eight clinch. He felt winded.

However, he still had a lead on them and so when he turned at the end of the alley, he broke into a run despite gasping from the impact of the rock. He could sense them running behind him and then he heard their yells. A rock landed in front of him and rolled ahead of his pumping boots.

"You going to die, soldier man!"

"You dead, soldier!"

Cliff dodged between two shacks and was out of their line of sight, but only for a few seconds. He ran down a second alley, forgetting he now had the chance to draw his weapon. He was just running instinctively, in a desperate attempt to flee; escape being the only thought in his mind. A second rock made contact, smashing into his elbow, and he knew immediately his arm was broken as it dangled limply at his side.

The pain made him gasp as he tried to hold his arm steady while running at the same time. He wanted to stop and fall to his knees so that the additional pain caused from moving would subside a little.

He had reached a few small brick buildings now. He headed for one, with the thought that if he could just get through the door, he could barricade himself inside and have the time to draw his weapon. That was as far as his thought process got, however, as a third rock smashed into the back of his head. He wobbled once before crashing into the little gate protecting the small front garden.

Lying face down, head twisted to one side, his last image before he lost consciousness was of a row of plants running up the side of the path; the sound of the rock, which had just bounced off his leg, rolling across the paving stones that led to the front door.

When he regained consciousness, he discovered

two strong hands wedged firmly under his armpits, dragging him over the threshold of the cottage in front of which he had collapsed. He screamed in pain as his boot caught momentarily on the bottom lip of the doorframe, twisting his body awkwardly in the process.

He lay on his back, holding his damaged arm. He could feel the blood running down his temple and into the pool that was forming on the concrete floor of the cottage. His eyes focused on a woman who was peering at him with concern.

Cliff felt comforted by the kindness in her face. Through his blurred vision he saw the same worried expression his mother might have had on her face had she been there. This stranger was much larger and stronger than his mother, however, strong enough to have dragged him to safety from her garden where he would have died had she not done so.

She knelt beside him, turning him gently onto his side. Cliff felt the softness of her large bosom as she leant over him to look closely at his head wound, murmuring in Zulu as she did so. Her face disappeared from his vision for a few seconds, and when it returned, he could feel the warmth of her breath as she gently wrapped a cloth around his bleeding head.

Her face kept blurring in front of his eyes and Cliff wondered if she actually *was* his mother. Had she known he was in danger? Found out where he was and had come to nurse him? In his concussed state, he thought perhaps he was dying. *I didn't realise Mom was a black woman. Am I black as well?* he wondered. His mind cleared when he heard the loud clang of a rock bashing against the corrugated iron wall, and then a second crashing through the glass window. The rock bounced across the concrete floor and some of the shattered glass landed on him.

"Izingulube (pigs)!" the woman shouted towards the door.

She stood up and yanked the door open. The gang stood at her gate, with rocks in hand.

"Is this how you treat your own grannies?" she yelled at them, hands on her hips. "Hhhawu, you are brave boys for sure. Tonight you can go home and tell your mother a proud story: 'Mama I am very brave; I threw rocks through a granny's window today; I am so strong I can even make an old granny scared of me; we went in a gang of us just in case the old granny was too strong!' Go on. Run quickly and tell people what brave soldiers you are."

Some of the gang started to look down self-consciously as she spoke, kicking the lose pebbles in the road.

One said, "I don't have a granny."

"Because she ran away! I am sure she was afraid of such a bad boy." The woman dispatched them with a final burst of wrath. "Go, run home now. Say to your mother, 'Mama, mama, where's your mother? Where's my granny? I want to throw rocks at her. I am a brave boy'."

The leader tried to maintain his menacing posture as some of his gang members started to move away from the gate. "We won't go until we can have the soldier. You must let him come out so we can take him," he threatened, but with little conviction now.

"He is my visitor. I don't throw my visitors out into the dirt." She turned on her heel and slammed the door shut.

*

When Cliff next opened his eyes, he found himself lying on a small bed, his head swathed in bandages. A boy of about five was sitting next to Cliff's bed, holding his hand. He smiled.

"I am going to be in MK one day. I will be a soldier like you. Granny said I must hold your hand so you don't die; so you will feel better."

"Thank you. Your warm hand makes me feel much better," Cliff managed to reply.

He tried to move but the shooting pains down his arm and back stopped him from doing so. He cried out in pain, which frightened the young boy who was beside him. He raised his head slightly to look at his arm and saw that it too was bound tightly in bandages. His leg was tightly tied to a broomstick; the brush head resting on his stomach.

"You need to get to the hospital, and soon," the woman said, from where she stood at her kitchen window. "But they are all around the house waiting for you to leave," she said, looking back at the scene outside. She brought Cliff some water. "You need to drink," she said, kneeling down and lifting his head gently.

He gulped down some water, surprised at how thirsty he was. Eventually he was able to speak. "You saved my life. Thank you. What is your name? I am Cliff."

"My name is Mable," she said. "And this is Jonjon," she added, patting the boy's head. "He thinks he's a warrior, like the little general."

"That's Midgy Batwana," the little boy informed Cliff with a grave face, thinking he was enlightening his new soldier-friend. "Midgy's army is called the Under Fourteens. I will join it so I can get ready for Umkhonto we Sizwe and then—"

Jonjon suddenly stopped talking as he ducked down to avoid a smack on the head from his granny.

"You will get ready for school. And that's the only thing you will get ready for umfaan." Mable tried to look stern but laughed instead. She turned her attention back to Cliff. "Now you are awake, tell me where your men are. We can ask them to come."

"They are not far – up at the police station – but how can we call them? The gang, you say, are still at the front of your house?" Cliff murmured, feeling sleepy again.

"Jonjon will call them – if it is not too far as you say. Those boys will not see him, he will go through my neighbours garden out the back. We share an outside toilet. If they do see him, they will think he is my neighbour's boy. Hey Jonjon?"

"I will tell your men what happened and show them the way here," Jonjon said, springing up ready for his mission.

Mable turned back from the window after watching to make sure none of the gang saw Jonjon, or if they did, weren't bothered with him appearing out of next door's front gate.

"Are you awake Cliff?" she asked.

Cliff had dozed off again; he could not seem to stay awake. Mable said he should not sleep too much, and insisted he listened carefully as she began telling her story:

Jonjon was her daughter's son. Her daughter had been killed in the Soweto riot of 1976 and she had looked after the boy ever since. She had no work but her son sent her money. He lived in Durban and had a good job.

*

Jonjon looked right and left as he walked down the

narrow lanes between the shanties. Although he knew his surrounding neighbourhood intimately, he was a lot further away from home than normal and so felt unsure of the way.

He was familiar with how to reach the police station from the main road – it was just a walk all the way up Seventh Avenue; its security lights sited on top of very high poles discernible even before one reached the top of the street. However, walking the back way between the shanties was not so easy.

He had decided he should stay off the main streets in case someone stopped him. His granny always warned him about strangers approaching him. She said they could be a sangoma (medicine man) looking for young boys to take for 'muti'.

Turning into an alleyway that opened out into a small clearing, there were a few older boys playing with a ball. They called to him.

"Hey, where are you going umfaan?"

Jonjon didn't answer. Instead, he broke into a run, in case they approached him. He could hear them laughing as he turned one corner then another before slowing down to a walking pace again. He turned into the next street and there the boys were again – in the same spot with their ball. He had walked around in a circle and now he was lost.

He didn't feel very brave anymore. In fact he felt like crying and fought fiercely to hold back his tears as he re-traced his steps. Suddenly he spotted an old ladder propped up against a shack. He ran over and climbed it quickly.

Sure enough he could see over the shacks. Casting his eyes from left to right, he saw the security lights and now knew which way to go. Before he climbed back down, he spotted something else; something that brought him great happiness as his body flooded with relief. In the neighbouring narrow road was a police Land Rover. He recognised it as such by the red and blue lights on its roof rack.

He tried to descend as quickly as he could down the rickety old rungs of the ladder, but he slipped on the bottom one, grazing his knee and landing on his backside with a *thump*. However, he got to his feet again in seconds and ran towards the Land Rover.

As he rounded the corner, he was surprised to see the policeman standing beside the vehicle was black. He was talking with two township people but that did not stop Jonjon from interrupting. He reached up and grabbed the policeman's hand.

"Mr. Policeman! Mr. Policeman!" he cried, tugging at his hand. "There is big trouble. You have to take me to the police station so I can call the soldiers. Quickly!"

Zeb looked down at the young boy.

"Hhhawu, slow down a bit. What's the trouble? What's your name?" he asked.

"My name is Jonjon Hani."

"Oh I see, Jonjon Hani. Well, my name is Zeb Hani. Maybe we are relatives? What do you think?" Zeb smiled.

"Mr Zeb Hani, we must go. The soldier in my house is hurt!"

That got Zeb's attention, and he realised that the young boy, who was still holding his hand, was on a mission. Having established from Jonjon that the house was surrounded by an armed gang, Zeb agreed with the boy that they did indeed need reinforcements. With Jonjon in the Land Rover beside him, he raced back to the police station. Zeb had radioed for back-up but decided the young boy would be safer left at the station than staying with him.

*

"Your soldiers are here at last," Mable said, looking out the window for what seemed to Cliff to be for the thousandth time. "Your Casspir thing is coming. Oh my father! And Jonjon is up there too!"

Cliff tried to get up as he heard the Casspir's thumping engine get closer; the vehicle moving slowly down the narrow gravel lane and almost touching the houses it passed between. Its wheels crunched to a stop just before the house, and high up in the cab occupying Cliff's normal seat sat Jonjon. The boy was peering over the dashboard, which he was holding on to, his grin splashed across his little face shining like a quarter moon.

Unlike Jonjon, Cliff certainly wasn't grinning and nor was Mable as she struggled to take his weight. He felt dizzy and his vision was blurred. His shattered elbow and injured leg strapped to the broomstick made him gasp with pain but still, he was determined to leave this weird township battle on his feet. A trickle of blood ran slowly down the side of his face as Mable's bandage was by now completely saturated.

The gang was still hanging around the cottage, glaring defiantly at Cliff's men – most of whom were not much older than them. Zeb had not been able to get his Land Rover past the Casspir so he parked behind it where the rest of the press corps had left their cars. For once, the Casspir had been the lead vehicle.

When the gang saw Zeb elbowing his way between the journalists and cameramen, they slipped away into the lanes between the shanties. Before leaving some pointed up towards where Jonjon was exiting through the Casspir's passenger door.

Taking in the scene, Zeb pointed at the Casspir. "Is there a stretcher in that thing?"

"Yes Major," said one of the squad, which had formed a protective ring around the house.

"Good," Zeb said. "Get your captain onto it."

Mable was now standing in her doorway with

Cliff still clinging to her for support. She was looking at Zeb with interest as he spoke to Cliff.

"You OK my friend? You owe this lady and the boy your life, I reckon. Although I wish that gang had not had the opportunity to see him with your men. They will put two and two together."

"I'll sort it out," Cliff winced, while not actually having any clue what Zeb's comment meant.

"That is Major Zeb," Jonjon yelled out to his granny, pointing at him. The boy reluctantly climbed down from the Casspir before continuing. "Your son's boy... your son in Durban. Major told me. You are his granny and I am his cousin!" Jonjon was still grinning, looking very pleased with himself indeed.

"Zeb? Is that really you? Umkhulu kakhulu manje! (you are so big now)" Mable cried out, as Cliff's men eased him off her shoulder and onto the stretcher. He could not say anything to her as he had lost consciousness once again.

"Hello ugogo wami (my grandmother)," Zeb said, raising his hand in greeting. "I have asked many who live here for a long time but nobody knew of you. I will tell my father. He will be happy I visited you," Zeb laughed, shaking her hand with both of his.

"Umkhulu kakhulu manje," Mable repeated, with tears in her eyes this time.

There was a growing thumping sound from an approaching helicopter, and everyone turned their faces upwards. Like a giant mechanical bird, its dark shape momentarily blocked out the sky as it came up from the valley beyond the houses and suddenly into view over the shanty roofs. Its nearness to the roofs made it feel like it was on top of them. In its down draught, the plastic shack walls billowed, and the corrugated iron roofs struggled against the boulders that held them in place as the helicopter thudded above them before slowly moving away without gaining height.

Zeb yelled to the squad. "You better get your captain over to the soccer field where the helicopter will land. Do you know how to get there? It is only a short distance."

"I will show them!" Jonjon yelled, running off in the right direction and beckoning Cliff's men to follow him.

Chapter 20

Recovery

Curled up on his lap, Sam's cat purred and rubbed his cheek against Peter's letter that Sam was holding loosely in his hand. He gazed over his English summer garden, reflecting on the news Peter had relayed in considerable detail. *What an amazing outcome. Who would have thought?* He marvelled at the many twists and turns fate had presented his friends and how their country's enforced army training could have had such an impact on their lives.

The sudden movement of his cat as it jumped down from his lap brought Sam's thoughts back to the here and now. The cat crouched down in the lush grass as it watched a squirrel descending from one of two large oak trees growing in the back garden.

Intrigued as usual, Sam watched as the squirrel dashed forward a few metres and then retreated to the safety of the tree's trunk. The cat tensed momentarily and then sank back down into the thick grass. Sam wondered if the squirrel was teasing the cat or just psyching itself up for his escape dash.

Suddenly the squirrel made its move. The cat tensed, seemingly waiting for the right moment when the squirrel would be exactly between the two trees and thus at the point of no return. However, at the same time, another squirrel took off from the opposite oak. The two passed each other at the midway point; forcing the cat to reconsider which to target as its eyes flicked between the two. By the time the cat reacted, he had lost a vital second and the squirrels ran free.

Beautifully orchestrated my bird-feeder thieves, Sam thought, smiling. He picked up Peter's letter and read it again:

Sam,
I have so much to tell you, I thought a letter would be better than a phone call, and anyway...

Zeb slipped his small bag into the overhead compartment and eased himself into the seat of the single-engine plane that would take him over the Drakensberg Mountains to Maseru in Lesotho, where his journey had started several years ago.

The first part of that original journey had found him cramped in the trunk of an old Ford car. Although this return trip to Maseru was somewhat more salubrious, he was, as in his first trip, lacking in information as to what awaited him at the end of the journey.

The MK leadership had decided it would be safer to get Zeb out of the country while they still could rather than have him face trumped up charges from the government. They were concerned that he had taken the little general into his confidence. Clearly it had been useful, but there were those in the MK leadership who were adamant that Midgy had allegiance to many sides.

Some even thought he was nothing but a snitch and feared the repercussions for Zeb. They decided they should quit while they were ahead and get Zeb out while they could. He had been working undercover for a long time, but now it was time to get him – whom they considered to be a valuable asset in their organisation – away from any potential threat of discovery and subsequent conviction. Leaders like Zeb would be invaluable once the ANC came to power.

*

For Zeb's father the telephone call from his son was bittersweet. On the one hand it was good to know that the rumours his son had turned against the people were unfounded, but on the other his son was leaving the country once again. Who knew when he would see him again?

At least he had visited his granny, and it would be some consolation to have Jonjon staying in the room they had built on for Zeb – her son being there would be like a little bit of his dear lost sister. A trusted friend would drive him down to Durban and only his granny would know where he was living now.

*

Opening the document folder he had taken from his jacket pocket, Zeb slipped out the passport he had received so he could complete the arrival document the cabin crew had given him. When he opened it, a confirmation slip for a bank transfer dropped onto his lap. He picked it up and read it. It confirmed two transactions – one to his father and one to his granny. The considerable savings he had accumulated during the last few years in the police force had now been split between them.

Whether ill-gotten gains or not, the government owed his family for the death of his aunt, and this would be just a drop in the ocean compared to what they had been denied. Leaning his head back against the headrest, Zeb sighed. Jonjon was safe and so was his granny but there was still much work to be done.

Raechel's eyes opened to see Mary staring at her intently. "Welcome back," smiled the nurse, as her eyes flicked away and across to the various screens surrounding Raechel's head. "How are you feeling girl? Any pain?"

Raechel pointed to the water glass beside her. Her throat was too dry to answer. She took a sip from the glass Mary held to her lips.

"No, I'm fine while you keep giving me that wonderful stuff of yours."

"Let me know when you need to go to the toilet," Mary murmured, as she concentrated on the angle of the glass at Raechel's lips.

"Well, isn't that the elephant in the room?" Raechel smiled.

She was no stranger to the challenges a person like her had to face going to a public toilet, but being in a hospital bed, unable to walk, was a whole new game.

Mary put her hand on Raechel's hand and smiled. "Well, let's send that particular elephant back to the bush. You just tell me when and I will handle it. You'll see girl."

Raechel squeezed her hand gently.

"Now you go back to sleep. That boy of yours will be back before you know it."

*

Josh's eyes fluttered open for a few seconds and saw the ceiling strip lights passing by overhead. The vibration of the hospital gurney transporting him to the recovery ward reminded him a bit of a train clattering over the joints in its tracks, particularly when they pushed it over the lift entrance. He noted that one of the neon tubes above him was out before he too was out cold.

When his eyes opened again, he was in bed, with multiple screens monitoring him and numerous tubes and wires attached to his body. Mary's blue uniformed body blocked his view of the room as she leant across him to fiddle with a switch on a monitor above him. He tried to see the time on her watch that dangled from her breast pocket just above his face, but it was too small and upside down.

"How're you feeling Josh? Sip of water?"

He shook his head slowly.

From the bed beside him he heard Raechel's voice. "Seen any kidneys lying around Josh? I seem to be missing one."

"Don't make me laugh – not yet," he groaned.

"Looks like you have your first visitors Cliff – Brenda, and I think her father, are here to see you. You up to it?" asked his nurse, Maggie.

"Father? Are you sure? Well that's interesting... Yes, I'm OK thanks."

She disappeared from sight but he could still hear the slight squeak of her rubber soles as she walked briskly down the hall back to the reception desk, where he presumed his visitors were waiting.

A visitor would be a pleasant distraction; distract him from what he had been re-playing repeatedly in his head. He had spent his entire time in hospital thinking about what had happened to him, as well as what hadn't.

Now that the threat of attack was over and he was lying in a secure hospital bed, his mind was no longer preoccupied with the basic human desire to just survive and escape his attackers. Only now, did the enormity of the events of the previous days become real to him.

He had been so close to losing his life; probably stoned unconscious first before being fatally stabbed. He shuddered, for the umpteenth time, feeling the sobbing welling up in him. Instead, he took a few deep breaths until he calmed down.

Cliff's head was swathed in bandages as a result of the fractured skull he had sustained from the rock attack. He had not required surgery but he had very deep lacerations. His shattered elbow meant his entire arm was in a plaster cast and held in a metal contraption beside him. He was also in a leg brace as a result of the rock that had hit him as he lay on the pathway of Mable's small garden.

He would be forever grateful for the sedatives they had given him throughout his first night in hospital. These would continue to be administered as the specialists had informed him that his recovery period was going to be a long one.

His face had severe bruising – located mainly under his eyes – and the mirror the nurse held up to him earlier had revealed a raccoon-like image. They had both laughed hysterically when he referred to himself as such although the resulting stabs of pain made him regret his attempt at humour.

The door opened and in walked Brenda. She looked radiant and to Cliff's astonishment she was followed by someone he knew but had not seen for a long time. Brenda's smile faded as she registered the extent of Cliff's battered and bruised appearance that was compounded further by his shocked expression at seeing who she was with. He barely heard her words of greeting as he tried to comprehend the scene confronting him. *He can't be, surely? The nurse must have misheard*, he thought.

"Cliff, you look terrible! I am so sorry," she said, taking hold of his hand. "I phoned Beryl to get your address and she told me what had happened. We came straight away," she said, glancing briefly at the man next to her who was smiling at Cliff. "Are you feeling all right to talk?"

"Yeah, it looks worse than it is. This drip keeps the pain at bay but forgive me if I sound a bit out of it occasionally," he smiled. "As bad as I look, it will be great that you can call Mom and tell her you've seen me with your own eyes, and I'm OK. She will be freaking out."

"I will – and yes, she is," Brenda replied. Her smile returned as she said, "The last few days have just been my best ever! Look who I found after all these years? My father, Cory Swartberg!" Brenda placed her hand on the arm of the man beside her. "Dad, this is Cliff."

Shaking Sergeant Swarberg's hand briefly and gingerly, Cliff searched his face for any sign of recognition. Yet the head bandages, raccoon eyes and the few years that had elapsed since their last encounter, seemed to have erased all chance of his erstwhile nemesis recognising him.

The conversation centred mainly on the last few weeks since their discovery of each other. Cliff only partly listened as his mind raced. He thought he probably hadn't ever mentioned the sergeant by name in his anecdotes to Brenda about him and Peter; rather simply referring to him as 'the sergeant'. Had she known who he really was, her life-changing reunion with him would have been rather soured, he believed.

*

Cliff remembered that she had devoted several scenes in her book to an 'overzealous instructor' although she had refused to go into detail on his near demise. "I don't want any sympathy for him Cliff, and anyway, it's too gory for me," she had said.

Just like Josh had with his scoop, Brenda too had wanted the previously untold side of the story published – in this case conscription and its potential effects on young people.

"People think it's right they do their duty but nobody thinks about the potential effect on these young people; most of whom are totally unsuited to a military regime, as you are seeing right now. Or even if they should be taking up arms against their fellow citizens. My God, it's the American Civil War all over again, except in this case the people they are shooting at are fighting for their own freedom!"

Brenda had said this to Cliff during their recent meeting at the café after he had updated her on what was going on in Alexandra.

*

As they talked, Cliff watched Sergeant Swartberg's facial expressions. Ignorant of who he really was, Cliff felt a bit like he was in a covert operation. It reminded him of the time he and Brenda had gone to a fancy-dress party wearing full face masks and had decided not to reveal who they were for some time. They had been surprised at how titillated they were to be unrecognised in the company of people they knew well; listening to their unguarded conversations unseen.

As they spoke, Cliff rapidly came to the conclusion that Brenda needed to be kept in the dark. He did not want to spoil this precious time for her. Clearly, he needed to make sure he had Sergeant Swartberg on board with such a strategy, even if it was only temporary.

"Brenda before I forget, could I ask you a huge favour?" Cliff smiled.

"Of course."

"This is embarrassing... I obviously did not arrive here very well prepared and I will get someone to bring me some clothes and stuff as soon as I can, but in the meantime, I need a few things. Would you pop down to the arcade I'm told is on the ground floor and get me some underwear and a toothbrush? Any old make will do. You know my size."

"Sure, I understand your predicament. I'll be ten minutes, OK? Heaven knows it's something I've done for you before?" she laughed, as she walked out the door.

Cliff felt happy for Brenda. Her whole demeanour seemed to have changed since discovering who her birth mother and father were and finally knowing the full story. She had parents now and even siblings, albeit *step* ones. It was the part of her life she had always missed.

"Well Sergeant, it's a small world, isn't it?" Cliff said, after Brenda had left the room.

Sergeant Swartberg's eyes widened with surprise at being addressed by his former military rank.

"Sorry Cliff, have we met before?"

Cliff saw his facial expressions switch through a range of emotions as Cliff enlightened him as to who he was. He also reminded him of Peter and Sam. The surprise on his face morphed into a look of concern as he recognised the threat his past might have on his relationship with his newly found daughter.

With eyes downcast from time to time, he relayed to Cliff what he believed had been behind his ill-tempered, mean attitude in the past; the reason for the anger he carried and how much he regretted some of his actions.

He seemed genuinely sincere to Cliff when he said he had been striving to change in recent years, and finding Brenda had lifted the huge weight of resentment and guilt from his shoulders. He told Cliff he was a different man now, thanks to her having found him.

Cliff suggested he and the sergeant keep what they had just disclosed between themselves for now; try to not spoil anything for Brenda. Cliff reasoned that sometimes white lies are for the best and Sergeant Swartberg agreed immediately with great relief.

Before either man could speak again, Maggie came in and busied herself checking all the monitors, telling Cliff she did not want him overdoing it. After she left Cliff looked back at Brenda's father. He was struggling to adjust to the sergeant's new status. He knew he was being belligerent but he couldn't resist asking the question hoping the answer would be the response he sought.

"By the way Sergeant, just out of curiosity – after your accident, we found a box of sunglasses in your Land Rover. Were you going to sell those to the guys, or just hand them out to whoever needed them on their Golden Highway journey?" Cliff asked, with a smile.

He didn't get an answer as at that moment the door opened and Brenda burst through.

"I couldn't find any flowers so I bought you a present instead," she winked, waving a packet in front of her. "What have you two been chatting about? Been getting to know my new dad have you Cliff?"

"OK that's it, good people. This young man has to rest now. Sorry," Maggie said, as she came back into the room.

"Sure, we'll be off then," Brenda said. "In fact

Cliff, I really did bring you a present but it means some work as I would like you to write a foreword. You'll see what I mean," she said, as she handed him a neatly wrapped package tied up with a ribbon. She bent over to kiss his cheek in farewell.

As they went through the door, the former Sergeant Swartberg looked back. "Army-issue Cliff – for the desert. The adjutant asked me to handle it, didn't want the CO to know." At Brenda's quizzical expression, her father said, "Just something we were chatting about – World War II stuff," he smiled.

*

Cliff laid back against his pillows, feeling physically drained of energy.

"I told you so. Too much, too soon," Maggie said, as she scanned his monitors. "Want me to open this for you?"

Cliff nodded and she tore the brown wrapping paper open and handed him Brenda's 'present' – a manuscript, A4 pages affixed with an oversized staple. He turned it over and looked at the cover page:

The First Canary by Brenda Tarrant – 2nd proof

The doctors and specialists were delighted with the progress Josh and Raechel had made in the weeks since their surgery. Both were now able to sit in their wheelchairs and even hobble a short distance to the toilet when supported by a nurse.

Peter was a constant visitor; relaying messages between them and the rest of the family. He had started bringing in the daily newspaper as well. This was how they had discovered the news about Cliff and subsequently learnt he was in the same hospital as them.

Coming through the door Maggie said, "You've got visitors. OK?"

"Who?" Cliff asked.

"Surprise," she said, and disappeared back through the door.

He heard some muted conversation from the doorway before Maggie gave the urgent instruction, "Go left! Go left, Peter."

Through the door there suddenly appeared two wheelchairs; one pushed by Peter the other by Maggie. Occupying the two wheelchairs were Josh and Raechel. Josh was holding open a newspaper towards him so he could see the second-page headline:

"'Hero captain in revenge attack by same gang'," Josh read out. "Is this how we get to hear what you are up to?" Josh said, grinning.

The little general lay still in his tiny bed. He had heard something and waited for the sound to come again. He could hear the breaths of the other three who shared the large bed in his room. The snores from the priest echoed down the hallway of the manse, just as they did every night.

There it was again – the sound of metal straining against metal. Slipping quietly out from under his blanket, Midgy got down onto his knees beside the bed and listened for the sound again. And there it was. He crawled silently across the floorboards, trying to remember if any of them creaked.

Robbers? Midgy wondered, as he edged closer to their open bedroom door where he would be able to peep into the lounge room. *But everyone knows the priest has nothing to steal. Maybe just his old TV*, he thought.

Midgy peered through the gap between the door and the wooden doorframe of the lounge room. He saw dark shapes at the window, working as quietly as they could as they levered the metal burglar bar frame from where it was anchored to the outside wall over the lounge window.

Not burglars. These guys want to get in quietly; they want surprise on their side, he thought.

Midgy crawled back across the room as quickly as he could. He leant over the other three boys who were still fast asleep in the bed like three sardines in a tin.

"Vuka. Vuka, wake up," he whispered urgently. "Vuka, abantu ababi (wake up, bad people). They come for us, I know," he said, shaking them gently.

The three boys woke and were instantly vigilant. As young as they were, they had long since learnt how quickly a threat could come when they least expected it and the need for a fast escape.

"Follow," he whispered, crawling as fast as he could back to the door.

This time he did not stop at the threshold. He kept going down the passage as fast and as quietly as he could, thankful that it was so dark in the house. The priest's snores accompanied the four boys as they moved quickly down the hallway on all fours.

At the front door of the manse Midgy reached up and switched off the porch light the priest always left on, as a welcome for stray souls, he always said.

Opening the door, Midgy crawled outside with the others right behind him. For a second, he thought of dashing to the fuse box to retrieve their stashed knives but decided every second was better spent on escaping. As they began making their way to the playground and the safety of the gum trees alongside, they were spotted.

Coming around the house to investigate why the porch light had suddenly gone off, one of the three intruders who had previously been at the window, saw the boys and started yelling to the others that they were running away.

The other two heard his call and came running from the other side, joining the pursuit of the boys as they reached the playground.

*

Rubbing his eyes, Gerry felt his way down the hallway until he reached a light switch.

"Who was shouting?" he called towards the boys' room. "What are you up to now?" he sighed, seeing what looked like empty beds in the dim light of the passageway.

At the door to their room, he reached around for the light switch. When it came on, he saw their beds were indeed empty. He shrugged and switched the light back off. "Who knows where they are? They come and go at all hours, these Under Fourteens," he said aloud.

When they all trundled off, Cliff picked up the newspaper Josh had left behind. Despite the metal frame that was holding his arm in position, he could at least still hold the newspaper up, albeit at a funny angle. He ignored the article about himself, feeling decidedly embarrassed by the use of the word 'hero' in the headline.

"It's how we sell newspapers Cliff. Those are the kinds of words the reader wants to see," Josh had explained. "'Captain' is not as appealing as 'hero captain' and nor is 'attack' as appealing as 'revenge attack' is it?" Josh had said with a smile.

"Anyway, you are one," Raechel said. "So stop cringing and enjoy your second fifteen minutes of fame."

He was shaken when he came across the story about the abduction of four boys from a church sanctuary in Alexandra: 'Young activist found dead in veld, three others badly beaten'.

He wondered if there was any link between the tragedy and the sudden disappearance of Zeb, which Josh had told him about, that had not been reported anywhere in the press. Josh had received a message from one of his sources though that Zeb was OK and had since left the country.

Reading the story, Cliff was shocked to have his worst fears confirmed: the body was that of Midgy. What did this have to do with Zeb and enlisting Midgy's help to track down the hit squad? He wondered what Josh knew about all this.

Suddenly Jonjon came into his mind. Was he in danger for helping to save his life? Zeb had seemed very concerned about the gang seeing him in the

Casspir. If someone as young as Midgy could be a target for revenge, why shouldn't Jonjon? He wasn't much younger in the Alexandra scheme of things. Cliff hoped Zeb would get him out of the township somehow.

*

Cliff's eyes opened, his chin was being tickled by the newspaper, it lay across his chest. He had dozed off, which he was prone to do with his medication. He thought he might have been dreaming about Jodie visiting him. It prompted him to reach for the mirror Maggie had left, to see if his facial injuries had improved, but they hadn't. Maybe it was a good thing he had not heard from her. One look at him would probably have sent her running away.

When asked, Peter had mumbled something about her trying to arrange something at work so she could come up and see all of them but he had seemed vague.

Cliff had been told he was due to be discharged at the end of the week, but there had been a delay. His specialist had insisted that if he wanted to be discharged from hospital, he must arrange to have a carer during his convalescence as he didn't want him overdoing things. He refused to discharge him until he could confirm he had such support.

The list of hospital-approved carers Maggie had given him lay unread on the table next to his bed. He knew he was procrastinating but what was he waiting for? Someone who wasn't a stranger from some list to offer support? In which case, that would be his mother.

Beryl had her bags packed in readiness to move in with him for as long as he desired (even though she hated Johannesburg, being under the impression that Afrikaans was the main language spoken there, which she could not speak). Telling her that the city's population was mainly English and that Pretoria was the Afrikaans dominated city didn't change her opinion of his city.

This thought process made him reach for the list Maggie had compiled for him at the specialist's request.

"You will see they indicate whether they are 'live in' or not. 'Live in' is what you will need Cliff – at least for a few weeks. Also, check their availability period, which for you should be a minimum of a month." She had said this days ago when she had first handed him the list.

He started at the top but after reading the details of just two of the named people, he became exasperated and called for Maggie.

"Yes General?"

"Don't you start!" he laughed.

"Part of your therapy – winding you up! Now, what can I do for you?"

"How am I supposed to choose a carer when I know nothing about them? Young or old? Easy going or strict? Likes to chat or is the silent type? This list tells me nothing!" he complained, waving it above his head.

"You've read through the whole list, have you?" his nurse inquired, frowning theatrically. "Read the *whole* list, please." she said with a smile before she left the room.

"How will that help? How do you know I haven't read the whole list already?"

"Just read it," she called as she strode through the doorway.

Mumbling to himself about how one might expect *nurses* to be a bit sympathetic, Cliff started again; this time reading each row right to left as he went down the list, ignoring those who were not offering a live-in service in the column on the right. He found one that was live-in but only for three days.

"Well, that's not very useful," he snorted to himself.

The next one on the list stated live-in and also 'as long as required'.

"OK, progress," he murmured, as his eyes flicked to the name on the left of the sheet. "Jodie Pike," he read aloud.

Epilogue

Pen in hand, Brenda smiled up at the young woman standing in front of the table as she handed her back the signed copy of her book. It had taken two years to advance from the manuscript she handed Cliff that day in hospital to publishing the finished novel and attending book signing events like the one she was at today.

The second proof had sat on her desk at home for nearly a year before her publisher threatened to abandon the project if she did not start working on the edits. She had been so involved with her newfound family that there had not seemed to be any time for her book.

Brenda's stepsisters, Janice and Catie, had been a revelation. The three sisters shared so many common characteristics, likes and dislikes – it was like they had grown up together. Halfway into the book's second year Janice had taken it upon herself to manage Brenda's final steps to becoming a debut author, persuading the publisher to let her help with the marketing of the book. That was why Brenda could see her now, at the rear of the room, whispering into the publisher's ear.

*

Brenda took the copy of *The First Canary* that was being held out to her. It was an elderly man who stood smiling down at her from across the other side of the table.

"What name would you like me to mention?" she asked, looking down and opening the cover.

He continued to smile, now down at her blond hair as she sat pen poised and said, "Oh I don't want an actual name, just 'grandad' would be lovely."

Brenda instantly looked up with an expression of astonishment.

"Grandad! I didn't see you in the audience," Janice said, arriving at the signing table.

"Sorry I haven't said hullo yet dear, I just arrived," he responded. "Decided it was finally time to come and meet my first granddaughter, make amends," he said, looking back to Brenda with a smile.

Before any of the three could say more, the publisher came up behind them, tapping a glass with a spoon. After getting everyone's attention, she said, "I am so sorry all. We must end today's reading and signing. I have just been reminded by Brenda's marketing assistant that she is due at the airport in a short while. There will be another signing opportunity next week at Limes Bookstore, in Eloff Street."

"My God that child is as beautiful as her mother," Josh said, standing arm in arm with Peter outside the tiny sandstone church located in the grounds of Sam's country hotel near Pietermaritzburg.

They were watching Jodie and Cliff mingling nearby with friends and family after the ceremony. Cliff seemed to have a permanent grin on his face as he gazed down at Hannah in the crook of his arm. Sam had offered the couple free accommodation for their extended family and the use of the church, and as most of their family were in Natal it made sense to them to have Hannah's christening down here.

"You'll have to get your own priest though, General," Sam had laughed. "I'm too busy with the hotel to do ceremonies nowadays."

With the imminent release of Nelson Mandela and conscription being a thing of the past, Sam and his family had returned to the country to begin taking over the hotel business from his parents, who were keen to retire.

Looking up at Josh, Peter smiled.

"And aren't *you* lucky you got the mother's twin brother," he said, giving Josh a gentle nudge. "Do you think we will ever have a child? You know, adoption. Surrogate. Whatever."

"OK, first, let me ask you this. Who gives up his career? You or me?" Josh said, deadpan.

"You two bickering again?" Brenda laughed, approaching from behind. "Can the godmother separate the two godfathers for a while," she laughed, squeezing between them. "You two are like Siamese twins."

"Brenda, the famous author. How are you? It's been a while," Josh said.

"Well other than the surprise visitor at my book signing this morning, things are going to plan. I read a review on the plane that suggested my book contributed to the end of conscription, but I think that's a bit of a stretch."

*

Jodie squeezed Cliff's arm in a quiet moment and after kissing him on the cheek briefly she leant over and kissed her baby daughter Hannah on the forehead.

"Come on," she whispered. "Beryl and Raechel are dying to hold Hannah again. You'll have to part with your treasure for a while," she smiled, as she led Cliff and their daughter across the immaculately kept lawn to where Cliff's mother and Raechel were talking to Gerry, who had officiated earlier.

Cliff was hovering near his mother, giving her instructions on how to hold Hannah while Jodie and Raechel laughed at his fussing.

"As I said this morning, I had some practice when you were a baby," Beryl informed her son.

He was just backing away from her, feeling a little guilty, when behind her he saw an official looking black Mercedes coming slowly up the driveway.

"Who is this, do you think?" he murmured.

"Beryl, did you invite someone important to Hannah's christening?" Raechel joked.

The vehicle came to a gentle halt on the driveway fifty metres from them, and a tinted rear window began to slide down as a large man with an earpiece attached to a cord that disappeared under his jacket collar climbed from the passenger seat.

The window was all the way down now and the face Cliff saw was unmistakably the same as the one he had seen in his semi-conscious state, grinning down at him from a Casspir over two years ago. Jonjon jumped off the rear seat as the door was opened for him and he ran towards Cliff.

"Captain Cliff. Captain Cliff," he called, coming to a skidding halt before them. Putting out his hand with a smile he greeted the ladies first, as Zeb had instructed him earlier. "My cousin Zeb fetched me in his big car. He's a very important man now. My granny told me," Jonjon informed them excitedly.

Behind him, Zeb approached, smartly dressed and with a grin, it seemed to Cliff, nearly as wide as the arms he held open in greeting.

Acknowledgments

The inspiration for this novel came from my son Kel. Over the years he has had to listen to many anecdotes from my younger days. He has yawned through some as a young boy, been open mouthed at others as a teenager and laughed at many over a beer with me as a young man himself.

It was during one of these latter occasions that his mirthful response to yet another army training camp anecdote was: 'Hey Dad, you should write your second book around some of these experiences. Share them maybe, I have learnt from them'.

And so arrived *The First Canary*.

I would also like to acknowledge my wife Dagmar for her tireless and astute editing of various drafts. Her eye for detail is unsurpassed and her suggestions invaluable.

I am extremely grateful to my brother Roy Baverstock and long-time friend Graham Ford who ploughed all the way through a very rough first draft to provide invaluable feedback that resulted in some significant changes for the better in structure and story line.

www.sheldonbaverstock.com

www.ingramcontent.com/pod-product-compliance
Lightning Source LLC
Chambersburg PA
CBHW010611100526
44585CB00038B/2511